Intertextuality 2.0

OXFORD STUDIES IN SOCIOLINGUISTICS

General Editors:
Brook Bolander
Monash University
Adam Jaworski
University of Hong Kong

INTERTEXTUALITY 2.0

Metadiscourse and Meaning-Making in an Online Community

Cynthia Gordon

OXFORD
UNIVERSITY PRESS

OXFORD
UNIVERSITY PRESS

Oxford University Press is a department of the University of Oxford. It furthers
the University's objective of excellence in research, scholarship, and education
by publishing worldwide. Oxford is a registered trade mark of Oxford University
Press in the UK and certain other countries.

Published in the United States of America by Oxford University Press
198 Madison Avenue, New York, NY 10016, United States of America.

© Oxford University Press 2023

Library of Congress Cataloging-in-Publication Data
Names: Gordon, Cynthia, 1975– author.
Title: Intertextuality 2.0 : metadiscourse and meaning-making in an
online community / Cynthia Gordon.
Description: New York, NY : Oxford University Press, [2023] |
Includes bibliographical references and index.
Identifiers: LCCN 2022029938 (print) | LCCN 2022029939 (ebook) |
ISBN 9780197642689 (hardback) | ISBN 9780197643440 (paperback) |
ISBN 9780197642702 (epub)
Subjects: LCSH: Intertextuality. | Weight loss—Electronic discussion groups.
Classification: LCC P302.45 .G67 2023 (print) | LCC P302.45 (ebook) |
DDC 306.44—dc23/eng/20220915
LC record available at https://lccn.loc.gov/2022029938
LC ebook record available at https://lccn.loc.gov/2022029939

DOI: 10.1093/oso/9780197642689.001.0001

9 8 7 6 5 4 3 2 1

Paperback printed by Marquis, Canada
Hardback printed by Bridgeport National Bindery, Inc., United States of America

In memory of my mother, Karen Gordon.

Her love, creativity, and ways with words—and even her appreciation of cats—shaped this book. I miss her.

CONTENTS

ACKNOWLEDGMENTS

The idea for this book took root at the Center for Advanced Study in the Behavioral Sciences at Stanford University, where I was a 2012–2013 Fellow and member of a research group on language and digital media organized by Deborah Tannen. I greatly benefited from the supportive environment provided by the Center, and especially from conversations with Deborah Tannen, Susan Herring, Naomi Baron, Michael Macovski, Dan Jurafsky, Michael Anderson, and Timothy Schroeder.

Over the years I have had productive exchanges with many colleagues and friends about my work-in-progress. I am particularly thankful to Diane Grimes, Melissa Luke, Richard Buttny, Najma Al Zidjaly, Miriam Locher, Sage Graham, Donal Carbaugh, Kristine Muñoz, Alla Tovares, Fred Erickson, Sylvia Sierra, Aisulu Raspayeva, and Charles Zuckerman. I also have benefited from conversations with HoFai (Viggo) Cheng, Hanwool Choe, Felipe Leandro de Jesus, Didem İkizoğlu, Jordan MacKenzie, Nicholas Mararac, Minh Nguyen, and Alexus Wells—who served as my teaching and research assistants as I worked on this book—and from interacting with students enrolled in my courses on the discourse of social media and language and food at Georgetown University. I thank attendees of our department's interaction analysis workshops. I am grateful to my colleagues in the Department of Linguistics for their support, especially Deborah Tannen and Heidi Hamilton, my long-time heroes who have become my dear friends.

I thank Deborah Tannen, Adam Jaworski, and Brook Bolander for their thoughtful and generous feedback on the entire manuscript. In addition, I thank Alla Tovares for her comments on several chapters, for our time together through the pandemic, and for her friendship.

I thank my family, especially Greg Gordon and Dina Giurini-Gordon, Sarah Gordon Leekha and Shya Leekha, and Whitney Gordon, for their love and support. Shad and Archie make every day brighter; I am grateful to have them in my life.

CHAPTER 1

Introduction

Intertextuality and metadiscourse online

THREADING THE NEEDLE: A CAT MEME AND THIS BOOK'S THEME

On an English-language online discussion board hosted on the website of a popular health and weight loss application that I will refer to as "FriendInFitness" (FIF), a poster started a thread with a post in which she inquired how to make a plain, low-sugar breakfast cereal (Cheerios) taste better. She indicated that she liked the honey nut variety of the cereal and wondered if there was a way to improve the taste of the plain variety, which she did not like as much. Other posters suggested that she add honey, or add nuts, or add honey and nuts, or just eat the honey nut variety instead (later, the original poster explained that she wanted to eat the plain variety because it had more iron, so replacing the plain with the honey nut was not a good option). Participants in the thread also recommended, with varying degrees of seriousness (especially given that the discussion boards largely focus on weight loss), that to enjoy the plain cereal more she should add cinnamon, or put it on ice cream, or blend the cereal into a milkshake with honey and nut butter, or add chocolate-hazelnut spread. To address the original poster's interest in increasing her iron intake, posters recommended (again, with varying degrees of seriousness) that she take an iron supplement (which the original poster subsequently explained that her stomach could not tolerate), eat high-iron foods such as kidney beans, mix the plain cereal with the honey-nut cereal to balance iron richness and good taste, or eat the honey nut cereal from an iron skillet. Some thread participants accused the original poster of being immature and ridiculous for not simply learning to enjoy or at least tolerate the plain cereal, of being misguided for

Intertextuality 2.0. Cynthia Gordon, Oxford University Press. © Oxford University Press 2023.
DOI: 10.1093/oso/9780197642689.003.0001

treating breakfast cereal as a primary dietary iron source, and of being a troll (i.e., of posting for the sake of stirring up trouble on the discussion boards, including engaging in the practice of posting similar inquiries across multiple boards on the same website, which it turns out that she did). In the unfolding of all of this, one discussion thread participant posted a meme, or circulating image macro; these are "captioned images that typically consist of a picture and a witty message or catchphrase" (Dynel 2016:663). This meme is shown in Figure 1.1.

This post encapsulates, in a basic way, two interconnected theoretical concepts that are fundamental to our understanding of online discussion board discourse and are at the core of this book. The first is *intertextuality*, which captures the idea that all texts and conversations—and by extension, other creations such as photographs and songs—are linked to other texts and conversations (and creations), and that people, through making and interpreting such links, create and infer meanings. The second is *metadiscourse*, which broadly refers to discourse about discourse and captures the notion that one function of language is to communicate about itself. Scholars have long recognized that the two theoretical concepts are related: when a speaker or writer makes connections to a prior conversation or text (intertextuality), some message is necessarily communicated about it (metadiscourse), and when a speaker or writer produces discourse about some prior utterance, text, or interaction (metadiscourse), this creates connections between a current and past utterance, text, or interaction (intertextuality). However, existing studies have tended to focus on one notion or the other, thus leaving underexplored the specific ways in which these phenomena are intertwined at the

Figure 1.1. "I LOVE THIS THREAD" meme.

micro-interactional level, especially online, and for what purposes. My inter-actional sociolinguistic study contributes to filling that gap by demonstrat-ing how intertextual linking strategies, both linguistic and multimodal, are mobilized in discussion board discourse on FIF as a resource to accomplish the metadiscursive activities, targeted at various levels of discourse, through which participants define group interactional norms and facilitate engage-ment in the group's primary shared activity: exchanging information about, and providing support in, weight loss, healthful eating, and related issues. In this way, the analysis I present illuminates the importance of intertextuality and metadiscourse in the context of an online "community of practice" (Lave and Wenger 1991; see also Eckert and McConnell-Ginet 1992).

Intertextuality is illustrated in, and greatly shapes the meaning of, the "I LOVE THIS THREAD SO MUCH" cat meme post. While intertextuality—so named by Kristeva (1980), following Bakhtin's (e.g., 1981) theorizing—has been long used to refer to the idea that all texts are linked to and derive meaning from other texts, the term has been expanded beyond written and spoken texts to include, in Deumert's (2014:77) words, "anything spoken, written, filmed, danced, painted or sung *that can be interpreted by an audience*" (italics in the original); this includes memes that combine images and words. The meme shown in Figure 1.1 is intertextual in several senses. First, the term "intertextuality" applies to various types of repetition in discourse, including lexical, syntactic, stylistic, and myriad more (Tannen 2007b:9), and by defini-tion, memes are, in Wiggins and Bowers' (2015:1886) words, "remixed, iter-ated messages which are rapidly spread by members of participatory digital culture for the purpose of continuing a conversation" (the term itself can be traced to Dawkins 1976). This meme has traveled across many websites—as a quick reverse Google image search shows—and has a rich and varied history of use; its use in the thread, whether the poster intends it or not, intertextu-ally references those prior uses (I do not trace those uses here; that could be a book unto itself).

Second, by using the meme, its poster indexes (again, even if not inten-tionally) the broader genres to which it belongs. This kind of intertextuality, or what Fairclough (1992:104) calls "constitutive intertextuality" or "interdis-cursivity," refers to "the configuration of discourse conventions that go into [a text's] production," and this applies to any type of text, written, visual, spoken, or multimodal. Briggs and Bauman (1992) call this "generic intertextuality," which highlights, as Bauman (2004:5) explains, "orienting frameworks for the production and reception of particular types of text." In other words, generic membership shapes how a text is used, and identifying the genre of a text (such as a fairy tale or a memo) helps interlocutors interpret its meaning. This particular Internet meme, like all memes, can be said to belong to at least one "family" of memes, which Segev, Nissenbaum, Stolero, and Schifman (2015) define as a group of interrelated memes that are connected by specific recurring features and structural patterns (i.e., by repetition). Identifying a meme's family—the other memes to which it is intertextually connected in generic terms—is part of interpreting it. The meme displayed in Figure 1.1 belongs to multiple meme families, as illustrated by the examples provided in Figure 1.2, and the intertextual connections it makes to such examples affect the meanings the meme takes on in the thread about cereal and dietary iron intake. Perhaps most evidently, the meme shown in Figure 1.1 is identifiable as a member of the (extremely large and diverse) genre of "cat memes," or memes that center on cats and various aspects of their appearance and personality, in particular their cuteness as well as their oft-cited aloofness and grumpiness, as encapsulated in 1.2a, which features the well-known Internet character Grumpy Cat and provides a negative assessment of the year 2016 (as might be expected, an identical version featuring the year 2020 also exists). Links between the "I LOVE THIS THREAD" meme and the category of cat memes support a lighthearted and playful interpretation of the meme; cats are generally treated as humorous in online contexts (see e.g., www.lolcats.com; Zappavigna 2012:103–104; worth noting, however, is that they also emerge to construct ideologies about serious topics such as body shaming and sexism [Fryer 2021]).

The meme also belongs to a group of memes that are metadiscursive; memes in this family evaluate others' discussion posts and entire threads, usually using the syntactic frame "I like X" or "I love X" (rather than, for instance "This thread is Y"). As a pun (a play on the dual meanings of "thread" as a plaything for cats and an online discussion), the meme's text evaluates the discussion thread in a humorous and playfully appreciative way. Most likely the appreciation is directed toward the silliness of many of the posts (such as the one suggesting, on a weight loss discussion board, mixing cereal and ice cream to increase iron intake), and not toward the quality of the discussion content in terms of dietary information and support. The example shown in

Figure 1.2. Examples of memes related to the "I LOVE THIS THREAD" meme. 1.2a., cat meme; 1.2b., meme (positively) evaluating a discussion post; 1.2c., meme (negatively and humorously) evaluating a discussion thread (i.e., indicating it is time to abandon the thread).

Figure 1.2b functions to praise a specific post playfully and engage in word-play with the dual meaning of "post" (similar to Figure 1.1's play on "thread"). The meme shown in Figure 1.2c, which involves the phrase "I like where this thread is going," is sarcastic in tone: the meme's image shows train passengers viewing their own train's derailment in progress (which cannot possibly be good for the passengers), and "I like this thread" is typically used to indicate that it is time to abandon a thread because the quality of discussion has degenerated (http://knowyourmeme.com/photos/690148-abandon-thread).

The meme posted in the cereal-focused thread of the cat hugging the ball of yarn (Figure 1.1) is thus intertextual in multiple senses: it echoes previous uses of the exact same meme elsewhere online and may derive meaning for readers of the thread who recognize that; it links to the broader meme families to which it belongs, also potentially recognizable and a source of meaning-making for other posters (e.g., they might recognize the meme as a cat meme and recognize that cat memes often cue humor); and it is a single post that creates links to the thread as a whole and among the thread's posts (i.e., it ties all the previous posts together by using image and language to comment on them).

This brings us to the fact that the "I LOVE THIS THREAD SO MUCH" meme is also an example of metadiscourse: it is used in the cereal-related discussion thread to comment on the thread itself; it is discourse about some discourse ("this thread"). This general phenomenon—which is as diverse as intertextuality is in its empirical realizations and potential functions—has been studied in various guises and using various terms, including not only *metadiscourse* (e.g., Craig 1999, 2005; Fairclough 1992; Hyland 1998, 2005, 2017), but also *metacommunication* (e.g., Bateson 1972; Verschueren 1995), *metalinguistic messages* (Bateson 1972), *meta-talk* (Schiffrin 1980), *reflexive language* (e.g., Lucy 1993b), *metalanguage* (e.g., Hanks 1993; Jaworski, Coupland, and Galasiński 2004a, 2004b), *metapragmatic discourse* (e.g., Silverstein 1993), and *metapragmatics* (e.g., Blum-Kulka 1997; Tanskanen 2007; Verschueren 1995, 2004). This extremely diverse body of research emphasizes that human language can be used to communicate about itself; it demonstrates how people use language to communicate about the linguistic system, specific instances of language use (immediate or displaced), and language in use more generally; and it shows how, in using language to communicate about language, interlocutors simultaneously communicate about relationships and the nature of social situations (an idea captured in Bateson's 1972 concept of *metacommunicative messages* or *metamessages*).

Metadiscourse, like intertextuality, plays a role in the construction of meanings, as well as of social groups or communities. Cameron (2004:313), for instance, observes that "[m]etalinguistic resources seem very often to be deployed to connect various aspects of linguistic behavior to a larger moral order" or set of beliefs shared by members of a group. As Jaworski, Coupland,

and Galasiński (2004b:3) explain, how people use language to communicate about language illuminates "how social groups value and orient to language and communication" and may come to "constitute structured understandings, perhaps even 'common sense' understandings—of how language works, what it is usually like, what certain ways of speaking connote and imply, what they *ought* to be like" (italics in the original). This means that metadiscourse not only conveys information about ideas and interpersonal relationships but also contributes to the construction of social groups and their ideologies. The "I LOVE THIS THREAD SO MUCH" meme metadiscursively marks the thread as a recognizable type on the boards, and one that has entertainment value for some members of the group, making it worthy of playful, positive assessment. Another example is how some of the posters to the thread to which the meme was posted labeled the original poster's post as "trolling" (which evaluates her participation negatively and suggests that she should be sanctioned, as this activity is not allowed on the boards). Jaworski, Coupland, and Galasiński (2004b:3) emphasize the importance of exploring metadiscourse as part of any study of "language as a form of social action" in order to understand better not only meaning-making but also phenomena such as the construction of social groups and boundaries. This study, by focusing on the language of the FIF discussion boards as well as the accompanying image-based content, advances this call and line of research.

My title, *Intertextuality 2.0*, zeroes in on my analytical and theoretical goals by signaling a double meaning. On the one hand, it refers to the discourse I examine and the phenomenon I focus on: intertextuality in the context of interactive, multimodal digital communication (i.e., intertextuality in what has been called "Web 2.0"). On the other, it signals the primary argument I advance in this book: intertextuality is not one theory, but two at once, in the sense that its companion, metadiscourse, must be elevated in studies of intertextuality if we are to fully understand its role in Web 2.0, particularly regarding the functioning of groups of people who gather online and engage in a shared endeavor. While it is widely understood that intertextuality (often explored with a focus on the concept of repetition) and metadiscourse are interconnected phenomena, the details of their interconnection remain underexplored. Taking an interactional sociolinguistic approach (as articulated by, e.g., Gumperz 2015 and Tannen 2004), I show how intertextual linking strategies facilitate engagement in activities or frames (Goffman 1974; Tannen and Wallat 1993) that center on discourse about discourse. This metadiscourse serves what might be identified as "practical purposes" (Craig 2005), such as helping to overcome a misunderstanding; it is used "in goal-directed ways" and for "strategic communication" (Jaworski, Coupland, and Galasiński 2004b:3,4), such as to influence how a particular stretch of discourse is to be interpreted. Far from being unusual, such uses of language are essential to human communication, as has been observed by many scholars (e.g., Lucy 1993b; van Leeuwen 2004). I demonstrate how through "practical" or "strategic" metadiscursive activities—that, as is common in contemporary digital interactions, are necessarily multimodal in nature (e.g., Herring 2013)—members of the group define what specific terms mean, indicate what types of posts are appropriate and valued, advance competing perspectives, solve problems, and create shared ideologies regarding how communication and relationships work both offline and online (and how communication and relationships relate to weight loss).

Returning to Figure 1.1 with this in mind, it is clear that to understand the "I LOVE THIS THREAD SO MUCH" cat meme as a contribution, by way of a single post, to an online discussion about the palatability and nutritional value of breakfast cereal, it must be examined through the lenses of *intertextuality*—which captures the idea that meaning-making happens through connecting texts (broadly construed) to other texts, both specific texts and those generically similar, to weave a comprehensible web of meaning—and *metadiscourse*—which acknowledges that discourse about discourse is common, productive, and worthy of examination in everyday (online) interaction. Intertextuality, in the form of intertextual linking strategies, is the "thread" that makes metadiscourse possible and interpretable in (online) contexts.

While metadiscourse and intertextuality are omnipresent across all types of online discussion boards (and indeed, in all types of interactions, online and face-to-face), here I explore these interwoven notions in one specific context: online discussions among people who in general are seeking information, advice, and support regarding weight loss and related issues, such as kinds of foods to eat and to avoid, effective exercise routines, how to maintain motivation, and the challenges of making healthful choices part of one's everyday life. These discussions lie at the intersection of health, physical appearance (notably, body size and shape), and food. These are topics that are of interest to many laypeople and are discussed "across multiple arenas" (Kurtz et al. 2017) but may be identifiable as a "preoccupation" among people of a certain level of privilege, as observed by a number of food studies scholars (e.g., Guthman 2011) and sociologists (e.g., Gailey 2021). On the FIF discussion boards, it is taken for granted, for example, that participants have access to sufficient amounts of food (likely, too much), the time and energy to attend to what they eat and to engage in structured exercise activities, and the time, energy, and technological resources to communicate online with others who share their interests and goals. Much of the communication on the boards also reflects an underlying ideology about health: the belief that health—including food consumption and body weight and composition—is largely the result of individual willpower (as Guthman [2011] points out, this has interesting connections to neoliberalism and capitalism; gender also figures prominently in such discourse, as discussed by Weber [2009] and Gailey [2021], among others). While beyond the scope of my study, it is worth noting that the discussion boards I examine manifest many recognizable ideologies pertaining to health and body weight, such as the idea that being overweight is a moral failure (see Coupland and Coupland [2009] for a useful discussion of how women's magazines in the United Kingdom construct such ideologies; Gailey [2021] provides a compelling exploration of how 74 "women of size" describe their experiences with stigma, discrimination, and violence, thereby demonstrating the effects of such ideologies). In addition, the online discussion boards I study constitute one context among many—social media, advertisements, infotainment programming, and news media—that highlight a seeming fixation on health. In such contexts, idealized versions of embodied health are portrayed (see, e.g., Mishra's [2017] study of print weight loss advertising from 1930 to 1990, and Fuller, Briggs, and Dillon-Sumner's [2013] study of discourses of food and gender in health magazines targeted at women and men); food is given symbolic and ideological value (see, e.g., Mapes' [2020] analysis of "throwback Thursday" posts from the *New York Times* food section's Instagram account and the accomplishment of what Jaworski and Thurlow [2009] call "elitist stancetaking"); and embodied health and food ideologies collide (see, e.g., Gordon's [2015b] study of a reality TV show focused on improving [overweight] children's health by altering their families' food procurement, preparation, and consumption practices). Thus, while the discourse I examine is specific to the discussion boards providing the source of my data, and I approach it as a case study, connections to communication about similar topics and issues in other contexts cannot be ignored.

With this in mind, I note that the existence of the online interactions from the FIF discussion boards, as well as my analysis of them, reverberates with the increasing public recognition that communicating about health- and food-related communication can help improve communication and ultimately health (note that this too emphasizes the agency of the individual, rather than systemic economic or other issues). This communication ideology is evidenced, for instance, in (social) media, including a podcast episode on the topic of "How to Talk to Kids about Picky Eating & Good Nutrition" (Silverman 2017); a health blog titled "5 Things Not to Say to Your Partner about Losing Weight" (Sass 2017); and a newspaper essay called "How to Talk to Your Doctor about Awkward Men's Health Issues" (Dabaja 2019). In addition, scholars in communication, linguistics, and related fields have long understood that valuable insights can be gained by studying health- and food-related conversations, such as in doctor–patient interactions (e.g., Hamilton 2004; Speer and McPhillips 2018) and in mealtime conversations among family members (e.g., Paugh and Izquierdo 2009; Wiggins 2013). In other words, there is ever-increasing interest in how people communicate about health, food, and related topics, not only but especially online, and this book aims to weigh in while also interweaving intertextuality and metadiscourse as theories.

MOTIVATION AND OVERVIEW

The posting of the "I LOVE THIS THREAD" cat meme serves as a simple (albeit, in the discussion, rather decontextualized) example of metadiscourse and intertextuality, the two interlinked, twin theoretical concepts at the core of this book. Online communication is an ideal area in which to explore these notions: early on in the study of computer-mediated communication (CMC), Herring (1999) suggested that the "persistence" of online textual communication—the fact that what is posted online often stays there, available to read and reread later—not only assists in cognitive processing but also heightens what Cazden (1976) calls "metalinguistic awareness"; in improving accessibility to the language of a text, it encourages reflection upon that language. Put differently, persistence fosters, and facilitates, awareness of linguistic and discourse features, and this awareness becomes manifest in metadiscourse, such as in assessments of one's English language competence on Flickr (Lee 2013), in representations of German dialects on YouTube (Androutsopoulos 2013b), or in creations of Ukrainian language ideologies in YouTube comments (Tovares 2019). Persistence also expedites the creation of intertextuality: a persistent digital text—be it a string of words, the entire text of a post, an image, a meme, or a video—is easily cut and pasted, quoted, responded to, moved, and modified online, as many scholars have observed (e.g., Adami 2014; Adami and Jewitt 2016; Severinson Eklundh 2010; Herring 1999, 2013). Research on online and digital discourse has identified numerous forms of intertextuality that involve linking texts or recontextualizing some part of an "old" text—or what Becker (1994) calls "prior text"—into a new context. Forms of online intertextuality that have been examined by discourse analysts and scholars in related research areas include the reproduction of words (e.g., as indirect or direct quotation), syntactic frames, memes and other image-related content, and hashtags, as well as uses of hyperlinks and direct or indirect references to cultural texts such as proverbs. Functions identified by such forms of intertextuality are also extremely diverse, ranging from refuting another participant's argument, to constructing a coherent identity for oneself, to creating "community" in various senses.

Building on this foundation (which I introduce in more detail in the next section), my examination of the discourse of online discussion board threads illuminates how intertextuality is mobilized in the engagement of various social activities—or what Goffman (1974) calls "frames" and Tannen and Wallat (1993) term "interactive frames"—that are inherently metadiscursive and facilitate the construction, and work, of the online community of practice: providing support for weight loss and related goals. Coupland and Jaworski (2004) suggest that while language use is infused with, and inextricable from, the "meta" (metalanguage, metapragmatics, etc.), it can be valuable to isolate and analytically focus on it "for the sake of theoretical argument when it offers distinctive sociolinguistic insights" (p. 23). My study is grounded on this premise: metadiscourse is spotlighted in this book not only due to its prominence and patterned appearances in my data set (and my interest in understanding its forms and functions), but also because it allows empirical investigation into interconnections between metadiscourse and intertextuality, both of which are key concepts in sociolinguistic studies of language. Further, my study lends insight into how posters use metadiscourse to collaboratively define norms of interaction and facilitate participation in the exchange of information and provision of support, and the role of intertextuality in these phenomena, thus contributing to our understanding of language in/as social life through a case study analysis of one online support community's discourse.

The threads I analyze, like the one about cereal discussed in this chapter's opening, are drawn from health, weight loss, nutrition-related, and sociability-oriented discussion boards hosted on the website of the popular weight loss application that I refer to using the pseudonym FriendInFitness (or FIF—users often abbreviate the name when referring to it and I will use the same practice). I identify and explicate six metadiscursive activities, or frames, that emerge repeatedly on the boards, and, I argue, work together toward the community's functioning. Four center around discourse about an unfolding online discussion and about online communication more generally: posters establish shared definitions of key terms and negotiate shared "rules" for the discussion (Chapter 2), posters "fix" another participant's contribution (Chapter 3), and moderators cut off communication by "locking" threads (Chapter 4). Through these activities, participants shape the shared online discursive space they use to exchange health and weight-loss-related information and support. The remaining two activities involve online communication about offline health communication-related problems: posters work to solve an original poster's problem of a troublesome interaction she had with her doctor and thereby simultaneously address broader communicative responsibilities in physician–patient interaction about body weight (Chapter 5), and they define the roles of communication and technology—not only the discussion boards, but also the calorie-logging app that is affiliated with the website—in offline interpersonal relationships (Chapter 6). Through these discussions of the "offline" world and its discourse, posters simultaneously create meanings, and their social group, online.

My analysis of these activities demonstrates that and how metadiscourse and intertextuality are fundamentally intertwined and can productively be explored as such: I identify and explicate the various forms of intertextual linking that intertwine to accomplish online metadiscourse in the form of metadiscursive activities or frames. Specifically, I show that intertextual linking is accomplished in the ways participants draw upon specific linguistic features (e.g., deictic pronouns), medium affordances (e.g., using the boards' quotation function to reply to a previous post), and semiotic resources of the type that Kress (2010) calls "multimodal affordances" such as graphic features (e.g., symbolic ways of pointing to or striking out text) and image-based content (e.g., photos in memes; short looped videos [or GIFs]; emojis). In demonstrating how these intertextual linking strategies facilitate and indeed are fundamental to metadiscursive activities, I both illuminate the interconnectedness of intertextuality and metadiscourse and show how understanding them as interconnected explains how online support communities such as FIF function.

In examining intertextuality in the context of online metadiscourse, I aim to contribute not only to our understanding of intertextuality and metadiscourse as key concepts for explorations of discourse in online and social media contexts, but also more broadly to the growing body of scholarship in an area alternately described as "computer-mediated discourse" (Herring 2004), "discourse 2.0" (Tannen and Trester 2013), "discourse in Web 2.0" (Herring 2013), "discourse and digital practices" (Jones, Chik, and Hafner 2015), or "digital discourse" (Bolander and Locher 2020; Thurlow and Mroczek 2011). In this context, as Bolander and Locher (2020:2) explain, "different modalities and practices" are intermingled "within the same virtual environment"; according to Herring (2013:4–5), these might include (among other possibilities), "text comments on photo-sharing sites; text (and video) responses to YouTube videos; text (and voice) chat during multiplayer online games; and text messages from mobile phones posted to interactive TV programs." Bolander and Locher (2020:6) note that if we consider language to be part of a multimodal collection of communicative means, "scholars might choose to start their analysis not by focusing on a single mode, but rather on 'action.'" In other words, sociolinguists and other researchers might begin their analyses by asking what action is (or actions are) being taken in a given moment (this is a tenet of mediated discourse analysis; see Scollon 2001, Norris and Jones 2005). In this study, I focus on actions—or more accurately, sets and sequences of actions: activities or frames—that are metadiscursive. As digital media continue to permeate everyday life, linguistics and discourse scholars find opportunities to bring insights to the larger scholarly conversation about digital communication media, including its multimodal nature, a goal of this book as well.

In addition, as Androutsopoulos and Beißwenger (2008) note, findings from studies examining computer-mediated discourse extend to other contexts, having "important implications for understanding key concepts in discourse studies, such as interactional coherence, participation frameworks, intertextuality, language-identity relationships, and the notion of community" (p. 2). In a related spirit, and quite early in the study of discourse 2.0 (in fact, before the term was coined), Katriel (1999) suggests that ethnographic studies of technologically mediated communication allow us to revisit old and enduring "questions of interactional patterning" while also lending insight into "radically new contexts of communication" (p. 100). Further, as argued by Walther (2012), research into uses of digital communication technologies contributes to language and social psychology research (and I would suggest discourse scholarship more broadly) by raising questions that "can generate theoretical understanding of how humans communicate both with and without machines and, sometimes, help illuminate the nature of social life, in general, in ways we might not have seen without technological lenses" (p. 398). Investigating intertextuality and metadiscourse online thus provides a window into these concepts and how they are related in a particular virtual space, while also suggesting the need to examine more closely their role in other contexts both online and offline, and the space between.

THEORETICAL BACKGROUND

The vast bodies of research on intertextuality, metadiscourse, and the discourse of online discussion boards provides the grounding for my research. In what follows, I review studies in each area, highlighting those that bring at least two of these three areas together.

Intertextuality (online)

In this section, I first introduce the notion of intertextuality and discuss explorations of it in face-to-face conversations as well as public news media, wherein scholars have long studied links between texts and those prior (and/or those that follow). Then, I summarize prior research on intertextuality in digital contexts—such as websites, email, and various platforms such as Facebook and Twitter—as my work builds on these foundations.

Intertextuality: Tracing the term

Extant research on digital discourse highlights the prominence of intertextuality, or how meaning is created through various forms of textual repurposing and interlinking. However, the term has a much longer history: indeed, intertextuality is a feature of all discourse, not only discourse online, and its study (though not the term) can be traced back to scholars whose theorizing is fundamental to contemporary understandings of language, among them Saussure (1916), who identified meanings produced in language as relational, wherein the meaning of signs derives from relations to other signs and the sign system; Bakhtin (e.g, 1981), a language and literary theorist who wrote in the 1920s until the 1970s and offered an understanding of discourse (especially novelistic discourse) wherein all words contain echoes of prior uses; and Kristeva (1980), who coined the term "intertextuality" (see Allen [2000] for a discussion of the genesis of "intertextuality" and its use in structuralism, psychoanalytic theory, and other research areas).

"Intertextuality" as it is used in discourse analysis and sociolinguistics is generally traced to Kristeva (1980), a philosopher, literary critic, and psychoanalyst; she devised the term in her presentation and interpretation of theorizing on *dialogicality* by Bakhtin (1981, 1984, 1986). Following Morson and Emerson's (1990) reading of Bakhtin, this concept captures three senses of dialogue: language is context bound and continually unfolding, meaning all words have a history; utterances are co-constituted by speaker and hearer (or writer and reader) and thus not only hark back to the past but also anticipate future responses; and in some cases, speakers use words from the past with the intention that the words be heard as if they are enclosed in quotation marks (which Bakhtin refers to as *double-voiced words*). The focus of linguistic studies that use the term "intertextuality" has been on two of these three meanings—the history of a word's use across contexts, and its use to evoke some aspect of this history, and how previous instances of language use are placed in literal or metaphorical quotation marks. While sometimes described as "intertextuality" (e.g., Erickson 1986:315), the speaker–hearer relationship in meaning-making has generally been taken up using concepts such as "recipient design," "co-construction," and, as Tannen (2007b:9) remarks, "joint production."

Bakhtin's theorizing on discourse, and Kristeva and Morson and Emerson's interpretations of it, intersects with linguist A. L. Becker's (1995) conceptualization of language use, or what he calls *languaging*. Languaging consists of "taking old texts from memory and reshaping them into present contexts" (Becker 1995:9). Citing both Bakhtin and Becker, and providing an integrated review of various studies of intertextuality in linguistics, Tannen (2007b:9) describes intertextuality as "the insight that meaning in language results from a complex of relationships linking items within a discourse and linking current to prior instances of language." Tannen's analysis of conversational and literary discourse demonstrates how various forms of repetition—including repeated words, syntactic structures, rhythmic patterns, and sounds—create coherence in a text as well as *conversational involvement*, which refers to "an internal, even emotional connection individuals feel which binds them to other people as well as to places, things, activities, ideas, memories, and words" (p. 27). To refer to the phenomenon of quotation, one of the more widely studied forms of intertextuality (and a phenomenon discussed by Bakhtin), Tannen introduces *constructed dialogue* as an alternative to the oft-used term "reported speech": when one participant quotes something that was previously uttered, it is impossible to provide a neutral, exact "report" of what was said (word-for-word; with the same pitch, amplitude, and stress patterns; in the same sequential slot of conversation; and so on). Even if that were possible (and, in the online context, exact replications of sequences of words are facilitated by cut and paste and the quotation function offered by many discussion boards), transporting previously used language into a new context changes its meaning. Thus, quoting involves reshaping and recontextualizing previously uttered words, which (building on Bakhtin, Becker, and others), Tannen remarks, fundamentally alters their meaning, thereby making the dialogue "constructed." Bauman and Briggs' (1990:73) framework of "entextualization" conveys a related idea: this is the process of "rendering discourse extractable, of making a stretch of linguistic production into a unit—a *text*—that can be lifted out of its interactional setting"; the text becomes "decontextualized" and can be "recontextualized" to create new meanings. The "I LOVE THIS THREAD" meme shown in Figure 1.1 can serve as an example: the meme is itself an extractable text, and when it is recontextualized, the meaning of "this thread" and "I" change (further, the meme would have a different meaning if instead of being posted on an online discussion board, for example, it were printed out on paper and affixed to a ball of yarn in a craft store).

Tannen's study is a highly influential example of research examining the forms and functions of repetition in verbal and written communication through the lens of intertextuality. This is a very diverse area, as evidenced by studies that have explored the role of repetition and intertextuality in how people accomplish everyday activities through talk, including working through disagreements (e.g., Tannen 2006); creating playful and humorous interactions of various types (e.g., Gordon 2002, 2008, 2009; Howard 2009; Norrick 1989; Sierra 2016, 2021); performing socialization of other people (e.g., Wortham 2005; Gordon and Luke 2013); telling stories (e.g., Bauman 2004; Schiffrin 2006); constructing identities for oneself and others (e.g., Gordon 2006; Hamilton 1998; Nguyen 2021; Sierra 2019); and reinforcing cultural stereotypes (e.g., Hill 2005; Mendoza-Denton 2011; Sierra 2019).

Particularly relevant for the current study are analyses focusing on how intertextuality is used by members of a group to create shared meanings, negotiate relationships, and construct identities (including a shared group identity), along with studies that "trace" the circulation of public (especially media) texts. Multiple studies stemming from an interactional sociolinguistic research project directed by Deborah Tannen and Shari Kendall to examine how dual-income couples with at least one child balance the demands of work and family have explored intertextuality as a feature of the conversational interactions of a type of social group (family; see Tannen, Kendall, and Gordon [2007] for more on this project). This project's methodology—having members of four couples audio-record their own conversations (with each other, their children, extended family members, and their friends, as well as at work) over the course of one week—provides a rich data set for exploring various forms of intertextuality, because the relatively long-term recording captured both an "original" uttering of some word or linguistic string, and its repetition, whether immediate (such as people repeating what they just heard on television, as examined by Tovares [2007]) or displaced (as in the examples I describe next). In Herring's (1999) terms, recording (and then transcribing) increased the "persistence" of each family's talk—making examples of intertextuality readily identifiable to the researchers, although they themselves were not members of the participating families. (Note that many other approaches to the study of discourse that collect data over time—either by recording, ethnography, or collecting historical documents, or by some combination of these—also facilitate the study of intertextuality; see, e.g., Verschueren's [2013] analysis of international diplomacy documents regulating warfare from 1856 to 1939; Hall's [2005] study of the discourse of a community of transgender individuals in Northern India; and Bauman's [2004] exploration of intertextuality and oral genres in various communities.)

In Gordon (2009), focusing on the interactions of one family that took part in the family discourse study and using the discourse of two others as points of comparison, I analyze how family members repeat words, strings of words, paralinguistic features, and other discourse structures (e.g., speech acts, narratives) in their everyday interactions, and I demonstrate how this creates shared meanings and constructs the family as a social group. For example, in the interactions among the focal couple and their nearly three-year-old child, Natalie, the parents and child use and demonstrate recognition of terms from the family's "familylect" (Søndergaard 1991) that are related to the child's various kinds of misbehavior: "shenanigans" refers to when the child talks to herself at nap time instead of going to sleep, for instance, while "boppy" (which also occurs with the pronunciation "buppie") is a term that signals that a serious tantrum is forthcoming from the child. In repeatedly using these terms both within and across conversations, family members construct the family as both child-centered and playful. And, when Natalie's aunt demonstrates lack of recognition of "boppy" in one conversation that was captured by the recorder, it momentarily positions her as an outsider (though Natalie's father—her brother—quickly fills her in). This speaks to the role of intertextuality in establishing a social group's membership.

Further, drawing on theorizing on framing in discourse (e.g., Bateson 1972; Goffman 1974, 1981; Tannen and Wallat 1993) and integrating it with the notion of intertextuality, my analysis of the family discourse data showed how family members recontextualize (in Bauman and Briggs' [1990] sense) particular strings of words from one conversation in a later conversation to create layers of meaning. For instance, in a second family, the father, Sam, who is at home with the couple's two-year-old child, Kira, is on the phone with his wife, Kathy, who is at work. Sam tells Kathy that Kira fell down while they were outside and split her lip, and Kathy sighs and says, "How come a disproportionate amount of injuries and accidents occur when she's under your care?" (and Sam chuckles). Several hours later, when both parents are home, Kathy is in the kitchen with Kira while Sam is in another room, and Kira falls off her chair and starts crying; Sam comes into the room to check that she is okay. Once it is clear that Kira is fine, Sam utters, using a smile voice, "How come she always seems to have an inordinate amount of accidents with Mom?" Sam's utterance invokes two contexts of enunciation: on the one hand, it is a response to the ongoing interaction in which Kira fell off her chair while her mother was minding her, functioning to criticize Kathy's parenting teasingly. On the other, it serves as an echo of, and comment on, Kathy's earlier criticism of his own abilities to look after their child. In this way, the use of similar wording and exact word repetition (*How come . . . disproportionate amount/inordinate amount . . . of accidents)* serves to layer meanings; these layers, which I understand as frames, are only discernible if both speaker and listener have access to the relevant prior text.

Examining the discourse of this family and of two others who also participated in the study, Tannen (2006) highlights intertextuality by tracing the development of conflicts about domestic responsibilities across disparate interactions. She demonstrates how topics are "recycled" (closed and then opened later in the same or in another conversation, as when an argument about who will take a package to the post office resurfaces in a later interaction between members of one couple); conversations are "reframed" as topics shift (as when a conversation about the package becomes a wider discussion of the provision of support among spouses); and interactions are "rekeyed" (as when the package is first discussed with anger, and later jokingly). Tannen thus shows how various transformations create new meanings and serve as a means to negotiate relationships among family members.

In a study that traces texts across public contexts and examines the meanings and ideologies that arise, Solin (2004) analyzes how, in an environmental debate about air pollution among scientists, the press, government, and pressure groups, an "intertextual chain" (Fairclough 1992) is created in research articles, news reports, and press releases. Solin shows how explicit references to prior texts (such as a magazine article that cites a research article), various kinds of repetition (such as citations of facts and claims), references to other institutions involved in the debate, and other strategies create links between the texts that constitute the chain, while also highlighting the "clear shifts in the strength of expressions of causality" between pollution and health that occur as research articles are filtered into the press (p. 288). She suggests that the transformations that occur relate not only to generic conventions, but also the ideologies of the stakeholders involved, as well as the power relations among them. Also exploring intertextuality in public discourse, Hodges (2011) traces the circulation of what he terms the "Bush 'War on Terror' Narrative," which emerged after the attacks on the United States on September 11, 2001. He explores how this narrative was constructed, maintained, and contested across contexts, including in President George W. Bush's speeches, the media, and focus groups conducted with politically active college students in the United States. For example, Hodges analyzes how talking points and sound bites—such as "terrorists and tyrants," "weapons of mass destruction," and "war on terror" itself—are used repeatedly by politicians, in newspapers, on television news, and so on. Circulation of these key concepts worked to reinforce (and sometimes, to resist) the "War on Terror" Narrative, which advocated for a particular understanding of 9/11 and of the relationship between Al Qaeda and Iraq, thereby working to "subsume disparate foreign policy objectives" under the narrative (p. 17).

Various studies have also investigated how material from public texts, such as news and entertainment media, is utilized in more private everyday conversations. These include Tovares' (2007, 2012) exploration of how words and phrases heard on television resurface in family talk as members share and negotiate knowledge and construct alignments; Fägersten's (2012) examination of how members of one polylingual family make media references to establish common ground; and Sierra's (2019, 2021) study of how material from online memes and entertainment media is recontextualized in conversations among a group of young adults to create humor (which has the simultaneous, unintended effect of reinforcing ethnic stereotypes).

In summary, the studies reviewed in this section thus far explore intertextuality in private talk, across various modes in public discourse, and across the boundaries of what we typically conceive of as public versus private. They emphasize how having an interactional and textual record, including academic publications, recordings and transcripts of speeches, news media reports, TV shows, and recorded conversations, facilitates intertextuality as a research topic.

Intertextuality in digital discourse contexts

As mentioned previously, Herring (1999) observes that the "persistence" of online communication—the fact that once it is "out there," it is usually retrievable—facilitates intertextuality (and scholarly explorations of it). In fact, studies have identified numerous and diverse forms of intertextuality online, which, in the spirit of contemporary terminology such as "discourse 2.0" and "Web 2.0," I call "intertextuality 2.0." As Adami (2014:224) points out, "[d]igital technologies afford multimodal representation and re-use of previously existing texts in new contexts to an unprecedented extent and number of sign makers"; in digital contexts, "any text can be linked to another, forwarded into another space, embedded in some other text." This is a modern echo of previous research that highlights repetition in discourse (e.g., Tannen 2007b) and entextualization and recontextualization (e.g., Bauman and Briggs 1990); it also identifies online and social media communication as ideal for the exploration of intertextuality.

Indeed, examples of studies of online intertextuality abound. In what follows, I review select studies that are especially relevant for my analysis in that they highlight the range of forms of intertextuality online and/or functions that pertain to the creation of meanings, identities, and communities.

Hodsdon-Champeon's (2010) examination of racially antagonistic discourse in an online discussion forum identifies five types of intertextuality, pointing to the relatively broad definition of what constitutes intertextuality: references to other texts that are made directly, such as through paraphrase; naming the source text, or pointing to it using the word "this" or a symbol such as the caret (^); direct quotations from other texts, for instance, sections copied from online articles or quotations from previous posts; references to texts that are hypothetical, meaning a poster refers to a text that does not exist but is treated as if it did; references to proverbs, common phrases, and other cultural texts; and references to other texts that are made indirectly, where based on context it is evident that the information provided in the post could not have come from the participant who is posting but must have some outside source (this category is necessarily vague). Hodsdon-Champeon finds that when a participant in the online debate attempts to contest another participant's claim, direct references and quotations tend to be used; in contrast, when building authority for their own claims, participants typically do not do this, backgrounding the source of information, which she suggests can make it more difficult to discredit. While not explicitly focusing on intertextuality as a concept, Herring (1999) and Severinson Eklundh (2010), in their explorations of the related subject of discourse coherence online, identify various strategies that participants use to create coherence across turns or posts; these strategies involve connecting one text to another and thus can be classified as intertextual. For example, Herring (1999) finds that in asynchronous group discourse, such as online discussion boards, coherence is enhanced by linking—"the practice of referring explicitly to the content of a previous message in one's response"—and by quoting—"copying portions of a previous message in one's response." Severinson Eklundh (2010) focuses on quoting in email and in Usenet newsgroups; her analysis highlights how the properties of the technological systems and the social context both affect the quoting strategies used by participants. Quoting in email serves as a linking mechanism, facilitating the construction of a coherent conversational thread. Quoting is facilitated by the design of the system; as Severinson Eklundh remarks, for instance, some email systems by default include the whole message in the reply. In addition, systems may mark quoted material through indentation and/or pointers (i.e., ">"). She also notes that practices involving quoting may differ across contexts, such as in a user's private email messages versus in Usenet newsgroup discussions; she found greater use of quoting in the newsgroup. Baym (1996), who analyzes the discourse of a Usenet discussion group, finds that quotations generated through the affordances of Usenet were used to link agreeing and disagreeing posts to those to which they were responding. West and Trester (2013) examine intertextuality on Facebook; they demonstrate how it is used to accomplish the basic actions of the site—tagging photos, "liking," friending, and commenting on others' posts—and how these actions accomplish facework (in the sense of Goffman [1967] and Brown and Levinson [1987]).

Al Zidjaly's (2010) case study shows how intertextuality is used in one Muslim man's construction of his complex religious identity in chat room discourse. Relevant forms of intertextuality that she identifies are reshaping words (such as by quoting or paraphrasing words from the Quran, or from messages of other chat participants), actions (such as praying), and events (such as the aftermath of Salman Rushdie's [1990] book *The Satanic Verses*). Vásquez's (2015b) exploration of online consumer reviews of a range of products, including hotels, recipes, and common consumer goods, highlights both intertextuality and the related phenomenon of interdiscursivity. Vásquez found that the most common form of intertextuality in her data was when reviewers reference other reviews posted on the site, generally to show agreement (though sometimes to display disagreement). In addition, reviewers also make references to other online texts (such as Wikipedia entries or YouTube videos) and draw on offline textual sources (such as a product label) and material from popular culture (such as a TV sitcom). The author also identified instances of interdiscursivity, such as a review written in the form of a haiku, or when language from advertising was incorporated into reviews. Mitra (1999) explores hyperlinks as a form of intertextuality online that, through linking web pages to other web pages, helps members of the Indian diaspora (immigrants to the West) construct a cyber community that affirms their connections to India.

While not explicitly using the term "intertextuality," Zappavigna's (2012, 2014) corpus-based study identifies hashtags, retweeting, use of the "@" symbol (which addresses a tweet to another user), and expression of matching evaluations as serving a similar linking function on Twitter. Zappavigna (2014) demonstrates how, in tweets about coffee, these strategies accomplish fluid groupings of people, or what she calls "ambient affiliation": some tweeters belong to a group of Coffee Connoisseurs who appreciate high-quality coffee as part of living the good life, and others to a group of Coffee Addicts who express needing coffee just to survive the day. Making a direct link to the concept of intertextuality in her later work, Zappavigna (2018:73) observes that hashtags help "amplify" the "semiotic 'reach'" of tweets by making them visible to wider audiences and increase "the scope of potential intertextual relations" (in Kristeva's [1980] sense). According to Zappavigna, "[i]ntertextual meanings are particularly important in social media environments given the tendency of images, video, and written text to be replicated, modified, and recontextualized at rapid rates of high volume" (p. 73). Intertextuality is also relevant in thinking about tweets in terms of the layering of voices, such as discussed by Bakhtin (1986) and White (1998), and manifest intertextuality, as discussed by Fairclough (1992); for example, a hashtag can indicate a source of a quotation (Zappavigna 2018:88) and put voices in relation with other voices, including for accomplishing mockery (p. 143) and social bonding (p. 144).

Also analyzing online discourse and suggesting that intertextuality serves as a resource for creating alignments or connections among interactional participants, Ho (2011) examines requests made in professional email discourse among language teachers. His analysis reveals that the inclusion of parts of previous email messages in a group exchange is a form of intertextuality that serves to "foreground mutual prior agreement" (p. 2540), thereby reducing possible resistance to requests and convincing recipients to comply, ultimately helping to create group harmony. Ho also examines interdiscursivity, finding, for example, that the use of an informal register in part of an email message created connection among participants. Nguyen (2021) shows how members of an online Asian American Pacific Islander activist group on the messaging platform Slack use intertextual references, for instance by referring to other activist groups and describing their own offline activist activities, to construct themselves as "good" and knowledgeable activists, as well as to create their online community. Nguyen highlights how Becker's (1994:165) observation that "social groups seem to be bound primarily by a shared repertoire of prior texts," showing how an assertion that was previously explored in offline conversations (e.g., Gordon 2009) extends to online discourse as well.

Recently, scholars of digital discourse have given increased attention to intertextuality that happens across online contexts or social media platforms. For instance, Adami (2014:226) examines "crossposting" by a food blogger, a phenomenon she defines as when "an artefact uploaded to an online platform is re-posted, shared, embedded, or copied-and-pasted into another one," such as when the blogger reposts her blog to Google+ or Twitter, or embeds one of her YouTube videos in her blog. Cross posting creates "multiple pathways" for audience members to reach an artifact and "augment[s] the possibilities for reading/viewing it" (p. 233). While "each artefact [produced by the blogger] can stand and make meaning on its own" in one space, "a larger picture" can be "constructed by accessing all of them" (p. 237). Tovares's (2020b) analysis of an elite rock climber's tweets and Facebook posts during a multi-day climb underlines this point; Tovares shows how the climber begins some longer posts on Twitter and then (due to Twitter's character constraints) completes them on Facebook. Such studies demonstrate how having an understanding of the social media landscape and the history of use and intertextual connections of an artifact, be it a chunk of text, a meme, or a video clip, shapes its interpretation.

Adami also points out that as an image, chunk of text, or other artifact is moved between platforms, its genre may shift; in her data, photos laid out sequentially in the blog to depict an event appear with other photos in a type of "family album" format on Instagram. (I earlier gave an example of this phenomenon: printing out a hard copy of the "I LOVE THIS THREAD SO MUCH" meme and adhering the piece of paper to an actual skein of yarn that is for sale at a shop changes the meme's meaning. Of course, embedding the meme in this book, and repeatedly discussing it, has altered its meaning, too.) This speaks to the idea that while every website and social media platform has what might be called affordances in Gibson's (1979:127) sense—what it "offers" or "furnishes" users, "for good or ill," creating a "complementarity" of the user and the digital environment—these affordances differ. Such affordances, which are not unique to technological objects and programs, "allow human beings to *perceive* possibilities for action" (Deumert 2014:34, italics in the original); they do not determine people's actions. In another study looking across platforms, Giaxoglou (2017) explores one journalist's release of a leaked draft of a Eurogroup statement on Twitter, Facebook, and Scribd. The author highlights how the journalist, in making such cross-postings, makes "adaptations in line with the platform-specific formats and audience" (n.p.). Further, she suggests that this cross-posting activity demonstrates "the use of social media as a communicative environment of affordances rather than as discrete platforms" (n.p.), a phenomenon Madianou and Miller (2012) also describe in their ethnographic study of new media use in transnational families, referring to it as "polymedia."

It has also been observed that intertextuality exists between interactions that occur "online" and those that occur "offline." For instance, bits of online discourse (such as the language of memes), similar to other forms of media discourse, appear in offline conversational interaction (e.g., Sierra 2021), and offline activities and discourse are brought into online contexts, such as through telling stories (e.g., Gordon 2015a) and by making intertextual references to events and people displaced in time and space (e.g., Al Zidjaly 2010; Nguyen 2021). Androutsopoulos (2014:5) explains that the practice of "sharing" online and in social media involves not only users' "transformation of spoken discourse to written text," but also how users entextualize social activities by employing what Jones (2009) calls "technologies of entextualization"—for instance, using keyboards, video cameras, and the like to capture various types of moments from everyday life. Indeed, multiple scholars have advocated for the idea that what we think of as relatively distinct offline and online social worlds are in fact interconnected (e.g., Aarsand 2008; Jones 2004; Kurtz et al. 2017; Wilson and Atkinson 2005), and some have suggested that the online–offline dichotomy is a false one (e.g., Bolander and Locher 2020; Jones 2004). With this in mind, "intertextuality 2.0" as I understand it does not strictly reside online, even though my analytic focus is what appears in my data set, the discourse that is posted to the discussion boards (i.e., words, images, and so on). In Chapters 5 and 6, I aim to highlight connections between this discussion board discourse and discourse that seemingly originates in "offline" contexts, specifically focusing on online depictions and evaluations of face-to-face communication.

Androutsopoulos (2013a:237) proposes that researchers of computer-mediated communication should not only view online and offline as interconnected and inseparable but also acknowledge that written language "is closely related to various semiotic resources, including typography, still and moving images, and screen layout" and that the resulting richness plays a fundamental role in meaning-making. With this in mind, my study highlights multimodality as a fundamental part of intertextuality 2.0. Memes have emerged as an especially interesting example of multimodal intertextuality (as pointed out earlier in my discussion of the "I LOVE THIS THREAD" meme); Internet memes are necessarily intertextual; they are "artifacts" that hold "both cultural and social attributes as they are produced, reproduced, and transformed to reconstitute the social system" (Wiggins and Bowers 2015:1891). They are, to use Bauman and Briggs' (1990) terms, "extractable" and subject to the process of "recontextualization." In line with Herring's (1999) discussion of the persistence of online material, Wiggins and Bowers (2015:1892) note that memes' tendency to "persist" owes not only to the nature of memes as movable but also "the dynamic interaction among members of participatory digital culture." Knobel and Lankshear (2007:209) similarly remark that "the internet itself greatly facilitates meme longevity (not to mention meme distribution as well)." As multimodal texts, memes interweave words, images, and graphic features, and memes can not only be recontextualized in whole, but also in part.

There is also another form of intertextuality present in memes, as it is present in texts: Wiggins and Bowers (2015) suggest that memes are a genre (following how Bakhtin and Medvedev [1978] discuss genres). As mentioned previously, Segev, Nissenbaum, Stolero, and Shifman (2015) propose that memes can be grouped into what they call families and that family members have recurring features in common. Knobel and Lankshear (2007:217) argue that memes can be "organized into different categories of *kinds* of memes" in terms of main purpose (e.g., social commentary, hoax, absurdist humor). Thus, multiple scholars have noted that memes can be productively analyzed not only as they are used intertextually in different online contexts, such as to disagree with a discussion board post or to match playfully another just-used meme, but as they are more broadly interrelated to other similar memes. Like memes, GIFs are also continually circulated online. "GIF" stands for "graphic interchange format"; GIFs are defined by Tolins and Samermit (2016:76) as "looped animations of embodied actions" that are "typically drawn from movies or television." Like memes, GIFs are intertextual by definition. The authors observe that, in text messages, one participant matching another's GIF in terms of content or theme can serve an affiliative function in that the link between the two GIFs can be considered as a form of repetition and intertextuality. Like memes, GIFs can arguably be organized into groups, families, kinds, or generic types, an idea I explore more thoroughly in Chapter 4.

In summary, intertextuality is a prominent feature of spoken, written, and digital discourse, and it is clear that the general affordances of the Internet (such as creating an ongoing textual record), as well as the specific affordances of platforms, applications, and systems, shape how intertextuality manifests online. Its forms are diverse, ranging from quoted posts to reproduced images, from hyperlinks to symbols that create textual connections, and from references to shared cultural texts to hashtags. The functions of intertextuality are also diverse: while its underlying purpose is one of connection between words, texts, posts, video clips, websites, images, ideas, and people, this connection allows the construction of agreement and disagreement, multilayered meanings, identities, and social group boundaries. And, intertextuality creates a "discourse-deictic relationship" between the current text and the "original" source of the discourse (as noted by Severinson Eklundh 2010:3, regarding quotation in email messages); there is thus much conceptual overlap with metadiscourse, considered next.

From intertextuality to metadiscourse (online)

As Hyland (2017:16) pointed out several years ago, while metadiscourse "is a concept which seems to have found its time," it is nonetheless "a hard term to pin down and is often understood in different ways." In this section, I first give an overview of existing studies that focus on "metadiscourse," broadly construed (including various "metas" such as "metalinguistics," "metapragmatics," and "metacommunication"), working toward an understanding of what scholars have understood to constitute the "meta" of language, how and why it has been studied, and how it relates to intertextuality. Then, I briefly discuss key studies that have highlighted metadiscourse, sometimes in conjunction with intertextuality, in the exploration of computer-mediated or digital discourse.

Studies of the "meta" of language and communication

Just as intertextuality is a fundamental, inexorable aspect of language use, so too is language's reflexive or "meta" capacity, and this has long been recognized by scholars in linguistics and related fields. Coupland and Jaworski (2004) observe that "metalanguage" emerges in the work of scholars in functional linguistics such as Jakobson (e.g., 1960), Hockett (e.g., 1958), and Halliday (e.g., 1978), and that the idea is traceable to Saussure's (1974[1916]) observation that language is a system that can be used to communicate not only about objects and phenomena in the world, but also about language itself as an empirical phenomenon or an abstract idea. They also note that the concept figures prominently in linguistic anthropology and related approaches; this includes the work of Gumperz (e.g., 1982), the founder of interactional sociolinguistics, as well as of linguistic anthropologists Briggs and Bauman (e.g., 1992). As Tanskanen (2007:89) notes, "[t]he reflexive capacity of language has been the object of active study from several different viewpoints"; she cites as examples Lucy's (1993b) work on metalanguage, Hyland's (1998, 2005) and Ifantidou's (2005) examinations of metadiscourse, and Verschueren's (1995) exploration of metacommunication and metapragmatics. Other examples include Blum-Kulka's (1997) analysis of metapragmatic discourse, utterances, and comments, and Schiffrin's (1980) study of meta-talk. Tanskanen (2007:89) highlights the centrality of the "meta" of language in the work of Bateson (1972), who distinguishes *metalinguistic messages*, which are messages about language, from *metacommunicative messages* (or *metamessages*), which communicate about the relationship between participants and how messages should be interpreted. Bateson's notion of metamessages in particular has played an important role in microanalyses of conversational discourse, especially in interactional sociolinguistics (for discussions, see Gordon and Tannen 2021; Gumperz 2015; Schiffrin 1994; Tannen 2004; for examples, see Gumperz 1982; Tannen 1993, 2005, 2007b; Gordon 2009). In other words, at every moment of communication, people co-construct their sense of the unfolding social situation as well as their relationships. This is one omnipresent "meta" aspect of language use. In taking an interactional sociolinguistic approach in this book, I necessarily consider metamessages; however, the book's focus is oriented toward "metadiscourse," or what Bateson calls "metalinguistic messages." This is a vast area of research, as illustrated through my provision of brief overviews of three influential edited volumes, and then by my description of basic areas of research as well as specific studies of particular relevance for this book.

Lucy's (1993c) edited volume, *Reflexive Language: Reported Speech and Metapragmatics*, outlines the wide and cross-disciplinary acknowledgment of the importance of examining the reflexive nature of language use as well as various reflexive uses of language. As Lucy (1993b:11) observes, "speech is permeated by reflexive activity as speakers remark on language, report utterances, index and describes aspects of the speech event, invoke conventional names, and guide listeners in the proper interpretations of their utterances." Lucy (1993b) also uses the term "metapragmatics" to refer to "explicit reflexive uses of language, such as when a speaker characterizes or comments on some regularity or pattern of speech use" (p. 2), and he notes that such uses of language involve "trying to characterize the 'appropriateness' or the 'effectiveness' of using some linguistic expression" (p. 42). Prominent functions of reflexive language that are highlighted in the volume include reporting and evaluating language, constructing culturally shaped performances and texts, and constructing identities and shared meanings.

In their edited volume *Metalanguage: Social and Ideological Perspectives*, Jaworski, Coupland, and Galasiński (2004a) demonstrate how the metalinguistic function of language is realized in how people talk about their own talk and the talk of others, in how speakers create "reported speech" (or what [Tannen 2007b] calls "constructed dialogue"), and in how stylization (as discussed by Rampton, e.g., 1995) is accomplished. In addition to highlighting how analyses of metalanguage find grounding in various research traditions, including linguistic anthropology, folk linguistics, and critical discourse analysis, Jaworski, Coupland, and Galasiński (2004a) openly acknowledge the challenges of exploring a phenomenon as multifaceted as metalanguage, and the volume's chapters demonstrate key functions, notably constructing ideologies, identities, and communities, across diverse contexts. What is more, their volume offers a discussion of "what range of 'meta' processes need to be recognized and theorized in sociolinguistics, how we should view them in relation to each other, and how we can approach these dimensions methodologically in different social contexts of language use" (Jaworski, Coupland, and Galasiński 2004b:5). As they explain, "language about language" "is too literal a formulation" of the perspectives their volume encompasses, and they propose that a better one might be: "Language in the context of linguistic representations and evaluations". (p. 4).

Metapragmatics in Use, co-edited by Hübler and Bublitz (2007b), examines, in the editors' (2007a:1) own words, "how interactants actually employ meta-utterances to intervene in ongoing discourse." The book's contributors show how people "use metalanguage to frame their own or their interlocutors' utterances as true or false, precise or vague, cooperative or uncooperative, straightforward or misleading and so on, to secure or change the direction of the current talk, to create or maintain expedient social relationships" (Hübler and Bublitz 2007a:3). In this view, metapragmatics may pertain to Grice's (1975) maxims, cultural norms (including rules of politeness), specific speech acts, illocutionary functions, reference, organizational matters of discourse, and nonverbal and prosodic behavior, and it can occur in relatively explicit or relatively inexplicit ways. Like the volumes of Lucy (1993c) and Jaworski,

Coupland, and Galasiński (2004a) before, Hübler and Bublitz's (2007b) edited book demonstrates the prominence, diversity, and multifunctionality of the "meta" in language use.

An important note is that in exploring metalanguage, metapragmatics, and related notions in depth, the volumes also acknowledge the connection of intertextuality and metadiscourse. However, intertextuality as a theory, and the depth of its connections to metadiscourse, is not a major focus: searching "intertextuality" in Lucy's (1993c) volume (using Google Books) turns up two results, and it turns up five in Jaworski, Coupland, and Galasiński's (2004a) volume, as well as five in Hübler and Bublitz's (2007b). In focusing on meta-discourse, these volumes, individually and even more collectively, reveal the richness of research focused on the meta of language, including what exactly "meta" refers to as well as the functions of the meta, and thus provide foundation for my study, which extends them to incorporate theorizing on intertextuality more directly.

Studies of the meta of language and communication can also be organized by context of study and the types of metadiscursive functions highlighted, and, again, while many studies acknowledge intertextuality in some way, it is not a centerpiece of the analyses presented. For instance, one group of studies focuses on learning and socialization (both formal and informal), which is important for my purposes in that the studies highlight how metadiscourse is used to evaluate and shape the language use of an individual person or members of a social group. For example, in applied linguistics, there is focus on "metalinguistic feedback" provided to second language learners, including its form, uptake, and pedagogical implications, such as the effectiveness of such feedback for learning specific target forms (e.g., Bryfonski and Sanz 2018; Mackey, Park, and Tagarelli 2016). Discourse analysts have examined "meta-discourse" (Gordon and Luke 2016), "metapragmatic statements" (Vásquez 2010), and "talk about talk" (Lapadat 2003) in education and professional socialization. For instance, Gordon and Luke explore how in class discussion, counselors-in-training talk about address terms and the speech act of requesting information as a means of creating their transitional identities (from student to counselor) and animating the transition's tensions (such as regarding negotiating workplace relationships in terms of power and solidarity, as Tannen [1994] has discussed these terms). Blum-Kulka (1997) explores "metapragmatic discourse" in family dinners, specifically parental utterances designed to socialize children directly or indirectly into culturally appropriate linguistic and interactional behaviors while also facilitating and accomplishing sociability among family members. In her data, metapragmatic discourse includes comments regarding discourse management (e.g., "wait until your brother finishes talking"); comments regarding violations of Grice's conversational maxims, such as regarding manner (e.g., "say please"); and metalinguistic comments such as "queries and responses about word meanings, as well as comments topicalizing language," which she found especially prominent in the talk of bilingual families (pp. 181–182). Such comments not only (attempt to) shape the behaviors of individual children but also (re)create a family's norms of language use.

As Thurlow, Aiello, and Portmann (2020:531), point out, citing Woolard and Schieffelin (1994), "[m]etadiscursive commentary is inherently a matter of ideology." Metalanguage and metadiscourse thus figure prominently in studies grounded in critical linguistics and critical discourse analysis that focus on language (and other) ideologies and how they are created, along with their social and societal effects, such as how they contribute to the construction of social hierarchies and understandings of morality. For example, Cameron (1995:vii) identifies what she calls "verbal hygiene"—people's practices and attempts to regulate, beautify, or "clean up" language as an outgrowth of the reflexive nature, or metalinguistic capacity, of language. She considers a range of issues, from the teaching of grammar in schools to political correctness; as Cameron (2004:319) points out, the study of metalanguage "encompasses both the implicit and the explicit ways in which people define what language is, what it is for, and what it is worth," but she emphasizes that this is "about far more than just language." Jaworski, Thurlow, Lawson, and Ylänne-McEwen (2003) consider the representation of local languages in British television shows that focus on travel to other countries, and specifically on how traveling presenters interact with locals, animate or quote the languages spoken in the destination country, and make metalinguistic and metapragmatic comments (which they refer to as "metacomments") about language. The authors find that these practices accomplish ideological work: for example, how locals are shown speaking lends authenticity to TV show episodes and exoticizes destinations (and people); in how presenters evaluate foreign language use, English is constructed as the international communication medium (to be accommodated to by locals, regardless of their language backgrounds). British (native) speakers of English are positioned as global citizens, as tourists with potential access to the whole world. Further, a privileged, "tourist" class of people, one that spans international boundaries, is constructed, with local languages being treated as a mere background to cosmopolitan tourists.

A number of linguists have focused on the role of "meta" elements of language in structuring text and/or social interaction. Scholars who focus on written discourse, and academic writing in particular, have considered the role of "metacommunication" and "metadiscourse" in constructing a text, as well as author and reader relationships and identities (e.g., Hyland 1998, 2005; Abdi 2002, 2009; Ifantidou 2005; Zhang 2016). Sociolinguists have focused on conversational interaction; for example, Schiffrin's (1980) analysis of "meta-talk" considers subtle strategies that accomplish "talk about talk" and thereby organize both discourse and understanding. *Meta-talk* is a broad term and includes meta-linguistic references such as demonstrative pronouns that point to items in the text (e.g., "That's a lie"), meta-linguistic operators that modify or interrelate propositions (e.g., "For example"), and meta-linguistic verbs (e.g., "say," "argue," and "assert"). Maschler (2009:1) identifies discourse markers as a means of "using language in order to communicate about the process of using language," which she calls "metalanguaging" (building on Becker's [1995] term "languaging," which he introduced to emphasize language as a process). Maschler demonstrates, for example, how Hebrew discourse markers tend to cluster in conversational moments where there is a shift in frame (in Goffman's [1974, 1981] sense), communicating not only about discourse structure, but also about referential content, interpersonal relationships, and cognitive processes. Schiffrin (1987) also highlights the bracketing function of discourse markers, though she does not use a "meta" term for this. Van Ninjatten (2006), analyzing the discourse of child welfare meetings, shows how professionals use "meta-remarks" to evaluate and manage clients' contributions, thus structuring the institutional encounter. Scholars in communication studies have highlighted how metadiscourse is used to support one's position in, and to help structure, public hearings and meetings (Buttny 2010; Buttny and Cohen 2007; Leighter and Black 2010); how it serves as an "organizational sensemaking" tool in the context of crisis communication, specifically Hurricane Katrina teleconferences (Castor and Bartesaghi 2016:3); and how it functions as a means of accounting for acknowledged tensions between cultural groups in focus group discussions (Buttny and Hashim 2015).

In addition to having functions related to learning, constructing ideologies and identities, and structuring discourse, metadiscourse also works to structure alignments between participants; in the aforementioned studies, for example, it structures alignments between family members in everyday talk, between academic authors and their readers, and between people holding different roles in institutional encounters. Related, numerous studies have considered how meta aspects of language also create "communities" of various types and sizes. Some studies in this area focus on how members of a community label the types of discourse that take place in their community, the meanings of such labels, and the structure of the talk that bears them. Many of these studies grow out of, or are influenced by, the ethnography of communication and linguistic anthropology and generally conceptualize community in the sense of "speech community" as the term has been discussed by Hymes and Gumperz: a speech community consists of a group of people who share "rules for the conduct and interpretation of speech, and rules for the interpretation of at least one linguistic variety" (Hymes 1972:54); a speech community can be described as "[a]ny human aggregate characterized by regular and frequent interaction by means of a shared body of verbal signs and set off from similar aggregates by significant differences in language usage" (Gumperz 2009/1968:66).

For example, Carbaugh (1989:93) examines "cultural terms for talk as they occur in various systems of communication." Specifically, he considers data drawn from seven ethnographic case studies representing 11 different societies (in places including Panama, the Philippines, Fiji, the United States, and Israel). He finds that "indigenous labels for speaking"—terms members of a community themselves use to label speech, which are inherently metadiscursive—are used to capture different "levels" of communication, including individual performances, co-constructed performances, styles, and functions. This framework is useful in that it notes that labels for speaking—such as calling a stretch of talk "a fable" or as "being honest"—are not equivalent, even though all, importantly, are "used by natives not only to refer to aspects of their talk itself, but further to refer to social relations and persons" (Carbaugh 1989:103). In other words, a community's terms for talk convey messages about relationships, for instance, pertaining to relational dimensions of talk such as relative orientation to cooperation and competitiveness. They also convey messages about personhood, for example, through assigning motives to speakers (e.g., "lying"). In Carbaugh's (1989:112–113) formulation, people "use cultural terms for talk as a way to speak directly and literally about words and as a way to talk more metaphorically about interpersonal relations, social institutions, and models for being a person."

Other ethnographic studies of specific speech events and activities also highlight metadiscourse as community constituting, including of *dugri* speech (roughly, "straight" or "direct" talk) in Israeli Sabra culture (Katriel 1986); *communication* as a cultural category of speech used for interpersonal bonding and self-definition in the United States (Katriel and Philipsen 1981); and the language of a Mexican market's sales pitches, which occur in the form of a *grito* or *pregon* (roughly, a "call") or a *propaganda commercial* or (*plática) commercial* (roughly, "spiel") (Bauman 2004, ch. 4). In how members of a community label and enact different types of speaking, they create identities, as well as group norms, values, and boundaries. As Philips (2021:13) observes, research in anthropological discourse analysis has considered "relations between forms of discourse and how humans make sense of discourse in part by thinking and talking about how the talk they are involved in is related to other instances of talk." She notes that theoretical concepts used to address this topic include "metapragmatics" (as discussed by Silverstein [1993], as talk about language use) and intertextuality, along with the related notions of indexicality and interdiscursivity. In her study of a County Superior Court in Tucson, Arizona, in the United States, Philips (1998) found that judges' practices regarding how they took guilty pleas differed in structured ways (correlating with their differing political ideologies), and that judges were aware of such differences and shared ways of conceptualizing and talking about them. In short, they enacted "metapragmatic interpretations of the written law that were personal, yet also shared with other judges, through how they took admissions of guilt from criminal defendants," and such interpretations not only structured how they handled such pleas but also gave each procedure coherence (Philips 2021:14).

Philips is one among a number of scholars in linguistic anthropological and related approaches to the study of discourse who, in exploring metadiscourse, explicitly discusses its theoretical interconnections to intertextuality; as mentioned, this connection has long been acknowledged (sometimes indirectly) in existing research, but few studies explore it by way of microanalysis. For example, in the first chapter of the edited volume *Repetition in Discourse*, Johnstone and a group of scholars who participated in a conference focused on this topic observe that repetition—the centerpiece of linguistic studies of intertextuality, as noted by Tannen (2007b)—is inherently "metalinguistic" in that its function is "to point, to direct a hearer back to something and say, 'Pay attention to this again'" (Johnstone et al. 1994:13). In other words, as they explain, repetition "puts the utterance in brackets, making it impossible to treat the language as if it were transparent, by forcing hearers to focus on the language itself," and in that sense, "repetition is metalinguistic, even though it's not conscious talk about talk" (p. 13).

An observation made by van Leeuwen (2004:109), that metalanguage can be understood as "the recontextualization of linguistic practice" (such as when scholarly articles necessarily recontextualize political interviews as they provide analysis of them), also highlights connections between metalanguage and intertextuality (though he does not use the latter term). His analysis of three such scholarly works uncovers, for instance, a tendency toward "utterance autonomisation" (van Leeuwen 1996), or "cases where the writer or speaker is replaced [in the writing of the scholarly author] by his or her utterance, something which is often done to lend a kind of impersonal authority to the utterance" (van Leeuwen 2004:118). When "formal terms" are used as utterance autonomisations, this has the effect of attributing them agency and backgrounding the agency of the person doing the uttering or writing (e.g., "Negative assertions evoke . . ."). Through this (what can conceptualized as intertextual) practice, scholars communicate about the interview discourse they analyze (and the interviewees whose discourse is considered).

Fairclough (1992:122, and building on Maingueneau 1987:66–69) makes similar but more explicit connections between repetition and intertextuality on the one hand and metadiscourse on the other by defining "metadiscourse" as a "form of manifest intertextuality." This means that a text explicitly (and seemingly intentionally) contains some other text and "the text producer distinguishes different levels within her own text, and distances herself from some level of the text, treating the distanced level as if it were another, external, text" (an idea similar to Bakhtin's concept of double-voiced discourse). Paraphrase is also a form of metadiscourse; here "the speaker is situated above or outside her own discourse, and is in a position to control and manipulate it" (Fairclough 1992:122). These are both ways of indicating "pay attention to this" and accomplishing evaluation.

Related, Coupland and Jaworski (2004:29) observe that repetition "stands out as a prime example of a metalinguistic resource available to speakers (and writers)." The authors explicitly connect metadiscourse (or what they term *metalanguage*) to Bakhtin's theorizing (e.g., 1981, 1984, 1986); doing this links metadiscourse to the phenomenon that has come to be known as intertextuality. The authors do this primarily through the lens of Bakhtin's notion of heteroglossia, which emphasizes that language use is always comprised of a mixing of multiple linguistic forms and past and present voices that bring with them different social meanings. Coupland and Jaworski highlight how, through metalanguage, speakers and writers demonstrate reflexivity, make evaluations, and (re)construct language ideologies. As Coupland and Jaworski (2004:27) explain, linguistic choices are always "'meta' choices as they copy, approximate or contrast with other language forms." Following Bakhtin, these choices can be made with more or less awareness or intentionality, and for different functions. In other words, there are "instances of language use which invoke the 'meta' level more overtly than in others" such as in cases of speech representation (e.g., in "direct reported speech" or what Tannen [2007b] terms "constructed dialogue"). Indeed, the many explorations of instances of "quotation" (broadly construed) are among the scholarly studies where intertextuality and metadiscourse most often (implicitly) collide: in examining a phenomenon that is inherently intertextual (recontextualizing some old text into some new context), scholars uncover how this move is evaluative (the speaker, in doing this, makes some comment on the recontextualized material, which constitutes metadiscourse).

My own exploration of intertextuality in family talk (Gordon 2009), like Coupland and Jaworski's (2004) discussion of metatalk and ideology, draws on Bakhtin's (e.g., 1981, 1984, 1986) theorizing. As part of my study of intertextuality and framing in everyday family conversations (that were audio recorded over the course of one week), I examined how family members take linguistic material previously uttered by another family member in a specific prior conversation and reproduce it in a new context (Gordon 2009, ch. 4). I demonstrated how, in recreating "prior text" (Becker 1994, 1995)—i.e., by recontextualizing—family members layer meanings in interaction, which I conceptualized as a layering or "laminating" (Goffman 1974, 1981) of frames that I termed "overlapping frames." This lamination is created as family members, in repeating strings of words uttered by other family members (specifically, their spouses), comment on them in some way (often teasing about them or criticizing them) while also accomplishing another ongoing activity (as in the earlier "disproportionate/inordinate amount of accidents" example). In focusing on intertextuality as theory (and its relationship to framing in discourse), in Gordon (2009) I drew heavily on only one "meta" term—Bateson's

(1972) "metamessages." I briefly identified repetition as "metalinguistic," following Johnstone et al. (1994), but did not explore this idea in depth. Instead of focusing on the metalinguistic functions of intertextual repetition, I highlighted how intertextuality is mobilized as a resource to negotiate family meanings and relationships, such as, for instance, how by repeatedly using family-specific words, family members evoke a history of use and send a meta-message of "familyness" (Gordon 2009, ch. 2). In this book, I shift perspective to engage with the connections between intertextuality and metadiscourse, which I increasingly have come to see as inextricable theoretical perspectives, and as empirically powerful for the study of online discourse.

My analysis necessarily builds on existing research that highlights intertextuality as metadiscursive and/or metadiscourse as an intertextual phenomenon, in other words, on research that makes explicit the importance of these two concepts' application in tandem either empirically or through direct discussion of the interconnections. One such study is Inoue's (2003) analysis of "Japanese women's language" as it occurs in two translated works of fiction. Inoue focuses on quotation and reported speech (i.e., on how fictional characters are voiced), describing these phenomena as both "metalinguistic devices" and "intertextual practices" (p. 315). Her analysis illuminates and helps explicate women's language as language ideology: while most Japanese women do not speak "women's language," they recognize it as their own language. In Inoue's words, "one 'hears' Japanese women's language not so much from living bodies of Japanese women, as from imaginary voices," including the voices of fictional characters such as Scarlett O'Hara and Minnie Mouse (p. 315). "Women's language" is thus a "metapragmatic category" created through the "relentless metalinguistic dislocation and relocations of the imaginary voice of Japanese women through quotation and reported speech" (p. 316), a perspective that acknowledges both metadiscourse and intertextuality as fundamental for understanding how, through quotation, ideologies about language use are constructed.

Meinhof's (2004) analysis of British television commercials also explicitly acknowledges intertextuality and metadiscourse as related theoretical notions that are usefully applied in tandem. Drawing on Bakhtin's (1981, 1986) notion of double-voiced discourse as well as theorizing on style and stylization (e.g., Coupland 2004; Rampton 1995), Meinhof observes that commercials being recognized as humorous "directly depends on the viewers being prompted to imagine a certain set of meanings as a result of intertextual references" (p. 277)—similar to what I argue in Gordon (2009) regarding family talk—however, she goes on to argue that in making such references, the commercials "create metadisourses which playfully comment on, and comically subvert the narratives of the source material" (p. 280). In other words, the commercials not only parody some previous commercial or other text but comment on "a form of linguistic or paralinguistic behavior which needs to be consciously recognized for its metaphoric value" (Meinhof 2004:283). Also relevant for my study, the author emphasizes that metacommentary or metadiscourse must be understood as a multimodal phenomenon; it is not realized through language alone, but also through features such as music and images. For example, in one commercial Meinhof examined, exotic and beautiful settings set up expectations for the people who populate the scene (which appears to be a canal in Venice but is later revealed to be a Manchester shipping canal), expectations that are subverted when one of the characters speaks using an inner-city working-class accent, resulting in humor as well as metacommentary on language, social class, and culture. (I discuss multimodal metadiscourse in more detail in the next section.)

In summary, research on metadiscourse and related notions (e.g., metapragmatics, metalanguage, and meta-talk) has a long history and reveals how important to human communication it is that language is self-reflexive. It shows how the "meta" of language serves multiple functions in terms of creating meanings, relationships, identities, social groups, and ideologies. It also shows that different "levels" of meta have been explored—metapragmatic comments, produced in one or more utterances, function to evaluate lexical choice (e.g., failure to say "please") and create a group's norms of interaction; a single term may label an entire way of speaking (e.g., "being honest"); a metalinguistic feature (e.g., a deictic pronoun) structures discourse and creates meaning; metalinguistic comments create larger ideologies (e.g., constructing English as the language of cosmopolitanism). Studies of metadiscourse in digital contexts, reviewed next, accomplish similar functions, though metadiscourse there is created in different ways, shaped by the affordances of Web 2.0.

Metadiscourse in digital discourse contexts

Analyzing a corpus of print media articles and essays that address language use in computer-mediated contexts (such as in text messages), Thurlow (2006) finds that instances of what he calls "metadiscourse" and "metalanguage" create several ideologies regarding the changing nature of language use online. By examining "people's explicit, conscious, and articulated reflections about language—in other words their talk about talk" (Thurlow 2006:669), the author finds that online language is constructed as a "linguistic revolution" (new and distinctive), a "statistical panic" (ubiquitous and spreading), and a "moral panic" (as a "mania" responsible for declining literacy standards). Squires (2011) investigates how text messages that were part of a political scandal (primarily involving former Detroit Mayor Kwame Kilpatrick and his chief of staff Christine Beatty) are embedded in TV news broadcasts as a form of direct reported speech, and how such embeddings construct new meanings and reify ideologies by commenting on "language, technology, and the social actors involved" (p. 7). Both Thurlow and Squires identify news media as sites for discourse about digital discourse. Thurlow and Mroczek (2011:xxvii), citing Cameron (1995), observe that that metalanguage exposes ideologies related to what constitutes "good" or "normal" language, expectations regarding literacy, and the categorization of language users, and that this is true in both "face-to-face" and "digitally 'mediated'" contexts. Accordingly, recent studies have focused on digital discourse as a context for metadiscourse (and some subset of that research highlights metadiscourse regarding digital discourse specifically). In what follows, I summarize key studies of metadiscourse online, highlighting those that address the connections between metadiscourse and intertextuality and are thereby especially relevant for my study.

Existing studies of metadiscourse in discourse 2.0 contexts suggest that it serves similar functions to metadiscourse that occurs in (offline) written and spoken discourse. For example, it functions to create ideologies, including those related to language. Bogetić (2016), for instance, examines "metalinguistic comments" made by teenage bloggers on an English-language teen dating website, and shows how teens, in making these, "perpetuate many aspects of existing ideologies about the value of Standard English" while also "reworking" these ideologies for their own purposes (p. 262). Examining "metalinguistic comments" in a multilingual (Ukrainian-Russian) online context, Tovares (2019) demonstrates how YouTube commentators communicate about language in Ukraine and thereby construct identities, create and contest ideologies, and negotiate inclusion and exclusion. Lenihan (2011) explores "the metalinguistic discourse of *Facebook*'s 'translations' application and the metalinguistic commentary of the *Facebook* 'translators' as a community" (p. 48). She suggests that metalanguage "inevitably works at an ideological level" in this context, in that it serves as a kind of language policing (p. 48). This is evident, for instance, when members of the community discuss how to translate English technological terms, such as "mobile phone," into Irish (p. 58). Metadiscourse also emerged regarding standard versus nonstandard varieties, and translators' language choice in discussions among themselves.

Zappavigna (2018), drawing on a social semiotic approach, systemic functional linguistics, and multimodal discourse analysis, focuses on hashtags on Twitter as a type of "metadata" and "metadiscourse"; a hashtag "encapsulates, at a higher order of abstraction, the interpersonal meaning being made" in a tweet (p. 2), and it also functions as "textual metadiscourse" in the sense that it does work pertaining to discourse organization (p. 15). The author also observes that hashtags are "inherently heteroglossic" in Bakhtin's (1986) sense; they are an "explicit way of linking a social media text to other potential perspectives construed by other texts in the social stream" (Zappavigna 2018:12). Because hashtags link texts together "via metadata," they highlight texts' "intertextual dimension" (p. 37). Zappavigna observes that her definition of "metadiscourse" is "very different to how it has traditionally been used in linguistics where it remains an ambiguous term, particularly in terms of its scope"; she notes that common uses of "metadiscourse" in the field refer to both "discourse about discourse" and "the whole gamut of interpersonal resources available for managing how a text positions itself in relation to its real or potential audience" (p. 37). For Zappavigna, the definition of "metadiscourse" in the context of hashtags captures the range of "second order" meanings of multimodal texts linked by metadata (p. 37). One of the functions she focuses on is the interpersonal function: hashtags allow users to produce evaluative metacommentary; they are used to display affect, assess, and make moral judgments. Put differently, hashtags do ideological as well as interpersonal work on Twitter.

Taking a broader view of metadiscourse, Vásquez (2014) highlights one type of metacommunication in Yelp reviews that functions to link disparate posts, and thereby different posters, together. She explores how online reviewers intertextually refer to (and thus communicate something about) previous reviews by other reviewers. This practice highlights that people participate in the online community both as readers and writers and helps create engagement. Vásquez (2015a:20) further delves into metadiscourse that functions to "include" readers of online reviews "as active participants in the discourse" by examining phrases such as "oh, and don't even get me started" and "let me tell you," pronoun use, discourse markers, and other strategies. Related, Ho (2018) explores metadiscourse that connects online writers to readers, specifically in workplace requests communicated over email. He finds that metadiscursive strategies such as self-mentions (e.g., "I hope," "we all know"), hedges (e.g., "I guess"), and boosters (e.g., "really") accomplish persuasion by appealing to the recipient's reason, constructing the writer's credibility, and playing to the recipient's emotions (*logos*, *ethos*, and *pathos*, in Aristotle's terms).

Tanskanen (2007:89) remarks that participants in online discourse, and especially asynchronous forms of it, may have "better opportunities to reflect and comment on their own and their fellow participants' contributions than participants in real-time discussions" (a point related to Herring's [1999] discussion of textual persistence). Tanskanen examines metapragmatic utterances in online discussion forums, specifically "how participants comment on their own as well as their fellow participants' contributions to the discussion, thereby offering information as to how they would like their contributions to be interpreted and what they perceive as appropriate or inappropriate use of language" (p. 88). The author finds that metapragmatic utterances often occur in sequences and are used to anticipate potential problems, showing an adaptation to their fellow participants' perspectives. They serve as judgments of appropriateness of contributions, such as regarding message length or style, or whether a contributor is qualified to participate. They also play a role in controlling and planning an unfolding discussion (e.g., "I'd like to hear what others think about this"), and in providing feedback on it (e.g., "Interesting and valuable discussion!") (p. 101). Also examining discussion forum discourse,

Myrendal (2019) highlights a metalinguistic activity in which posters "compare and calibrate their individual understandings of key words following disagreement concerning word meaning" (p. 337).

Tanskanen (2007) differentiates between metapragmatic utterances that are intratextual (i.e., commenting on the current message) and those that are intertextual (i.e., commenting on an earlier message). She thus draws important links between intertextuality and metadiscourse. In Tanskanen's data, the majority of metapragmatic utterances were intratextual and initiated on one's own talk; the most typical function she identified was to judge appropriateness. In general, in fact, the posters whose discourse she examined, "seem quite reluctant to comment on their fellow communicators' contributions" in terms of appropriateness (p. 102).

Exploring comments on the appropriateness of others' online contributions in more depth, Boromisza-Habashi and Parks (2014) examine how members of an online academic community (a newsgroup) negotiate the community's boundaries through criticisms of one another's communicative practices ("natural criticism," in Carbaugh's 1989/1990 terms). As part of this, participants use "metadiscursive terms," such as "scholarly debate," "intellectual debate," and "intellectual fascism," to regulate others' forms of participation. The authors also found instances of what Boromisza-Habashi (2013) calls "adversarial mirroring": one poster alleges "fascism," and that action itself is in turn labeled as an act of "fascism" by another poster. Through such "critical metadiscourse," the exchange itself becomes an object of scrutiny; this shift of critique to metacritique, Boromisza-Habashi and Parks (2014:208) argue, helps "make transparent the process of normative regulation in the self-organizing systems of practice that sustain the intelligibility, appropriateness, and accountability of participation in the community of scholars" who subscribe to the newsgroup. Shrikant (2020) examines posts to an academic listserv to investigate how metadiscourse that "overtly comments on communicative actions" is used to manage "relational tensions" in the context of a conflict. Following Buttny (2010), as well as Boromisza-Habashi and Parks (2014), Shrikant demonstrates how metadiscourse is often used to problematize the communicative actions of others; this works to create "consensus about communicative norms and managing relationships" (p. 530).

Lanamäka and Päivärinta (2009), in their analysis of the discourse of two online communities (a support community for Multiple Sclerosis, and a group of contributors to the Finnish language Wikipedia website), identify six patterns of metacommunication online. They found that metacommunication can be used to comment on (1) community-level user roles and relationships, (2) community-level communication practices, (3) metacommunication genres or patterns, (4) individual metacommunicative utterances, (5) genres that organize the site's primary communication, and (6) individual utterances of the primary communication (p. 239). Thus, for example, ordinary users as well as site administrators can metacommunicate about the rules of the online community (pattern 2), about some specific user's utterance (pattern 6), or even about other metacommunication on the site (patterns 3 and 4). Indeed, such patterns can also be identified in other studies reviewed in this section; for example, Tanskanen (2007), Boromisza-Habashi and Parks (2014), and Shrikant (2020) consider communication about specific users' contributions (pattern 6), as well as about community-level communication practices (pattern 2).

Jones, Schieffelin, and Smith (2011) examine instant messaging exchanges among teenagers in which they assess their peers' online (Facebook) practices. Instead of occurring in the form of "reflexively elaborated metadiscourses," the assessments that the authors consider "emerge through and within meta-communicative gossip, that is morally motivated stories about others' online communication" (p. 26). For example, two girls exchange messages about a third girl's "prudish and socially inept" Facebook behavior (p. 33). Users of instant messaging also evaluate others' behaviors on Facebook (and, playfully, their own) by using terms such as "stalking," "lurking," and "creeping" (these three terms all capture the general practice of reading others' pages—sometimes constantly—but rarely or never posting on those pages; in other words, they describe a kind of voyeuristic practice). Jones et al., building on Bauman and Briggs' (1990) discussion of *decontextualization* and *recontexualization*, observe that such gossip is "not only metacommunicative; it is also metasemiotic insofar as participants incorporate materials from one new media channel into another through circulatory processes of decontextualization and recontextualization" (p. 26). Examining discourse produced on Facebook, Bryant, Marmo, and Ramirez (2011:13) use the term "metacommunication" to describe "comments made in regard to other users' wall posts, status updates, and notes," as well as Facebook's "like" feature; these examples exactly map onto what others have explicitly called intertextuality while acknowledging that all of these strategies in some way communicate about communication.

Bryant, Marmo, and Ramirez's (2011) identification of the "like" button as metacommunicative is but one example of a non-linguistic resource being recognized as metacommunicative; other studies that do this include Zappavigna's (2018) identification of the metadiscursive functions of hashtags and Meinhof's (2004) recognition of music and images as resources for metadiscursive commentary in television commercials. In fact, Coupland and Jaworski (2004:32) observe that multimodality is necessarily part of metapragmatics in general, and this idea has emerged across multiple studies. Jaworski and Galasiński (2002), for instance, analyzing British press coverage of U.S. President Clinton's nonverbal behavior during his testimony regarding his relationship with Monica Lewinsky, uncover how Clinton's behaviors are not so much described as they are portrayed through metapragmatic commentary that conveys "a particular version of reality" (p. 644), allowing newspapers "to pass moral judgments" (p. 645). Thus, metapragmatic comments made in text shape interpretations of gestures that are depicted in photographs. Hyland (2017) also notes that metadiscourse extends to the visual realm in the sense that design features guide readers through texts; this is described by Kumpf (2000) as "visual metadiscourse." PowerPoint, as examined by Stoner (2007), provides a clear example of how visual elements of modern communication technology—such as provided templates—metacommunicate in ways that affect interpretation and understanding. This general idea is also captured in Kress and van Leeuwen's (1996) "grammar of visual design," although the authors do not actually use the terms "metacommunication" or "metadiscourse." Kress and van Leeuwen explain, for example, that different modalities convey different levels of credibility—we often trust photographs over words, for instance (whether or not such trust is warranted), and that placement of words on a page (or screen) conveys information about their importance and relationships to other material that appears there.

Moving into the realm of social media and its role in an institutional context, Ehrlich (2021) examines the "meaning potential" that different communicative modes that appear in digital contexts have when recontextualized into the discourse of a rape trial. While she does not use the notion of "metadiscourse" explicitly, Ehrlich finds that photos and videos that were shared on social media that captured the event were given more truth and evidential value by lawyers and witnesses than were text-based instances of digital communication that were exchanged (text messages and tweets). In other words, the modes communicated something about themselves, and semiotic ideologies helped shape the trial's outcome: visual evidence of the victim's inability to consent led to the defendants being found guilty. Thurlow (2017), analyzing news media coverage of the digital media phenomenon of "sexting" as a case study, demonstrates how social meanings about digital discourse are multimodally "metadiscursively framed," thereby constructing ideologies. For example, the images that newspapers use for stories about sexting blur bodies, hide faces, and show silhouettes, creating a sense of illicitness, which is evaluative. Gordon (2019) explores metadiscourse as part of "repair" as it occurs in the comments on health and fitness blogs written by experts (housed on the same website as the discussion boards considered in this book). The study finds that both text and images are evaluated and repaired, and that repair activities, which are inherently metadiscursive, serve as resources for enforcing ideologies or "cultural discourses" (Carbaugh 2007) about expert blogs as a genre. Building on studies such as these, in this study I necessarily attend not only to the language of posts but also graphical and other visual elements.

Metadiscourse in online and other contexts is of interest not only to scholars, but to users of language in a variety of everyday contexts; as Jaworski,

Coupland, and Galasiński (2004b:6) observe, "metalinguistic sensitivity is, in a certain sense, a hallmark of contemporary social life," and they cite Chouliaraki and Fairclough (1999) for the argument that "nowadays people are generally more aware not only of their practices but of the discourses underpinning them," such as what language is understandable as sexist or racist. Related, Craig (2005:661), in his Presidential Address to the International Communication Association, recognizes both a "cultural preoccupation with communication, with its emphasis on problems, breakdowns, and remedies," as well as the pervasiveness of metadiscourse in everyday discourse (e.g., someone uttering in a conversation, "that's a promise"; a public service message indicating to parents, "talk to your kids about drugs"; a newspaper headline that comments, "Health Messages Not Getting Through"). This preoccupation with communication is reflected, as Craig notes, in Cameron's (2000:viii) description of "communication culture," an idea that emphasizes that our culture is "particularly self-conscious and reflexive about communication" and is one "that generates large quantities of metadiscourse about it." It also helps explain, Craig suggests, the existence of communication studies as a large and influential academic field. In daily life, people use metadiscourse for "practical purposes," such as to overcome communicative difficulties or problems (Craig 2005); "meta-communication" is often "called upon in cases of special communicative needs or problems," although it is also "part-and-parcel of everyday communication" (van Leeuwen 2004:118,127); people deploy "metalanguage" "for what might be considered communicative necessities— like retrieving meaning when communication misfires"—but also for arguably more "frivolous" purposes such as in arguing about how to translate the Bible into the made-up alien language Klingon from *Star Trek* (Cameron 2004:312; the Klingon example is discussed in Cameron 1995).

This book sets out to examine metadiscourse as it occurs in online discussion boards centered on weight loss and health. This metadiscourse orients to functions that are more "necessary"—such as achieving shared understanding of a particular lexical item that figures prominently in the discussion—and to those that are perhaps understandable as more "frivolous" (such as engaging in language play—though of course, play is a means of creating relationships and in that sense is not at all "frivolous"). The metadiscursive activities I explore target a range of aspects of communication, from "small" (e.g., a specific word's definition) to "big" (e.g., the role of communication in interpersonal relationships). They also illuminate various "levels" of the "meta" of metadiscourse; for instance, a moderator in her thread-locking message (to shut down a thread's unfolding) produces meta-commentary on the discourse of an individual thread, and posters start a thread that praises the moderator's general thread-locking practices. While I build on a range of studies that examine the "meta" of language and communication and these studies use different terms to do so, in this book, I use "metadiscourse" because it explicitly addresses the structural level I am analyzing (discourse, or language and other semiotic systems in use) and the term has also been associated with the idea that discourse about discourse has practical value: it helps people accomplish everyday sense-making and group building and provides scholars with insight into these phenomena. My analysis shows how metadiscourse, along with the intertextual strategies that facilitate it, accomplishes key activities in an online discussion and support forum where users come together primarily to discuss weight loss and related issues: they define the terms and guidelines for their online discussion, "fix" other participants' posts, cut off communication when it becomes problematic, engage in collaborative problem-solving, and define offline interactional "rules" and relationships as they relate to users' participation on the site and their use of the app. I briefly review studies that have explored the discourse of online support communities next, as my data set is also drawn from one such context, and several existing studies have highlighted metadiscourse.

(Meta)discourse of online support communities

For over two decades, the Internet has been a key resource for people seeking support for diverse issues and challenges, and scholars have considered the discourse of forums focused on motherhood (e.g., Kinloch and Jaworska 2020; Kouper 2010; Matley 2020) and parenthood (e.g., Haugh and Chang 2015), divorce (e.g., Morrow 2012), disabilities (e.g., Finn 1999), bipolar disorder (e.g., Vayreda and Antaki 2009), self-harming behaviors (e.g., Smithson et al. 2011a, 2011b), suicidal ideation (e.g., Lundström 2018), sexual abuse recovery (e.g., Weber 2011), cancer (e.g., Sharf 1997; Demjén 2018), and bone marrow transplantation (e.g., Hamilton 1998). Especially relevant for this book, research has also delved into online discussion boards that give attention to food consumption, including those focused on celiac disease (e.g., Veen, te Molder, Gremmen, and van Woerkum 2010), diabetes (e.g., Armstrong, Koteyko, and Powell 2012; Pounds, Hunt, and Koteyko 2018), eating disorders (e.g, Stommel 2008; Stommel and Koole 2010; Wesemann and Grunwald 2008), veganism (e.g. Sneijder and te Molder 2004), and diet and exercise (e.g., Ba and Wang 2013; Matley 2020).

Studies in this area show how online support is accomplished, as well as how people involved in support discourse construct themselves as a "community," broadly understood. Online discussion boards (and previously, listservs) have been identified as sites where people can work through problems, find and share information, provide mutual support, and engage socially with others with whom they have something in common (whether it be a way of life, a disease, or a traumatic experience). Explorations of the discourse of online support communities reveal that many threads orient toward a problem that is initiated from a thread's beginning—80% in Wesemann and Grunwald's (2008) analysis of a German forum for suffers of bulimia, for example. In their examination of a Taiwanese online discussion board for parents, Haugh and Chang (2015) demonstrate how the meaning of any given "problem presentation" post is itself up for negotiation; for instance, the post could be seen as troubles talk, complaining, or advice seeking (or multiple at once). In this book, in two of the three chapters that focus on the discourse of a single thread, the original poster presents a problem (the other begins with an information-seeking post). Researchers have identified a range of speech acts and activities that characterize the discourse of online peer support boards, including not only complaining, commiserating, and advice seeking and advice giving, but also expressing empathy, suggesting, contradicting, and explaining. Many studies have highlighted advice as a prominent feature of such discourse (e.g., Harrison and Barlow 2009; Kouper 2010; Stommel and Koole 2010; Smithson et al. 2011a; Morrow 2012; Locher 2013).

Existing scholarship also reveals that to partake in online support discourse, participants establish shared understandings and ideologies related to the issue for which they are seeking support (and sometimes, they argue about them). For example, it is through discourse that members of a diabetes support community negotiate what constitutes a dietary lapse (Veen, te Molder, Gremmen, and van Woerkum 2010), that participants in a support forum for those suffering with bipolar disorder establish the meaning of "bipolarity" (Vayreda and Antaki 2009), and that posters to a veganism forum normalize the diet and construct it as a healthy one (Stommel 2008; Stommel and Koole 2010).

Posters also negotiate what constitutes appropriate and productive participation. For moderated boards, moderators play a key role in this. For instance, in the context of a support community for disordered eating, Stommel (2008) shows how, when a new member posts content that is seen as encouraging unhealthy behaviors, a moderator intervenes, and Stommel and Koole (2010) examine how, when another newcomer glamorizes disordered eating, regulars in the forum socialize the newcomer into the group's ideology that disordered eating is an illness. Related, Weber (2011) explores a dispute on a Usenet newsgroup for survivors of sexual abuse that occurred between a newcomer posting for the first time and group regulars, showing how the regulars reinforce the group's organization, appropriate forms of participation, and boundaries in response to the newcomer's attacking of an established member.

A small body of prior research has explicitly addressed metadiscourse in contexts that are, like FIF, online sites for support, though this topic is relatively understudied. Wesemann and Grunwald's (2008) study of the German online bulimia support forum finds that few threads focused on metacommunication, by which they mean the forum communication itself (about 2.5%); interestingly, however, these were read by significantly more users than were threads on other topics. Analyzing online counseling rather than discussion boards, Jager and Stommel (2017) explore how counselors use metacommunication to manage interactional trouble: to attempt to avoid having clients disengage and sign off, counselors self-criticize, question the client's openness to receiving advice and feedback, and explain their institutional responsibilities and tasks. The authors found that these strategies were generally unsuccessful. As mentioned, various studies of online discussion threads have noted that users and moderators comment on aspects of other users' discourse, either implicitly or explicitly, such as by tagging a post as off-topic or by modeling the proper way to communicate. These studies do not integrate theorizing on metadiscourse and intertextuality, however. This book aims to contribute to our understanding of metadiscursive activities and how they are created by way of intertextuality by providing a case study analysis of examples drawn from one website's discussion boards that focus on weight loss and related challenges.

In a number of the studies reviewed here and previously in this chapter, online groupings of people who come together are sometimes described, either very purposefully or more casually, as "(virtual) communities." While in some studies, it is explicated why and how a particular group is best understood as a "community" and what exactly "community" means, in others, this is not made explicit. "Community," while a common everyday notion, is an inherently complex scholarly concept. While its traditional use in sociolinguistics as "speech community" was groundbreaking (e.g., Gumperz 1982; Hymes 1972), the term has also been identified as lacking fluidity, over-centering norms, and marginalizing people at the community's borders (as noted by Eckert 2006). "Community of practice" (Lave and Wenger 1991) has been brought into sociolinguistics as an alternative (by Eckert and McConnell-Ginet 1992; see also Bucholtz 1999, among others). Eckert and McConnell-Ginet (1992:464) define a community of practice as "an aggregate of people who come together around mutual engagement in an endeavor"; through a shared set of practices, participants create the community. In this study, I draw on this notion while also considering Herring's (2004) outlining of the basic criteria to consider in identifying online communities (in line with Stommel and Koole's [2010] approach to an eating disorders forum). Herring (2004) outlines the criteria as follows:

(1) active, self-sustaining participation; a core of regular participants
(2) shared history, purpose, culture, norms and values
(3) solidarity, support, reciprocity
(4) criticism, conflict, means of conflict resolution
(5) self-awareness of group as an entity distinct from other groups
(6) emergence of roles, hierarchy, governance, rituals (p. 355)

Participation on the FIF discussion boards meets the "community of practice" definition: it involves a group of people who come together in the shared endeavor of exchanging information and support online as they (presumably) engage in offline practices to lose weight and improve their diet and exercise routines. This is meaningful to my analysis in that posters use a shared set of practices (metadiscursive practices, to be specific) to facilitate engagement in the community's shared endeavor. While the criteria Herring (2004) identifies are also present—for example, there is ample evidence of solidarity and there is evidence of shared norms—worth pointing out is that "community" in digital discourse contexts may be extremely fluid: people may come together into fleeting "light communities" (Blommaert 2019), they may briefly align into relations of "ambient affiliation" (Zappavigna 2011), or some group of people may be best understood as existing in networked relations around an individual person who is its central node (Seargeant, Tagg, and Ngampramuan 2012). Further, while an online community of practice might look a bit different than what we think of as a prototypical offline community of practice, offline communities too may also be more "transient" in nature (Mortensen 2017). That said, all communities of practice are distinctive, including the one providing the discourse I examine. I describe my data in more detail, and my methods, in the next section.

DATA AND METHODS

The data

"FriendInFitness.com" is the pseudonym for a website affiliated with a popular calorie-tracking weight loss application I call FriendInFitness (or FIF for short; the website's real name is often abbreviated by users). It is similar to other applications and websites related to weight and health, such as DailyBurn, Lose It!, SparkPeople, and MyPlate. FIF is very popular; as of late 2014, around the time when I did most of my data collection, the app reportedly had over 75 million users (as of 2020, 200 million users were reported, although it is hard to know how many users are active at a given time). Use of the app and website is free and available to anyone with Internet access. To facilitate calorie tracking, the website offers nutritional information for thousands of foods, along with calculations for calorie expenditure for various forms of exercise. It also has a page dedicated to blogs on topics including individual success stories, fitness tips, recipes and meal planning, and new research findings related to diet and exercise. There are places to shop and to find apps that can be used in conjunction with FIF. My focus is on the community-oriented feature of the website: the discussion boards (which can be accessed on the website by clicking on a button labeled "Community").

Originally offering only English boards, FIF discussion boards are now available in multiple languages, including French, Swedish, Spanish, and Korean. The English-language boards, the source of the data I analyze, include a range of intersecting topics about health, food, and exercise, including "General Diet and Weight Loss Help," "Goal: Maintaining Weight," "Goal: Gaining Weight," "Food and Nutrition," "Motivation and Support," and "Recipes." There are also boards that are more socially oriented, such as one for new users to get acquainted ("Introduce Yourself") and two for general socializing ("Chit-Chat" and "Fun & Games"). Thousands of threads appear across these boards, and participants appear to be from around the world, with many, it seems, in the United States and the United Kingdom. Users begin a new thread in the appropriate board and give it a title; all responses are posted sequentially in the order that they appear (newest on the bottom).

While anyone can read the discussion boards, to post, a user must join as a member (there are free and paid memberships available). As is typical on many discussion boards, users of the FIF boards agree to follow a set of "Community Guidelines" regarding appropriate conduct, including not flame-baiting or trolling (posting provocative posts intended to start emotionally loaded arguments), not using vulgar or sexually explicit language, and not promoting potentially unsafe weight loss products or procedures. Volunteer moderators, of which there were about six at any given time during my data collection period, help enforce these guidelines by giving warnings to violators of the policies, banning users who do not heed warnings, and locking (or disabling) discussion threads that have degenerated into trolling, personal attacks, and so on (thread locking will be discussed in more detail in Chapter 4).

Methods and ethical considerations

The data I collected and examine here were readable by anyone before they were included in this book. In other words, I analyze only publicly available discourse drawn from messages that are posted in the public areas of the FIF website. When users register with FIF so that they can post to these boards, they acknowledge that the boards are public; in multiple places on the site users are reminded to exercise caution in deciding what information they wish to disclose, and that once something becomes available on the Internet, it is nearly impossible to locate and take down all iterations of it later (in this way, the site shows awareness of the "persistence" [Herring 1999] of online discourse and acknowledges that this is something of which users should be aware).

While the users of the website, in registering to participate, necessarily acknowledge the site's terms and conditions (such as those above), the issue of how online data are used for research purposes is a complex (and interesting) one. An early cautionary tale comes from a Facebook study called "Taste, Ties, and Time" (N.A. 2008), which is discussed by Zimmer (2010). As Zimmer points out, the study longitudinally collected personal (though publicly available) information on individual Facebook users who attended the same college, and it made the resulting data set public on an open-source research data repository. It did not take long for interested parties to figure out which college these Facebook users attended; because the data set included information about each participant's race, ethnicity, hometown state, and gender, it was even possible to identify individuals (the data set is no longer publicly available). Since this time, there has been increased attention to online research ethics, but the issue still remains complex, as is apparent in the two most recent sets of recommendations from the Ethics Working Committee of the Association of Internet Researchers (presented in Markham and Buchanan [2012] and franzke, Bechmann, Zimmer, Ess, and the Association of Internet Researchers [2020]). For example, franzke et al. (2020:7) note that younger people tend to expect that "public or quasi-public" forums were somehow private, even though these expectations do not match the "technical realities." That said, the opinion of the committee is that it is generally appropriate to analyze publicly available online communication among participants who have been informed by the platform that their interactions are public. This guidance and perspective seems to have shaped the data collection of numerous studies, including Gavin, Rodham, and Poyer (2008), Stommel and Koole (2010), and Veen, te Molder, Gremmen, and van Woerkum (2010).

Existing studies have analyzed verbatim extracts from online support websites regarding a range of health issues, including veganism, celiac disease, and eating disorders. This book's study of one website's weight loss discussion boards fits neatly into such research; nonetheless, because "[p]rivacy needs to be understood as contextual and emergent and we need to evaluate each case in its own merits" (Deumert 2014:30), for this project I submitted my research proposal to my university's Institutional Review Board and received exemption of my study. As part of this, I indicated that I would observe but not participate in the boards or interact in any way with posters (which would constitute intervention with human subjects). This is a common methodological choice; for instance, Veen et al.'s (2010:34) examination of an online support group for celiac disease collected data "without the use of methods such as interviews or surveys in which the researcher necessarily interacts with the participants in one way or another." Some scholars take an integrated approach; for example, Stommel and Koole (2010) gained informed consent from the administrators of the site they considered and also contacted posters if they were going to use word-for-word material from their posts, and if participants' contact information was available. However, the authors also used pseudonyms and modified private information (such as a user's exact location and age), and the dates of posting, in order to create greater anonymity. While

Vásquez (2015b:78) points out that to study intertextuality in new media contexts, it can be useful to have "a sustained period of participant observation of the site/community," and while this is undoubtedly true, I chose only to partake in the "observation" element so as to have minimal effects on the community itself, in line with many other studies.

Despite the consensus that analyzing publicly available online discourse is an acceptable approach—and thus that the potential benefits for our understanding of online communication outweigh the (minimal) risks to those who post online and thereby directly or indirectly agree to take part in a publicly observable conversation—some researchers, such as Finn (1999), Locher (2006), Gavin et al. (2008), Vayreda and Antaki (2009), and Morrow (2012), have taken steps to reduce the already very small likelihood that participants in such discussions might one day encounter their own typed words in a scholarly article or book and feel uncomfortable to find their usernames present. Such steps include using a pseudonym for the website, using pseudonyms in place of usernames, and not using any screen shots or photos of users in published work. I incorporated all of these additional safeguards into my study as well (though this decision is not unproblematic; see, e.g., Kurtz e. al.'s [2017] discussion of anonymizing weight loss blogs). Given these safeguards and the fact that the website makes it abundantly clear to users that the data are public, I did not seek permission from the website or its users to analyze the discourse of the discussion boards. This (in a way) arguably also further protects the participants: as has been observed by Finn (1999) and Gavin et al. (2008), an unobtrusive approach does not interfere with the ongoing provision of support in the forums, and as Sixsmith and Murray (2001:425) remark, while some scholars view seeking permission to analyze online discourse (even publicly available discourse) as preferred, others argue that this can create new ethical problems, notably the possible disruption of the processes of the group whose discourse is under study. Despite my consideration of all of these issues, and being generally comfortable with my decision-making, this is not, of course, the only way my data could have been collected and presented in this book (or even the best way). As Stommel and de Rijk (2021) recently point out, ethics around collection and use of publicly available online data for academic purposes should be an ongoing discussion among discourse analysts, and ideally this discussion should do more to involve perspectives beyond the researchers', such as those of participants and journal editors.

To analyze my data, I draw on Herring's (2004) conceptualization of computer-mediated discourse analysis (CMDA), which involves bringing theories and methods from across approaches to discourse analysis and sociolinguistics into online contexts, being certain to pay special attention to the affordances of the medium and platform, including the various semiotic resources available (such as text, images, and sound). The term "affordances" can be traced back to Gibson (1979), who observed that all objects enable people to identify possibilities for action (see Hutchby 2001, Deumert 2014, and Ledin and Machin 2018 for discussions); Ledin and Machin (2018) point out that semiotic resources carry with them ideas and assumptions that also mold their use and meaning. Hutchby (2001) indicates that the influence of the medium on the interaction—how it shapes what people can do—should be treated as an empirical issue. Deumert (2014:36) states it this way: "the design of the platform and its technological affordances do not determine practices." However, it certainly may influence them, as she explains, such as by putting "multimodality at one's fingertips" (p. 79), by facilitating audience participation through likes and dislikes (p. 81), and by giving users the ability to "reach thousands of people across the world within hours" (p. 87). Given the need to study online discourse empirically, including how affordances— and the various semiotic resources users have access to—are mobilized by users, my overall approach is grounded in interactional sociolinguistics (e.g., Gumperz 2015; Tannen 2005), an approach that "is founded on the convictions that language can only be studied in context and that it is constitutive of context" (Gordon and Tannen 2021:181). In line with the nature of the data, I integrate concepts from the study of visual communication (e.g., Kress and van Leeuwen 2006; Ledin and Machin 2018) and additionally draw on concepts and ideas from across approaches to the study of discourse and communication that highlight culture (e.g., ethnography of communication, cultural discourse analysis), discourse structure and sequence (e.g., conversation analysis, narrative analysis), and power (e.g., critical discourse analysis).

My data sampling technique also follows Herring's CMDA approach. Herring suggests that selection of data can be, depending on one's interests and purpose, random, by theme, by time, by phenomenon, by individual or group, or by convenience. For this study of intertextuality and metadiscourse, I chose my data primarily by theme and by phenomenon. Sampling by theme occurred when I analyzed one discussion thread, in its entirety, that is focused on a particular topic. This allowed me to explore how meaning-making unfolds on that particular thread, how disparate posts on the thread are interconnected by users, and the role of metadiscursive activities in the context of the thread. This technique is used in Chapter 2, which examines a thread on the topic of "clean eating," and Chapters 5 and 6, which investigate individual threads wherein participants discuss some original poster's problem (a difficult encounter with a doctor in one, and a disagreement with a partner in another). I also selected my data by phenomenon, which means I looked across threads to identify multiple instances of one kind of metadiscursive action or activity, to get an in-depth understanding of how that action or activity works on the discussion boards. Chapter 3, on the activity of "fixing" another person's post, and Chapter 4, which investigates how discussion board moderators—and one in particular—"locks" (or makes it impossible to add any more posts to) threads, use the sampling-by-phenomenon technique.

PREVIEW OF THE CHAPTERS

Chapter 2 examines one thread started by a poster who wondered about existing studies that compare a "clean" eating diet with diets that are not "clean," and who remained active throughout the thread's unfolding. In this thread, posters discuss what the term "clean" eating means (very roughly: eating food that is not at all, or is minimally, processed, but this is up for debate), and my analysis demonstrates how, in so doing, they not only (re)define an expression and practice that is important to (some) members of their community but also (re)construct the informal guidelines of their particular discussion (and in the context of the boards' Community Guidelines). The chapter thus shows how participants use various intertextual strategies to engage in the metadiscursive activities of defining "clean" eating and food and of discerning appropriate content and form of posts to the thread. These strategies include quotation marks, the boards' quotation function, paraphrase and word repetition, deictic pronouns and symbols, labels for words (such as "vague") and speech acts (such as "bullying"), speech acts themselves (notably, complimenting and thanking), and image-based content (a photo, a GIF, an emoji). In other words, the chapter demonstrates how various forms of intertextuality are mobilized across one discussion thread as participants create and engage in important metadiscursive activities: they grapple with a concept that holds importance for many (but not all) users and negotiate what constitutes a useful and appropriate contribution to the particular discussion. What is more, they comment on these activities, adding another layer of metadiscourse.

In Chapter 3 I consider multiple examples from across discussion threads of a different metadiscursive activity: where one poster "fixes" another's post and marks the action as "fixed," as in "I fixed it for you." My analysis demonstrates that "fixing" another person's post is a highly structured online action that can be characterized by a pattern I summarize as *reproduce—replace—refer—remark*. To reproduce some prior post, or part of a prior post, a poster uses the quotation function of the discussion boards. To replace, the poster adjusts some aspect of the prior post via font manipulations (such as using strikethrough or bold) and/or by adding or deleting part of the post's text. To refer, posters use deictics—the caret symbol (^) and/or the pronoun "it"—which connect, via pointing, the fixer's text to the post being fixed. To remark, a poster produces metadiscourse that names what has taken placed (e.g., "fixed" or "fixed it"). Each part of this pattern is intertextual, serving to link online posts to prior posts, and text to prior text. The chapter shows how "fixing" has social and relational consequences on these boards: the trope serves to assist other posters regarding posting image-related content, to construct disagreement, and to joke and play. It is identifiable as a highly routinized practice in the community of practice.

Chapter 4 examines discussion board moderator participation, which has to date been understudied. I demonstrate how one moderator in particular accomplishes a single action across multiple threads: how she announces that she is "locking" a thread, or terminating the discussion by not allowing any more posts because one or more of the "official" rules or guidelines of the boards—such as not personally attacking another poster—has been violated by one or more users. My analysis shows the role of intertextuality in accomplishing the face-threatening metadiscursive action of announcing a thread's locking, specifically in how the moderator uses the boards' standard letter-like template, adjusts the text of that template, and uses GIFs in creative ways. My focus on how this moderator completes this administrative task using all of these strategies demonstrates how she simultaneously entertains users and constructs her own identity as creative, clever, and knowledgeable about pop culture. Thus, the face-threatening metadiscursive action, via uses of intertextuality, is framed as playful and builds solidarity among members of the group.

Whereas Chapters 2, 3, and 4 explore discussion board posters' discourse about the online discourse of the boards, Chapters 5 and 6 explore their online discourse about offline communication and relationships. Chapter 5 focuses on one thread wherein participants collaboratively accomplish problem-solving regarding an offline interaction reported by an original poster who describes how her doctor commented on her body weight in a way that she found inappropriate; she shares her story on the thread, seeking encouragement and support, and contributes repeated follow-up posts as the thread unfolds. I demonstrate how participants accomplish a "problem-solving activity" (Ochs, Smith, and Taylor 1989) in an online context. In working to address the original poster's problem, which entails producing discourse about discourse, participants draw on specific intertextual linking strategies: they pose information-seeking questions, paraphrase and reframe others' discourse, tell matching stories, create "constructed dialogue" (Tannen 2007b), use the boards' quotation function, point (such as through the "^" symbol), and give advice. Through these strategies, the participants collaboratively evaluate and make sense of offline communication—the original poster's described encounter, but also their own similar encounters with healthcare providers. They thereby accomplish online support provision for the woman who had the difficult interaction, while also producing metadiscourse that lends insights into how they expect doctors and patients to behave in order to have successful communication about body weight.

Chapter 6 investigates one thread started by a poster who reports having had an argument with her partner and asks how she should deal with the fact that he does not like her using FIF, as he finds it makes her "obsessive."

Posters to the thread discuss how use of the app to record one's food and exercise, as well as use of the online discussion boards, may influence offline communication with intimate partners. While, like Chapter 5, this chapter addresses a single thread that focuses largely on offline communication, it differs in several important ways: the thread examined in this chapter consists of discourse about intimate (couples') communication and relationships, the original poster does not contribute to the thread after posting her original message, and any "problem-solving" present is backgrounded to the activity of posters advancing competing ideologies and arguing about them. Focusing on how the discourse of the thread is intertextually linked to broader cultural assumptions via indexing (Ochs 1992, 1993), and drawing on theorizing on communication as a cultural phenomenon (e.g., Carbaugh 2007; Tannen 1994), my analysis reveals not only expectations about how partners should try to create a balance between using the app and discussion board on the one hand, and interacting with their partners on the other, but also more general expectations about communication in intimate relationships. In other words, I show how participants metadiscursively define and negotiate their media ideologies (Gershon 2010) in relation to ideologies about "communication" as a cultural category (Katriel and Philipsen 1981) as well as "interpersonal ideologies" (Fitch 1998). Specifically, posts collectively suggest that digital communication media are (or can be) potentially disruptive to private, face-to-face talk; that partners' different understandings regarding a single digital media technology can lead to interactional trouble; and that apps (re)animate tensions inherent in all relationships (which are realized in discourse). These in turn point to and (re)create three ideologies that I describe as cultural discourses (Carbaugh 2007) or Master Narratives (Tannen 2008): quality time and communication (that should not be infused with technology) are important to partner relationships; partners should communicate somewhat openly about their technology use; and partners should, in their relationships, strike a balance between autonomy and connection (as successful weight loss requires both self-focus and support from others, both online and offline).

In Chapter 7, I summarize the findings of my research and loop back to my larger goal of illuminating how intertextuality and metadiscourse are linked both in empirical online data and theoretically. I first discuss the range of intertextual linking strategies uncovered by this research—ranging from the very "small" and concrete (e.g., a deictic pronoun) to the quite big and abstract (e.g., indexing cultural beliefs), from the textual to the multimodal—that people draw on in engaging in metadiscourse in the context of online discussion board interaction. Next, I review the functions that these metadiscursive activities serve on the boards, such as defining, fixing, locking, solving, and indexing. Finally, I reflect on how, in investigating "intertextuality 2.0"—intertextuality in the context of "discourse 2.0" or the "discourse of Web 2.0"—this study has benefited from stitching together not only intertextuality and metadiscourse, but also other concepts and ideas from across disciplines and approaches to discourse, and how I hope it may contribute to creating intertextual connections between them.

CHAPTER 2

"Most 'evidence' that people post has nothing to do with 'clean' eating"

Negotiating word meanings and appropriate thread participation

In interactions among members of online (as in offline) communities of practice, people negotiate meanings, relationships, identities, and appropriate communicative practices. As discussed in the previous chapter, for example, an important norm regarding participation on an online discussion forum for people who suffer from disordered eating is orienting to anorexia as a disease (not as a glamorous lifestyle choice) (Stommel and Koole 2010); to group members, "anorexia" is a term that signals an illness. While such norms are sometimes enforced by moderators (as Stommel 2008 demonstrates and I investigate in Chapter 4), community members also enforce what it means to engage appropriately, as well as what the words and phrases they use mean. In this chapter, I examine posts drawn from one FriendInFitness discussion thread to demonstrate how participants mobilize intertextuality to negotiate both what it means to engage in "clean" eating, and what constitutes a productive contribution to their unfolding thread on the topic introduced by the original poster: research studies conducted about "clean" eating. Analysis illuminates how intertextual linking strategies facilitate engagement in specific metadiscursive activities—to problematize and define meanings of lexical items and to negotiate the appropriateness of particular posts and kinds of posts—while also providing an introduction into the community's discourse in that the notion of "clean" eating emerges across multiple threads on the boards and appears in data extracts analyzed in other chapters of this book.

Intertextuality 2.0. Cynthia Gordon, Oxford University Press. © Oxford University Press 2023.
DOI: 10.1093/oso/9780197642689.003.0002

When I first came across the idea of "clean" eating and foods on the FIF discussion boards, it seemed to me (based on uses of the term there and my exposure to it in other contexts such as on the menu of the fast-casual restaurant Panera) that it referred to generally (or perhaps always?) avoiding highly processed foods that are produced in mass quantities (such as a shelf-stable fried apple pie) and instead eating foods that are closer to nature (such as a raw organic apple). While this basic definition is fairly accepted as a starting point on the discussion boards, the idea of "clean" eating and food is continually up for discussion and debate there (seemingly to some users' chagrin and others' enjoyment). In fact, elsewhere on the Internet, ample evidence that the term is hotly contested also appears: articles include descriptions of it as a ruse people "fell for" (Wilson 2017), as a "sham" (Gillison 2018), and even as "BS" (bull shit) (London 2017); at the same time, a magazine exists that is entirely dedicated to it (*Clean Eating*), in 2016 clean eating was identified by *Today's Dietitian* as one of the major nutrition trends of the year (Thalheimer 2016), and advice on how to practice clean eating appears on multiple websites (e.g., Applegate 2016). On the FIF discussion boards, too, "clean eating" is deemed unclear and undefinable by some; as an accepted lifestyle by others; and as a harmful, moralistic notion by still others.

In the thread I examine, which involved 81 posters, the person who started the thread, or the original poster (commonly referred to as "OP" or "the OP" on the boards, a term I will also use), inquired about existing research studies regarding the benefits of "clean" versus "unclean" eating in terms of health and weight loss. In discussing this topic, the participants use intertextual strategies to communicate about not only what "clean" eating means, but also how to engage in discussion of this topic, given the particular focus as laid out by the OP (on scholarly research studies comparing "clean" and "unclean" diets) as well as the Community Guidelines provided for the FIF discussion boards (involving, for example, a prohibition on personal attacks). My analysis reveals that intertextual strategies and resources used by posters include quotation marks, the boards' quotation function, repetition of words from and paraphrase of other posts, deictic pronouns and symbols, references to language made as it is evaluated using adjectives (such as "vague") and speech act labels (such as "bullying"), references made in speech acts (notably, complimenting, thanking, and criticizing) that are directed toward discourse and discourse producers, and image-based resources such as emojis and GIFs. I thus demonstrate how participants take advantage of intertextuality-facilitating affordances of the medium and of language to grapple with a concept that holds importance for many (not all) posters, and to negotiate simultaneously what constitutes a useful and appropriate contribution to this discussion in terms of the specific thread focus, and also the wider community guidelines regarding civil dialogue. Participants thereby collaboratively negotiate and (re)affirm meanings of terms (that are key to the discussion), practices (that animate the discussion), and understandings of productive community engagement.

THE CHALLENGE OF DEFINING "CLEAN" EATING AND FOODS

Before turning to this chapter's data and analysis, I note that the discussions of the term "clean" regarding eating and foods serve as an example of the broader phenomenon of people co-constructing food-related meanings in everyday discourse. For instance, numerous studies emphasize that what tastes good, what is "normal" to eat, and what is healthful are negotiated moment by moment in social interaction, in particular during family mealtimes (e.g., Ochs, Pontecorvo, and Fasulo 1996; Wiggins, Potter, and Wildsmith 2001; Wiggins and Potter 2003; Wiggins 2004a, 2004b, 2013, 2014; Mondada 2009; Paugh and Izquierdo 2009; Aronsson and Gottzén 2011; Bova and Arcidiacono 2014). In an early and influential study in this area, Ochs, Pontecorvo, and Fasulo (1996) examine dinner table talk among middle-class American and Italian families and uncover how cultural food preferences are constructed. In the American families, for instance, parents affirmed the idea that children's food preferences differ from adults', whereas Italian parents emphasized that each person has individual food preferences, regardless of age. Further, in the American families the nutritional value of food was highlighted, whereas Italian families focused on food as pleasure above all else. Wiggins, Potter, and Wildsmith (2001:8), analyzing dinner table conversations among three families in the United Kingdom, observe that mealtime is "an interactive event" for family members, and that "there is a strong sense of involvement with each other's actions," including actions related to "urging, offering, and negotiating" food for consumption. In engaging in such actions, "it is not only the act of eating that is being negotiated, but also the nature of food *itself*" (p. 9, emphasis in the original). Thus, one young teenager and her mother discuss whether a food item that is part of their dinner—salmon—is enjoyable (the daughter describes it as "foul"); this constructs the nature of the food item itself while also serving to negotiate whether the daughter should be held accountable for eating it. In a similar spirit, Backett-Milburn, Wills, Roberts, and Lawton (2010) explore parental attempts to control teenagers' tastes (such as encouraging them to appreciate "adult" and "cosmopolitan" foods) and eating practices (such as limiting snacking) among middle-class Scottish families. Collectively, such studies suggest that parents endeavor to shape children's food preferences during family dinners from the time that children are young to at least their teenage years. Wiggins (2016) traces food preferences even earlier in child development, to interactions that occur during weaning. All of these studies support the idea that the meaning of foods, and consumption preferences and choices, are discursively constructed, which is an important underlying tenet for my exploration of how online discussion thread participants negotiate what constitutes "clean" eating and foods.

The meanings of foods and norms of eating are constructed in other, non-family contexts as well, such as in schools, physicians' offices, and (social) media. For example, Karrebæk (2012) examines food socialization in interactions between a Danish primary school teacher (who belongs to the ethnic majority) and her minority (e.g., Turkish and Moroccan) students (ages 5–7) regarding the foods packed in their lunchboxes from home. The author finds that the teacher treats traditional Danish food (especially rye bread) as healthful and superior to the foods in the minority children's lunchboxes, whether those foods have been packed for reasons of cultural or personal preference. In addition, the students negotiate the morality of their food choices among themselves and show evidence of having been socialized into the idea that traditional Danish food is superior; for example, a child who brings white bread in her lunch hides it under the table when she sees the teacher approaching, and another student chastises her, "where is your rye bread?" (Karrebæk 2012:14). Through their talk about food, the children and their teacher negotiate not only which students are engaged in nutritionally sound eating practices, but also which are properly Danish (and this simultaneously serves as a mechanism by which minority background students are marginalized).

Meanings of food are also constructed and negotiated in medical encounters and communication about such encounters (such as in post-appointment interviews and in focus groups). Studies by Hamilton (2003) and Koenig, Dutta, Kandula, and Palaniappan (2012), for example, uncover difficulties that patients with diabetes have complying to dietary restrictions and find that physicians typically fail to understand the meanings of foods in their patients' lives. This is because physicians commonly do not (have/make the time to) learn about the obstacles patients face, such as personal attributes, social/situational factors, and culturally shaped dietary values. Instead, physicians focus on, to use Koenig et al.'s (2012:822) words, the "biomedical dietary values of food." Put differently, there is an absence of shared meanings regarding food and food consumption in communication between patients and physicians.

Meanings of food and eating practices are additionally constructed in media discourse, such as in advertisements, commercials, and newspaper and magazine articles, as well as in social media contexts such as Twitter, Facebook, and online discussion boards; this includes what it means to eat in positive, nourishing, and socially appropriate ways. For example, Fuller, Briggs, and Dillon-Sumner's (2013) analysis of articles in *Women's Health* and *Men's Health* magazines found that while both women and men are urged to control their eating, gendered ideologies around eating practices are conveyed: for women, good foods are those that lead to weight loss and improved appearance; for men, good foods are those that lead to muscle development and improved performance. Linn (2004) discusses how marketing and advertising targeted at children construct certain foods, such as candies and breakfast cereals, not only as fun and entertaining, but also as a means of personal empowerment: ads and commercials send messages to children that eating a particular candy, for instance, is not only fun, but also an experience of freedom from parental control. Linn thus suggests that children encourage parents (at times via throwing or threatening to throw tantrums) to purchase such items not only because they enjoy sugar, but also because of the treats' larger social meanings. Food-related meanings and ideologies are also created on health makeover reality television (e.g., Gordon 2013b, 2015b), such as by equating certain foods (e.g., leafy greens and tofu)—along with certain (slim) body types (see Gordon 2011)—with moral superiority and upward social mobility, while other foods (such as pizza and ice cream) and body types (overweight bodies) are associated with moral and social failure.

Especially relevant for my analysis in this chapter, negotiation about the meanings of foods, along with the meanings of words, also occurs in online contexts. Sneijder and te Molder's (2004, 2006) analyses of veganism forum discourse show how posters use language to create meanings, negotiate morality and accountability, and construct identities. In the discourse the authors consider, health problems are not ascribed to a vegan diet or vegan food items, but rather to individuals' bad choices, such as not choosing to eat a variety of vegetables. In this way, users defend veganism against real and perceived critiques; veganism is normalized. Sneijder and te Molder (2006) investigate online email discussion threads among people who enjoy food and reveal how participants portray themselves as "gourmets" by claiming knowledge about what good food entails, rather than simply stating what they like. Zappavigna's (2014) corpus analysis of tweets about coffee shows how "ambient affiliation" is accomplished by way of the stances they take up toward the drink (as part of experiencing a good life versus as a necessity to get through the difficulties of life). Myrendal's (2019) study of online discussion forum discourse, while not considering food-related communication, reveals how negotiations about word meanings that emerge from disagreements serve as a resource for restoring intersubjectivity among participants.

One way of describing and evaluating foods is through use of the term "clean," which is prominent in contemporary communication in various contexts, a focus of this chapter, and a site for disagreement. Studies have revealed "clean" eating to be a problematic concept, with links to ideas about health, morality, privilege, and also disordered eating. For example, Musolino, Warin, Wade, and Gilchrist's (2015) analysis of interviews conducted with 25 Australian women who practiced some form of disordered eating revealed that four of the interviewees identified with characteristics of clean eating and pursued practices they identified as "clean eating" and "raw food diets," associating these with purity and cleanliness. More broadly, practicing "clean eating" and related restrictive diets reflects a trend or "new food regime" that has emerged (Musolino et al. 2015:19); by describing their engagement with "pure" and "healthy" eating, women (and men) are able to justify disordered eating practices. Similarly, Cinquergrani and Brown's (2018:9) ethnographic study of the online behavior of 30 people who broadly fit into the category of sufferers of "orthorexia nervosa," a disordered form of eating that involves only eating "clean" or "proper" foods, found that "eating clean," for these individuals, "is considered a symbol of good living, and has become a means of self-governing." Further, it is linked to ideas about self-worth, as well as to socioeconomic status and other aspects of identity; for example, as one participant noted, "there is a harsh form of economic exclusion that says that someone who can't afford wheatgrass or spirulina can never truly be 'well,'" and most sufferers are women (Cinquergrani and Brown 2018:14). "Clean eating" has also been found to be presented as a prominent example of healthful eating on Instagram, an influential platform for young people, though it remains ill defined in that context, too (Pilař et al. 2021).

Despite these fascinating findings, there is a lack of studies in discourse analysis that focus specifically on "clean" eating and food. The only one I was able to identify is by Smith (2020); she explores how internationally known food writer and popular television chef Nigella Lawson rejects this notion in her cookbooks. The reason Lawson has to do this is to be in dialogue with circulating ideologies about clean eating propagated in magazines, online, and so on. For example, Smith (2020:5) points out that in *Simply Nigella*, Lawson (2015:lx) explicitly states that "food is not dirty," thereby pointing out the morality-laden nature of the term "clean" (posters to the FIF thread I examine also point this out). Thus, when Lawson uses ingredients that are elsewhere widely touted as "clean," such as gluten-free flour and coconut oil, she discursively accounts for this by explaining that a gluten-free recipe was developed for a guest who has celiac disease, or that coconut oil was used due to its taste. She thereby attempts to avoid the morality-related meanings and "health-giving promises" of "clean" eating but simultaneously in some way normalizes the existence of it as a practice (Smith 2020:7).

In summary, existing research demonstrates that, to use Wiggins et al.'s (2001:9) words, negotiating "the nature of food" is "a continuous process, requiring the joint efforts of the individuals involved." This negotiation, which takes place in interactions both face-to-face and online, is shaped by broader sociocultural ideologies. "Clean" eating is an uneasy notion. It is thus not surprising that the term itself sometimes becomes a topic of discussion among those interested in food and health, as in the thread I examine.

THE DATA: " 'CLEAN' VS. 'UNCLEAN' EATING STUDIES?"

To explore the collaborative (and at times highly conflictual) construction of "clean eating" as well as of appropriate thread participation in a discussion on this topic, I examine one discussion thread titled "'Clean' vs. 'unclean' eating studies?" This thread, appearing on the "Food and Nutrition" discussion board, consists of 283 posts that were posted by 81 users. The first 281 posts occurred in a span of three days; the last two appeared about two weeks later. The OP (original poster), a woman whose pseudo-username is CuddleSmash, is very highly involved in the discussion, posting 52 times. Five other users posted between 15 and 22 times on this thread; 7 users posted between 5 and 9 times; 18 posted 2 or 3 times; and the remaining 50 users posted once each. I sometimes was able to discern posters' gender presentation using information gleaned from usernames, photos, and contents of posts (where users sometimes directly mention their own gender identities), helping me choose appropriate pronouns when discussing specific posts.

Evidence of the contentious nature of "clean eating" on the FIF website extends beyond the thread I analyze to others that address this topic in some way. For example, in a thread called "What is clean eating," the first response is "No such thing." A thread called "Clean eating with toddlers" includes the observation that "Clean eating doesn't have a singular definition which is why it is such an unhelpful term." A poster to a thread called "Clean eating help" remarks, "oh dear. You don't know what you stepped into . . .," and another sarcastically comments, "These threads always go well." Posters to these various threads acknowledge the fraught nature of discussions around "clean" foods and eating, and it is evident that metadiscourse surfaces from the outset (with uses of words such as "term," "definition," and "thread"). The thread I chose for analysis begins with an original post that explicitly calls attention to problems with the term and outlines what kinds of posts are desired; the ensuing thread is metadiscursive from the beginning. I turn to the original post now.

THE INITIAL POST AND THE OVERALL SHAPE OF THE THREAD

The thread begins as shown in excerpt (1a), in the initial post by CuddleSmash wherein she highlights the troublesome nature of the term "clean" but also makes clear that she is interested in learning about any existing research studies that compare "clean" versus "unclean" diets. This provides the groundwork for the thread that unfolds. The post also shows how uses of intertextual linking strategies—specifically quotation marks, labels for different kinds of contributions to the thread that she would like (versus what she expects), and a GIF drawn from a television show—begin the metadiscursive activities undertaken in the thread.

For this and the following extracts, in parentheses after the poster's pseudo-username I list the post number; I gave each post a unique number starting with 1, to give a sense of where the post occurred in the overall thread. Paragraph breaks, spellings, and punctuation appear in the original;

line breaks are dictated by this book's page width; and line numbers have been added for ease of analysis. Online, the poster's profile picture and name appear, along with their designation ("Member" in this thread; "Moderator" is also an option) and the number of posts they have made to date on the left (these are not shown here). The text of their post appears to the right of this information.

In the text of the original post, below, "macros" refers to macronutrients (such as protein, fat, and carbohydrates) and "bro-science" is in-group jargon referring to ideas about nutrition and health typically held by men who are bodybuilders (i.e., those focused on building muscle for strength and/or aesthetic reasons). "ETA" refers to "edited to add," which is used here and in other posts to tack something onto a message as a sort of "PS." CuddleSmash titles the thread "'Clean' vs. 'unclean' eating studies?"

(1a) CuddleSmash (post 1)

1   So I'm genuinely curious. Are there any studies out there on clean vs. unclean diets? For
2   example, something on groups consuming the same number of calories and macros, but
3   one group eating clean with the other eats processed foods? I've been unable to locate
4   such a study, and I'm deeply curious as to how much difference it actually makes. ETA:
5   Including a definition of "clean" in the study would also be very helpful, as that seems to
6   vary wildly from person to person.
7
8   I realize that many people feel very passionately about this issue, and that's fine. I have a
9   thick skin, and am willing to be swayed by facts, although I know there will be plenty of
10 bro-science and hyperbole to sort through.
11
12 Thanks in advance!

CuddleSmash ends her post with a GIF; however, before examining that, I discuss what the text of her post (1a) accomplishes: It lays out a path for a discussion that will necessarily engage with the complexity of the terms "clean" and "unclean" and describes what kinds of participation she would like to see (and not see) in the thread. The OP's metadiscourse paves the way for even more metadiscourse in the posts that follow, and this metadiscourse too is created by way of intertextual linking strategies.

First, in (1a), CuddleSmash highlights the terms "clean" and "unclean" as important for her post, while also indicating that they are complex. She uses quotation marks around them in the thread's title: "'Clean' vs. 'unclean' eating studies?" Gutzmann and Stei (2011) argue that quotation marks may have multiple simultaneous functions, depending on context, including drawing a reader's attention to some expression as a form of language, attributing an expression to some outside source (as in the case of reported speech or what

Tannen [2007b] calls constructed dialogue), and accomplishing emphasis. Thus, quotation marks serve to mark the "otherness" of the words they enclose, as noted by Shukrun-Nagar (2009). Similarly, Lay's (2014:12) analysis of quotation marks in blogs finds that they can be used to refer to "some other known text"—such as previous posts on the topic—while also "hint[ing] at some collective knowledge that is passed over, something that cannot (or will not) be fully discussed" on the specific blog post.

Broadly, Gutzmann and Stei (2011:2651) suggest that quotation marks "block the stereotypical interpretation of an expression, and thereby indicate that some alternative meaning ought to be inferred." Inferences could be that a word enclosed in quotation marks is important, as seen in some shop signage, especially handwritten, for example, *"Fresh" Lettuce* (these are often [not without controversy] called "greengrocer's quotes"; see e.g., Abbott 2003); that an expression has an external source (either named or unnamed, e.g., *Sally promised that the lettuce was "fresh."*), and thus ideologically distancing the writer from the expression; or that the applicability of an expression to a given context is being questioned (e.g., indicating something like "so-called" or "supposedly" as in, *The "fresh" lettuce was actually 8 days old*). This means that quotation marks are intertextual—one part of the text is marked as separate from the rest, and perhaps from some other source. In Fairclough's (1992) terms, quotation marks are an example of "manifest intertextuality." They are also metadiscursive; in calling attention to language they communicate something about language. As Gutzmann and Stei (2011:2650) note, quotation marks are part of what "marks what people do with words."

Interpreted in light of these studies, CuddleSmash's use of the quotation marks in the title of her post—"'Clean' vs. 'unclean' eating studies?"—not only draws attention to these terms, but also their prior history of use, including the fact that their use has been contentious in this and other online contexts. In addition, in the body of her post, CuddleSmash more directly addresses the complexity of defining "clean" (and by implication "unclean"), noting that, "Including a definition of 'clean'" for any study posters cite "would also be very helpful, as it seems to vary wildly from person to person" (lines 5–6).

Second, with the difficulty of defining "clean" highlighted, the OP also identifies what kinds of contributions to the thread she desires: CuddleSmash seeks posts that address "studies" that compare "groups" (lines 2–3, "groups consuming the same number of calories and macros, but one group eating clean while the other eats processed foods"), and the "groups" must consist of people who eat "clean" and those who eat "unclean." "Unprocessed foods" are juxtaposed with "clean" here, thus indirectly defining her basic understanding of clean foods (they are not processed). The reference to "calories and macros," terms that are commonly used on these boards, indicates that she is seeking posts that reference a very particular kind of study: one where people in two matched groups eat the same number of calories per day and consume the same distribution of macronutrients (e.g., carbohydrates and proteins), but one group's members get these calories and "macros" from "clean" foods, whereas the other's, from foods that do not count as "clean." CuddleSmash also indicates that she can be persuaded by "facts" (line 9) that are brought into the discussion, not by anecdote or opinion. In her original post, she thus provides very specific guidelines for the response posts she wants, and to preempt a more undesirable direction the thread might take—and to some extent, does take—as it unfolds (some participants provide anecdotes, offer opinions, and criticize other users, instead of identifying studies; many also do not explicitly define "clean" as CuddleSmash requests).

In addition to addressing what she is looking for in terms of post content, CuddleSmash communicates about the form and tone of desired posts, albeit less directly, as seen in the second paragraph of her post, reproduced below:

(1b)   CuddleSmash (post 1; second paragraph only)
    8   I realize that many people feel very passionately about this issue, and that's fine. I have a
    9   thick skin, and am willing to be swayed by facts, although I know there will be plenty of
   10   bro-science and hyperbole to sort through.

The OP here hints at the morally and emotionally loaded nature of this topic with her mention that people "feel very passionately" about the topic of clean eating (line 8), which indicates heightened affect and possible strong disagreement; her "I have a thick skin" (lines 8–9) anticipates face-threatening responses due to the contentious nature of the topic. While CuddleSmash is seeking "facts" (line 9), she also anticipates (and thereby makes intertextual, anticipatory reference to) non-factual "bro-science" and "hyperbole" (line 10), which indeed do show up in the thread.

CuddleSmash further sets the tone for the thread she wants by using language to attend to the issue of social image or face (Goffman 1955), or to accomplish what Locher and Watts (2005) characterize as relational work. In particular, she uses strategies to reduce the face threat of imposing on others (i.e., she mitigates threat to what Brown and Levinson [1987] call negative face), and she also lays the groundwork for solidarity with them (i.e., she appeals to what Brown and Levinson [1987] call positive face). She justifies her post by mentioning twice that her motivation is not to stir up trouble or start a contentious debate: her post is motivated by her being "genuinely curious" (line 1) and "deeply curious" (line 4). She also makes clear that she has already tried, on her own, to locate the kinds of studies she is interested in ("I've been unable to locate such a study," lines 3–4), which again justifies her posting (i.e., she has already made efforts, which explains her decision to "impose" on the discussion board). Further, and as is common in many thread-initial posts that request help, information, or advice, she offers a preemptive thanks to other users (line

12: "Thanks in advance!"). This can be seen as buffering imposition, but also creating solidarity; the exclamation point contributes to this effect.

The GIF, or what can be described as a short looped video animation (e.g., Bourlai and Herring 2014), that accompanies CuddleSmash's post also helps lay the social and relational groundwork for the thread in terms of its key (Goffman 1974) or tone (Tannen 2006). At the end of the text of her post, CuddleSmash includes a GIF from the science fiction television show *Firefly* where a character named Wash holds a toy dinosaur in each hand and animates them talking; the text of the dialogue appears as text on the GIF. (For the scene, search "Firefly Clip: This Land" on YouTube.) This scene is very GIF-able, and it seems to have wide circulation as a meme, as verified by a Google image search using the terms "Wash," "dinosaur," and "Firefly." The text of the GIF represents how Wash animates the dialogue between the toy dinosaurs, with the meat-eating dinosaur (standing on two legs and with large teeth) eventually attacking the herbivore dinosaur (which appears to be a stegosaurus). I reproduce the exchange Wash animates between the two dinosaur toys below:

(1c) Text of the GIF used in the OP's initial post (post 1)

Stegosaurus:	YES . . . YES. THIS IS A FERTILE LAND AND WE WILL THRIVE. WE WILL RULE OVER ALL THIS LAND AND WE WILL CALL IT . . . THIS LAND.
Meat-eater:	I THINK WE SHOULD CALL IT . . . YOUR GRAVE.
Stegosaurus:	AH! CURSE YOUR SUDDEN AND INEVITABLE BETRAYAL!
Meat-eater:	HA HA HA! MINE IS AN EVIL LAUGH! NOW DIE!

The GIF is represented in the nine still images in Figure 2.1, organized into three rows to be read from left to right.

This GIF depicted in the images of Figure 2.1 functions as a face work strategy that also communicates that the OP does not want serious conflicts and wants a friendly discussion. This is supported by existing research observing that there is a "division of labor" between verbal/textual and visual modalities: the verbal/textual tends to carry serious content, while the visual adds and expresses more comical and fantastical content (in print media: Machin 2004; on broadcast news: Machin and Jaworski 2006).

As the thread unfolds, in general, participants attempt to identify research studies that compare the efficacy of "clean" versus "unclean" diets for overall health and weight loss, discuss the relationship between these and other well-known diets (e.g., low-calorie, vegetarian), and repeatedly push to keep the thread focused on "scientific studies" and the "facts" these have

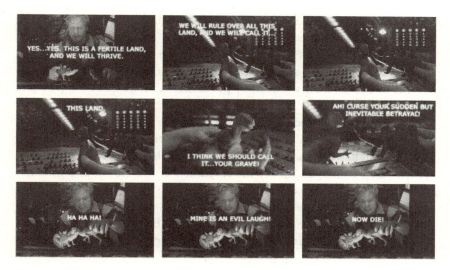

Figure 2.1. Still images from the GIF used in the OP's initial post (post 1).

yielded. Yet, there are also numerous playful and humorous moments. One such lighthearted moment occurs in the 69th message of the thread, when Salli28 intertextually refers to the initial post by writing, "Gotta say, I love that Firefly gif"; in the 70th, k8robin4 shows her appreciation of the GIF by using the quotation function of the boards to reproduce it and adding the comment "In for a Wash dinosaur GIF," along with a smiley face emoji. Use of the GIF in the original post thus facilitates relational work among the participants and shapes the discourse that follows: other posters also use GIFs in playful ways, affecting the tone of the thread as they simultaneously address the topic of "clean eating." K8robin4's use of the emoji, which can be said to function as what Gumperz (1982) calls a "contextualization cue," also contributes to creating a friendly tone (cf. Al Rashdi 2018). In addition, emojis are commonly used for "utterance ending," serving a phatic "'good-bye' function" (Danesi 2017:19), again continuing the friendly tone set by CuddleSmash.

Another layer of meaning in the GIF that CuddleSmash used in her opening post can also be identified, though it is not clear if this was her intention. I interpreted this GIF not only as an example of an "inevitable" fight between two parties who are different, and a humorous take on such a conflict, but also as an illustration of two parties who will likely never agree on eating practices specifically (in the GIF, the two parties are toys of an herbivore dinosaur and a meat-eating dinosaur). The OP's use of this GIF thus can be seen as especially clever, which accomplishes, following Locher and Watts' (2005) theorizing on linguistic politeness, facework and identity construction for her (GIF use and identity construction will be discussed in more detail in Chapter 4): just as two dinosaurs with different diets will at some point fight, so too will humans with different dietary practices.

While aspects of the OP's post anticipate a somewhat difficult discussion that might become clouded by participants' passion, in fact this particular discussion thread (overall) seems fairly productive (though there are examples that have elements that could be described as "hostile," as will be shown later in this chapter). As noted, the thread is fairly long; this means it garnered a great deal of interest while also being allowed to continue without moderator intervention (how one moderator "locks" threads that break forum guidelines is considered in Chapter 4). My interpretation of this thread as a generally productive one is supported by posts to the "clean eating" thread itself; several participants positively evaluate the thread. For example, the 191st post praises the quality of the discussion, and the fact that it has been maintained for eight pages of posts; it uses intertextual resources to do so.

(2)   <u>Trugeri (post 191)</u>

1 I just came in to compliment OP, and many others in here, because for 8 pages, this has

2 stayed relatively on topic, there seems to be a decent amount of friendly debate going on

3 with some minds open to considering alternate view points, and most have tried to stay

4 focused on science and less on anecdotal evidence. So far, this is one of the most neutral

5 discussions I have ever seen on this much lauded topic—from both sides.

6

7 I hope I did not just jinx this thread.

Trugeri produces the speech act of complimenting CuddleSmash (the OP) and many of the other posters for the quality of the thread. Her post is filled with intertextual strategies that accomplish metadiscourse: she uses the deictic "this" (lines 2-3, "this has stayed relatively on topic") to point to the thread; she uses "friendly debate" (line 2) and "one of the most neutral discussions I have ever seen on this much lauded topic" (lines 4–5) to label and characterize it as a text separate from her post, thus creating links between her post and the rest of the thread. While Trugeri mitigates her praise—noting that the thread "has stayed *relatively* on topic" (lines 1–2, italics added), that there is a "*decent* amount of friendly debate," that "*some* minds are open to considering alternate view points," and that "*most* have tried to stay focused on science and less on anecdotal evidence" (lines 2–4, italics added)—she generally indicates the success of, and her appreciation for, the thread and its contributors. Interestingly, Trugeri also shows awareness that she has produced metadiscourse (meta-metadiscourse); in calling attention to the positive features of the thread, she notes that she hopes she "did not just jinx this thread" (line 7), which refers to the idea that saying something aloud (or in this case, typing) about something may inadvertently ruin it.

In what follows, I will show how posters, including CuddleSmash, comment on the discourse of the thread, including the (in)appropriateness and (un)helpfulness of specific posts, as they engage in the overall metadiscursive activity of defining and discussing what exactly constitutes "clean" eating and food. While some posts both grapple with definitions of "clean" eating and convey the poster's opinion about what constitutes a productive contribution to the discussion, for analytic purposes I consider these phenomena—defining terminology and negotiating appropriate participation—in two separate sections. I first turn to "clean" eating as a concept and term and demonstrate how intertextuality serves as a resource to facilitate negotiating its meaning(s).

INTERTEXTUAL RESOURCES AND DEFINING "CLEAN" EATING AND FOODS

Posters use various intertextual linking and marking strategies to accomplish the metadiscourse needed to negotiate the meanings of "(un)clean" eating and "(un)clean" foods (along with other related terms like "processed," which was used in the original post of the thread). For example, in the thread's third message, k3smith indirectly advances an understanding of "clean" eating as a sometimes (or compensatory) activity, drawing on the strategies of quotation marks and lexical repetition.

(3) k3smith (post 3)
  1 "Clean" eating helps me hit my macro targets . . it would be difficult to hit them eating
  2 fast food. Although I eat ice cream every day. And McDonalds quite a bit.

Like CuddleSmash in her original post, k3smith uses a version of "macros" ("macro targets," line 1) to refer to macronutrients (such as protein and fat). This poster also uses the term "clean" and, as Cuddlesmash did in the title of the thread, situates it within quotation marks. This ties her post into the unfolding discourse of the thread, and the collaborative activity the thread entails.

In addition, k3smith offers a view of what "clean" eating means. Fast foods such as items served at McDonald's, which she reports to eat "quite a bit" (line 2), are widely understood to be highly processed (i.e., not clean); ice cream (which k3smith reports she eats every day in line 2) is not typically conceptualized as a "clean" food either. This conveys k3smith's understanding of clean eating as one component of a diet where one also eats processed foods; this contrasts with some others' views of "clean" eating as something that means avoiding certain foods entirely (as evidenced in other posts).

In the thread's 7th post, marmosetmeow21 quotes k3smith and more directly engages in the difficulty inherent in the term "clean." This poster uses multiple intertextual strategies—the boards' quotation function, the deictic pronoun "this," and paraphrase—to link her post closely to k3smith's. Further doing metadiscursive work, marmosetmeow21 uses quotation marks to set off the term "clean" and produces evaluations of it using adjectival phrases and expressive speech acts. (In this and other examples showing one poster quoting another post in part or whole by using the board's quotation function, quoted material is indented and highlighted in gray; this roughly reproduces the on-screen layout on the website. To differentiate quoted material from words typed by the present poster further, I do not add line numbers for quoted material.) In line 8, the poster mentions that she eats ice cream "when [she has] the calories," which refers to the FIF app's calorie tracking mechanism (i.e., she eats ice cream when she can do so without surpassing her daily calorie goal).

(4)   marmosetmeow21 (post 7)

> **k3smith (3)**
>
> "Clean" eating helps me hit my macro targets . . . it would be difficult to hit them eating fast food. Although I eat ice cream every day. And McDonalds quite a bit.

1   This gets into the fact that "clean" eating is completely vague and "processed" as usually
2   used by "clean" eaters is incoherent.
3
4   I don't like fast food, so I almost never eat it, but also I don't eat "clean" because I don't
5   believe in the concept (calling foods dirty, acting as if nutrition is about not eating foods
6   vs seeking out a nutritionally balanced diet). Another reason I think it would be silly for
7   me to give up processed foods is that they are extremely helpful for me in meeting my
8   macros. Greek yogurt, for example.
9
10   Oh, and I also like to have ice cream when I have the calories. I don't see why this is
11   bad if I don't skimp on my nutrition to do it.
12
13   A study that compared "clean" eating with sensible eating of the sort that seems to be the
14   usual alternative recommended around here would be interesting, but I doubt it's been
15   done. Lots of difficulties. There are efforts to compare vegetarians and not, but causation
16   is always a problem.

Marmosetmeow21's use of the boards' quotation function embeds k3smith's post into her own; she further uses "this" (line 1) to point to it ("This gets into the fact that 'clean' eating is completely vague and 'processed' as usually used by 'clean' eaters is incoherent," lines 1–2). These strategies create a relationship of intertextuality between the two posts. Marmosetmeow21's paraphrase of k3smith's mention of "McDonalds" as "fast food" (line 4) also contributes to this.

Using quotation marks around "clean" (lines 1, 2, 4, and 13) again places focus on the terms used for discussion, specifically pointing out the ambiguous nature of, and problematizing, the term "clean." Thus, for instance, the beginning of marmosetmeow21's post—"This post gets into the fact that 'clean' eating is completely vague" (line 1)—could be read as implying that there is no real "clean" eating. The quotation marks could also imply "clean" eating is only a so-called, not real, practice. Further, "'clean' eating" is contrasted with "sensible eating" (line 13); this undercuts the idea of "'clean' eating" in two ways: first, it is presumed to be the opposite of "sensible"; second, there are no quotation marks around the word "sensible," which suggests that while "clean" eating is a supposed practice, sensible eating is a real and definable phenomenon. The poster also uses quotation marks to indicate that there is no accepted definition among "clean" eaters—"and 'processed' as usually used by 'clean' eaters is incoherent" (lines 1–2); this is interpretable as questioning the validity of "clean" as a food-related notion, while also problematizing "processed." This traces back to CuddleSmash's original post that equated "unclean" with "processed."

While calling attention to the term "clean," this post also explicates its downsides. Not using the term "clean" but referring to "the concept," marmosetmeow21 explains in lines 4–6, "I don't believe in the concept (calling foods dirty, acting as if nutrition is about not eating foods vs seeking out a nutritionally balanced diet)." This supports her use of quotation marks around "clean" as implying "so-called." Further, she again communicates about some of the meanings she views as being built into "clean" by indicating that she does not understand why eating ice cream occasionally is "bad" (lines 10–11). In fact, many posters take issue with "clean" (as CuddleSmash, the OP, predicted) as a food-oriented term in that it invites a dichotomy wherein other foods are considered "unclean," or "dirty," or "bad," which has moral implications for everyone who eats (and thus is one reason some cookbook writers, such as Nigella Lawson as shown by Smith [2020], might not want to be seen as endorsing "clean eating").

In the next example, user BradGH_ also engages with the notion of "clean" and uses the intertextual linking strategies of the board's quotation function, quotation marks, and repetition. His post is the 29th in the thread; he first quotes the entirety of marmosetmeow21's post (which I elide below, as it was just shown in extract 4). He then comments on it ("This is the part that stuck with me," line 1) and addresses the impossibility of the existence of studies of the type the OP seeks.

(5)   BradGH_   (post 29)

((*uses quotation function to quote entirety of marmosetmeow21's post, shown in extract 4*))

1   This is the part that stuck with me. The study would be impossible to conduct because of
2   the randomness and vagueness of "clean eating." Studies need to be done with concrete
3   terms and conditions. Clean eating as it is so loosely defined makes that impossible.
4   To study a diet without processed foods we first have to define what a processed food is.
5
6   People who say they eat clean think that's simple. But many vegetables are processed in
7   some form before being sold. Should those be eliminated? Of course every clean eater
8   would say no, that's not what they meant.
9
10 Science would also assume given the conditions laid out that things like yogurt, cheese,
11 butter, seasonings, milk, etc. would need to be eliminated. Show me one self proclaimed
12 clean eater who avoids these foods and I'll mail you cookies. Clean cookies.
13
14 Every clean eater sets their own standards for what is considered "clean." And hey, that's
15 fine. More power to ya, best of luck in all your endeavors. But there's no way for science
16 to deal with that, much less test it.
17
18 It is a made up concept with no definition or clear guidelines. May as well try to study
19 what color unicorns are.

Here, BradGH_ uses the quotation function and the deictic "this" (line 1) to link his post to a previous one by marmosetmeow21. In addition, he uses quotation marks around "clean eating" and labels the term as entailing "randomness and vagueness" (line 2), which echoes marmosetmeow21's previous use of "completely vague" (excerpt 4, line 1) and is thus intertextual (though perhaps not intentionally so). In creating metadiscourse about "clean" (and mentioning the notion of processed foods as well) BradGH_ also metacommunicates about the meaning of "study": he notes that "Studies need to be done with concrete terms and conditions" (lines 2–3) and sarcastically remarks, "May as well try to study what color unicorns are" (lines 18–19). This links to and produces discourse about the OP's query, indicating that it cannot be responded to as asked.

Other posters also engage in the metadiscursive activity of discussing and defining the term "clean," remarking that its lack of definition means no scientific studies comparing "clean" and "unclean" diets exist, and that personal anecdotes are all the original poster will receive. This metadiscourse involves not only intertextual repetition of "clean" (often set off with quotation marks) but also intertextual links to discourse that does not yet exist: potential future posts to the thread. One such example is TuffTodd6's post (the 34th in the thread), which also mobilizes the boards' quotation function (to quote CuddleSmash's original post).

(6)   TuffTodd6 (post 34)

> ((*uses quotation function to quote OP's initial post,*
> *shown in extracts 1a–c*))

1   Don't know if you could do a study on that . . . .
2
3   Whose definition of "clean" is used?
4   And then whoever does win out in the "clean" definition, other people who have a
5   different definition will disregard the study.

Lexical repetition ("clean"—in quotation marks—lines 3 and 4; "study," lines 1 and 5) ties this post to CuddleSmash's initial post, as well as to the multiple other posts using these terms such as the post of BradGH_. TuffTodd6's use of a rhetorical question in line 3 ("Whose definition of 'clean' is used?") invites readers to recognize the problematic nature of the term "clean" regarding conducting scientific studies and highlights the unlikelihood that the thread will be able to meet the OP's hopes, thereby echoing and linking to the post by BradGH_, as well as the earlier post by marmosetmeow21.

Other posters are even more dismissive of "clean" as a concept that can be defined; to problematize and devalue the term, they use adjectival phrases, both attributive and predicative. Through this practice, they accomplish what Myrendal (2019:334) calls "a meta-linguistic objection," thereby "taking up a stance" in an ongoing negotiation of a word's value and meaning. For example, in the 141st message, marmosetmeow21 posts, "But I just wish people would get over the stupid term 'clean'"; and in the 165th post, she notes, "what I really wish is that we could drop the needlessly offensive and non informative term 'clean'" from the discussion." "Stupid" and "offensive and non informative" are used to evaluate "clean" not only as a concept or idea, but as a piece of language that is drawn in from outside of the post that comments on it—the practice of "clean" eating does not make sense, nor does the term. In the 206th post, LadyOink describes "clean" as "a marketing term" and in the 148th post, neanderslim remarks that the term has "no clear definition." Thus, participants across posts collaboratively point to and problematize "clean" as a concept and as a term that has now circulated throughout the thread. Their discourse is intertextual in two senses: their individual posts are linked to the term "clean" as used in other contexts, both those specified (e.g., in other posts on the thread) and nonspecified. Through engaging in the metadiscursive activity of discussing and attempting to arrive at a definition of "clean," these posters do not actually provide useful definitions but, rather, invoke unhelpful ones.

The meaning of "(un)clean" is also adapted for humorous purposes, perhaps in an intertextual nod to the friendly tone CuddleSmash's original post GIF helped set for the thread, while also calling the term "clean" into question. In the 241st post, LadyOink uses quotation marks and repeats the terms "unclean" and "processed" to make a joke that is reinforced by an image she contextualizes in her post. She also brings the topic of talk to the realm of alcoholic beverages, often invoked for humor on these boards (another example appears in Chapter 3). The textual content of LadyOink's post is shown in (7); the image she posted at the end of this text is shown in Figure 2.2.

(7) LadyOink (post 241)
  1 mmmmm . . . if I wasn't so full from processed food, I'd want cheese
  2
  3 Bloody Marys are processed and unclean.
  4 And by "processed" and "unclean" I mean "delicious" and "happy."

In this post, LadyOink self-identifies as a non-clean eater by indicating that she is "full from [eating] processed food" (line 1). She also continues to problematize and negotiate the meaning of "clean," emphasizing that every dieter may

Figure 2.2. Image of a Bloody Mary.

very well have their own definition. She first describes Bloody Marys—a drink which typically includes vodka, tomato juice, and Tabasco and Worcestershire sauce, along with olives and other items for garnish—as "processed and unclean" (line 3). In line 4, she uses the terms again, this time enclosing each of them in quotation marks ("And by 'processed' and 'unclean'") to comment on her own just-prior use of those terms, poking fun by assigning her own meanings ("I mean 'delicious' and 'happy.'"). In proposing that a photo of an alcoholic beverage represents "clean" eating, LadyOink brings the discussion to the realm of ridiculousness (alcohol is typically not considered "clean"). This is reinforced by the posted photo; the Bloody Mary depicted appears to be a lowbrow caricature of the drink. It is served in a large, somewhat dirty-looking Styrofoam cup, it includes a plastic straw, and there is an overabundance of olives filling the cup. A quick Google image search of "Bloody Mary" reveals that this is not the way an attractive or high-class drink is served (i.e., in a glass, with artfully arranged garnishes). The image contributes to the humorous nature of the metacomment LadyOink is making. But LadyOink's post also intertextually reinforces a serious point made by many other posters: different people define "clean" differently, and thus studying "clean" eating as a dietary practice is not possible. A similar effect is achieved in other posts that include joking about the term and idea of "clean," such as in post 195 by JenAngel2 ("If I get my mouth washed out with soap, does that mean I have a 'clean' diet?") and post 249 by violette ("If I drop an M&M on the floor, I eat it.").

In summary, posts across the thread use intertextual linking strategies to call attention to, problematize, negotiate, and even joke about what the term "clean" means when it comes to eating and food. Though not a focus here, they likewise engage in what related terms, such as "processed," mean, for instance arguing about whether bread counts as "processed," and whether cooking counts as a kind of processing. Uses of quotation marks, the quotation function, word repetition and paraphrase, deictic pronouns, adjectival phrases that describe language that exists beyond the specific post, and images contextualized within the thread collectively accomplish intertextual linking and create intertextuality, facilitating accomplishment of a metadiscursive activity that animates the unfolding discussion on the topic: while one accepted definition of "clean" is not identified in the realm of food and eating, many posters advance and support the perspective that "clean" is a tricky notion, and the term has shortcomings. This is fundamental to their collaboratively determining whether the studies of interest to the OP—"clean" versus "unclean" diets—actually exist (the OP eventually decides they do not, as will be shown in analysis of her later posts). However, "defining terms" is not the only metadiscursive activity in which the thread's posters engage. They also negotiate what constitutes productive and appropriate thread participation, meaning they produce discourse that evaluates individual posts, multiple posts, and the thread as a whole, considered in the next section.

INTERTEXTUAL RESOURCES AND DEFINING
PRODUCTIVE PARTICIPATION

So far, I have focused on how posts to the thread work to define "clean"—ultimately, the consensus is that there is no one definition, and thus there can be no "studies" on the topic of "clean" versus "unclean" diets. However, in discussing this term, participants metadiscursively engage beyond this lexical item, such as when Trugeri communicated about the entire thread by praising it (extract 2). Even more prominent in the thread is metadiscourse about the specific posts of other posters. This phenomenon already emerged in examples wherein a previous post is quoted: in quoting the post, the quoting party not only creates intertextuality but also necessarily takes a stance toward what is being quoted, following Bakhtin's (1986) theorizing; in Tannen's (2007b) terms, the quoted material's meaning is necessarily being changed in that it is brought into a new context; in Becker's (1994, 1995) terms, "pushing" "prior text" into a new context necessarily "reshapes" its meaning. Thus, for example, BradGH_ (extract 5) quoted marmosetmeow's post (extract 4) as means of advancing the idea that the concept of "clean" is problematic. Through the boards' quotation function as well as other means of intertextual linking, participants negotiate the appropriateness and usefulness of the posts to the thread: they address whether the posts fit in with the kind of discussion the OP, CuddleSmash, indicated that she wanted (a levelheaded discussion based on "studies" of "clean" versus other diets conducted by authoritative experts, not on anecdotes and opinions). In addition, posters address whether posts meet or violate the discussion boards' general guidelines, which encourage civility and participant comfort (e.g., by banning personal attacks on other posters). In this way, my analysis in this section intersects with previous research that explores the discursive negotiation and accomplishment of (im)politeness online among members of various groups (e.g., Angouri and Tseliga 2010; Darics 2010; Graham 2007; Graham and Dutt 2019). However, rather than focusing on theories of (im)politeness, I highlight how posters generate intertextual links to create the metadiscourse that evaluates whether a post, part of a post, or a group of posts is a productive and appropriate contribution.

As mentioned, the OP, CuddleSmash, is an extremely active thread participant; she is responsible for 52 of the 282 total posts (about 18%). She frequently intertextually references and evaluates others' contributions, often by thanking or otherwise expressing appreciation for their discourse. For example, in the thread's 136th post, she responds to a poster who has provided a hyperlink to a research study by thanking; she uses the quotation function and adds, "Thanks! That one hasn't been posted yet. And it is interesting . . .," using "that one" and "it" to refer to the post's content as separate from her own post. By issuing thanks for a post, she produces discourse that intertextually links to and (in this case, positively) evaluates prior discourse.

Other posters also flag other participants' posts as appropriate and valuable. For instance, the 126th post includes rhetorical questions that highlight the variety of issues that need to be considered in comparing studies—including whether food is "clean" and "unclean," whether study participants are "normal weight" or overweight, and whether they are healthy—and in the next post (127), indy3627 compliments the post, using the quotation function and writing, "I think you make some great points here. I've been curious about this as well." She thus suggests that the post she quotes and refers to was topically appropriate, as it was something about which she was also "curious" (and note that this echoes a term used in the thread's original post: CuddleSmash was "genuinely curious" and "deeply curious," as seen in extract 1a). Indy3627 also labels the post she quotes as accomplishing the activity of "mak[ing] some great points" and points to it with "here." In these ways, the post is intertextually linked to and communicates about the previous post. She goes on to add a hyperlink to a study that might be relevant, thus advancing the discussion. Later, Optimist315 also gives a compliment (in post 211), paraphrasing a previous post that addressed differences in how foods can be processed and validating its relevance to the thread: "Good point, not all processing is created equal."

Not all posts are identified as being interesting and appropriate for this thread about clean eating, however (as CuddleSmash predicted in her original post, pseudoscientific information is posted, for example). Intertextual links are also used in metadiscourse that problematizes other posts. The following post by k3smith, the second post to the thread, consists of a hyperlink to an article on CNN about a nutrition professor who lost 27 pounds eating a diet where two-thirds of calories consumed came from Twinkie snack cakes; in the sixth message of the thread, the OP uses the quotation function and critiques the post. In her comment, she refers to "CICO," a commonly used acronym on the boards for "calories in, calories out," or the idea that as long as you consume fewer calories than you expend, you will lose weight.

(8)   CuddleSmash (post 6):

> ((quotes k3smith's post, which consists of one hyperlink))

1   Ha! I know all about the Twinkie diet, as I'm usually the one who posts it. But that
2   doesn't really address the question, as there's no control group and tests to compare. And
3   I'm not interested necessarily in just weight loss, but also in general health markers.
4
5   I'm really curious as to whether this clean eating rage makes a real difference, as most of
6   those who tout it claim that while CICO works for weight loss, clean eating addresses
7   total health. Does it exist?

Here CuddleSmash not only quotes k3smith's post (consisting of one hyperlink) but also uses "the Twinkie diet" to paraphrase the gist of the material contained in the hyperlink. She uses "it" and "that" (line 1) to refer deictically to the posted hyperlink that she critiques; the "Ha!" arguably recognizes, however, that k3smith's post could have been intended as a joke. Continuing on, CuddleSmash characterizes the post by k3smith as one that fails to address the question she asked in her original post because the Twinkie diet does not meet the specifications of a scientific study ("there's no control group and tests to compare," line 2); further, the focus of the Twinkie diet link is weight loss only; i.e., it indicates that as long as a dieter lowers calorie intake, the result is weight loss no matter where those calories come from—which reiterates the weight loss idea of CICO and says nothing about "clean" eating. In lines 5–7, CuddleSmash reiterates the curiosity she outlined in her initial post and explicitly identifies the Twinkie post as relating to CICO but not "clean eating" or "total health."

Similarly, in post 17, ed_ab61 posted a comment along with photos, and his post was intertextually referenced by another poster (but not the OP). The images ed_ab61 posted were no longer visible online when I collected my data (and I could not locate them), but another poster describes one of them as being of a woman lighting herself a cigarette using the candles that light up her 100th birthday cake; basically, it seems the photos were of elderly people who were clearly exhibiting what are commonly understood as "poor" health habits while celebrating their advanced birthdays with cakes. The accompanying text ed_ab61 posted said, "I wonder if those cakes are clean, non-processed, sugar-free, gluten-free, flour-free, etc." In the 19th message of the thread, Optimist315 uses the quotation function to reproduce the entirety of ed_ab61's post and also adds commentary.

(9) Optimist315 (19)

> ed_ab61
>
> ((*images not included*))
>
> I wonder if those cakes are clean, non-processed, sugar-free, gluten-free, flour-free, etc.

1 That's not really helpful. There are always outliers. The OP has a legit question-whether
2 or not there are studies out there showing evidence. These pics are hardly evidence, and
3 certainly not studies. And gluten free has nothing to do with clean eating. That is for
4 people who are allergic to gluten.

Optimist315 uses "that" ("That's not really helpful," line 1) to point to the previous post that is quoted. This sentence indicates that the people pictured in the quoted post who happen to live a long life despite unhealthy practices such as smoking and eating cake are the exception, not the rule ("There are always outliers," line 1). Optimist315 uses "these pics" (line 2) to refer to the content of ed_ab61's post as well, further creating intertextual links. The poster also makes intertextual links to, and produces metadiscourse about, the original post by labeling it as presenting "a legit[imate] question" (line 1). The pictures posted by ed_ab61, Optimist315 suggests, do not meet the requirements of the thread, as they are neither "evidence" (line 2) nor "studies" (line 3). While Optimist315's uptake critiques the post as if it were posted seriously, that the images were intended to be humorous is also a plausible interpretation and could be seen as tracing back to the OP's playful-dinosaur-toys-arguing GIF, and as serving as prior text for later humorous posts that include image-based content, such as LadyOink's "clean" Bloody Mary post, which included a photo.

Many other posts link to, and evaluate, some other post (or part of a post) as helpful or unhelpful to the thread (though such posts may also accomplish other functions), thus contributing to the metadiscursive activity centered around determining what kinds of posts are welcome and appreciated. For instance, in post 63, CuddleSmash quotes part of post 57 by indy3627 in which she suggests that there is evidence that "clean" foods tend to be lower in calories, salt, and chemicals than other foods and provides a hyperlink; CuddleSmash adds a speech act expressing gratitude and uses the deictic "that" ("Thanks, I'll definitely check that out"). In post 97, the OP quotes post 93 by PicaSaver, which recommends a particular website and adds text that includes the deictic "this": "Thanks! This is exactly the sort of thing I've been looking for!!" In post 62, shown below, CuddleSmash performs the speech act of thanking multiple (unspecified) users for their posts; she acknowledges that users have posted useful material, though the posts do not completely answer her question.

(10)   CuddleSmash (post 62)
  1 Thank you guys for the informative articles. I'm still really confused though, and I think
  2 it has to do with defining terms, as previously mentioned.
     ((three additional paragraphs elided))

Here CuddleSmash performs thanking; she uses "the informative articles" (line 1) to reference others' positive contributions. In addition, she demonstrates how the unfolding thread has influenced her thinking about the thread's topic: while she remains "really confused" (line 2), she goes on (in text not shown in extract 10) to ask about terms she has seen in the thread, including "additives," "processed," "canned food," and "TV dinners." The content of the thread's posts has thus led her to call attention to, and wonder about, other terms (in addition to "clean," considered in the first part of this chapter). In the last paragraph of her post (again not shown in 10), CuddleSmash concludes that meeting the specifications of her original post is not possible, as "there is no such study, possibly because the definitions are nonsensical and random" (note, however, that the thread continued to develop, with 121 more posts being added).

Posts to the thread also negatively evaluate previous posts, both by CuddleSmash and others. As shown in excerpt 8, in CuddleSmash's second post to the thread (post 6), she problematizes an earlier post that provided a link to what is known as the Twinkie Diet. As was shown in excerpt 9, ed_ab61's post of elderly people in front of birthday cakes celebrating their advanced age (post 17) was problematized (by Optimist315 in post 19) with the sentence, "That's not really helpful." Much later in the thread, CuddleSmash by way of the quotation function reproduces a post wherein a documentary that presents "scientific evidence" and "quotes scientific studies" of various diets is recommended. She goes on to expresses skepticism, referring not only to this post but to a group of unspecified posts, as shown in (11) (lines 1–2 include the phrase used in the title of this chapter).

(11)   CuddleSmash (post 164)

  ((uses quotation function to quote a previous post recommending a documentary))

1 I'll check it out! What I'm finding, though, is that most "evidence" that people post has
2 nothing to do with "clean" eating, and has more to do with vegetarianism. If there's proof
3 of a difference in the health effects of "processed" veggies vs. fresh veggies, I'm
4 definitely interested . . . but that doesn't seem to be the case, mostly, I suspect, because
5 there is no difference.

In lines 1–2, CuddleSmash evaluates other posts, noting that "most 'evidence' that people post has nothing to do with 'clean' eating" (note the quotation marks on "evidence," suggesting it is not evidence at all) regarding her area of interest: "clean" eating. However, she mitigates her criticism by not selecting individuals (she refers to "people" in line 1) or specific posts; in addition, she explains this shortcoming by suggesting that the studies she is interested in do not exist (rather than, for instance, that other posters are too incompetent to find them or are intentionally being unhelpful).

As CuddleSmash predicted in her original post, this thread is a challenging one in that not only is the topic difficult, but there is also the potential for incivility and hurt feelings ("I realize that many people feel very passionately about this issue, and that's fine. I have a thick skin, and am willing to be swayed by facts, although I know there will be plenty of bro-science and hyperbole to sort through," lines 8–10 in extracts 1a and 1b). Intextextual linking strategies are used to create the metadiscourse that calls attention to, problematizes, and manages this. I show one multi-post example that also demonstrates that the line between being uncivil and joking can be unclear as participants intertextually reference, and attempt to police, other posters' contributions.

In post 28, Marianne_J offers a definition of "clean" and her post is later evaluated, in a quite hostile way, as not contributing to the thread, and as evidence that she is a repeat offender in terms of posting non-helpful content.

(12)   Marianne_J (post 28)

1   Our bodies were made to eat real food; so it makes sense that anything that is not "real"
2   would wreak havoc eventually. To me, real food, clean food, is anything that has not
3   been altered. Of course, that does not mean cooking.

This poster makes assertions while offering a personalized definition of "clean" food that equates it with the term "real." User Son_ofaBeach_22 takes issue with this post (and with Marianne_J herself, it seems) and quotes and comments on it three times (these posts represent three of his five total posts to the thread). First, in post 30 he uses the quotation function to quote the post and notes that most foods have been altered via uses of fertilizers, genetic modifications, and the like, thus implying that describing food as "real"—as Marianne_J does—is not useful. Second, in post 31 he again quotes her post and criticizes it, also referring what he expressed in his just-previous post, "See what I'm saying? Arbitrary, personalized, and random." In post 33, Son_ofaBeach_22 quotes Marianne_J a third and final time and adds another metadiscursive comment. Like the others, this is face-threatening and could be viewed as an example of "flaming," as he attacks Marianne_J personally, and multiple times (this phenomenon tends to be associated with the online discourse of men, according to Herring [1994] and other scholars, though it is not clear what role posters' gender identities play here).

(13)   Son_ofaBeach_22 (33)

((quotes Marianne_J's post, shown in excerpt 12))

1   So, no study then? Thank you for once again posting a conclusion with no support.

Son_ofaBeach_22 uses a rhetorical question to link to and comment on Marianne_J's prior discourse—her post does not mention a study, and further he suggests this is not the first time she has posted something that he views as being not productive. In addition, he (sarcastically) thanks her, characterizing her post as a particular kind of speech activity: it offers "a conclusion with no support" (which is not what the OP was asking for). This face-threatening post evaluates Marianne_J's post negatively as not meeting the criteria outlined by the OP (and is further face threatening as being but one of three posts he makes that criticize her). While it could perhaps be intended or perceived as humorous—as it is perceived by the final post of the thread, which uses the board's quotation function to quote this third post by Son_ofaBeach_22, adding "Hahahahahahahaha!!!!!!!!!!!!!!")—given the repeated critique of Marianne_J by this user, it unlikely that she interpreted it as humorous (as I did not; in fact it seems to violate the discussion boards' prohibitions against personal attacks and flaming).

Docorange2001 piles on this activity; he quotes the post by Son_ofaBeach_ 22 that quotes the post of Marianne_J, creating further intertextual links, and adds his own comment:

(14)   <u>Docorange2001 (post 41)</u>

   ((quotes Son_ofaBeach_22's post that quotes and criticizes Marianne_J's post))

   1   To be fair, you failed to give credit to the imminent authority "Itmakes Sense." "They
   2   Say" and "Mygrandma Who" are also important researchers in this area.

Docorange2001 addresses Son_ofaBeach_22's post by (jokingly) including constructed researchers' names that represent imagined, clichéd sources of dubious information. This provides additional critique of Marianne_J and her discourse, who had based her post on the idea that "it makes sense" (extract 12, line 1), and by using lexical repetition and quotation marks, Docorange2001 belittles Marianne_J's post (as he sees it, it is not relevant to a thread about research studies). It also can be seen as constructing humor in mixing more formal language ("failure to give credit," "imminent authority") with the ridiculousness of the invented authorities' names ("Itmakes sense," "They Say," and "Mygrandma Who"), constituting interdiscursivity. It is not entirely clear, again, if the post is intended or experienced as face threatening by Marianne_ J, but in any case it serves as an example of the ongoing negotiations about what kinds of posts are perceived as contributing to the thread (ironically, in evaluating Marianne_J's post negatively, Docorange2001's own post does also not meet the criteria outlined in the original post by CuddleSmash).

Finally, PoemBird, 12 messages later, quotes this entire exchange by way of recontextualizing it using the quotation function and comments on it, thereby contributing to evaluating what constitutes a useful and appropriate post on this thread.

(15)   <u>PoemBird (53)</u>

   ((quotes Docorange's post that quotes Son_ofaBeach_22's post that quotes and criticizes Marianne_J's post; these posts appear in extracts 12–14))

   1   ^^ word.

PoemBird's uses of the quotation function and the two carets (^^) that accomplish pointing facilitate metadiscourse about multiple posts at once. "Word" is an idiom for "agree," and PoemBird shows approval of what has transpired (the critique of Marianne_J's contribution, and perhaps, the antagonism toward her). As noted, the tone of this entire metadiscursive exchange is somewhat ambiguous between an attack on Marianne_J's contribution and play; it does seem notable, however, that the quoted and criticized post by Marianne_J was her only post to the thread.

Other posters evaluate others' posts negatively with similar or even greater levels of explicitness. As an example, I summarize an exchange that primarily involves two posters. An active participant on the thread, indy3627, a woman who posted 22 times, brought up the issue that contemporary prepared foods are designed to be "addictive" (post 72). In post 74, TuffTodd6 (a man) quotes parts of her post and responds; for instance, he writes (echoing her use of the term "addictive," and adding abusive language), "Are you an adult? Can you make choices on your own? So what if they do make it more addictive. . . . They ain't forcing it down your throat. . . . MY GOD, take some damn responsibility at some point, and stop blaming others or some big company (. . .) COMES DOWN TO CHOICES." (This post echoes many neoliberal ideologies about weight loss mentioned in Chapter 1). Indy3627 uses the quotation function to reproduce this and adds a metadiscursive comment.

(16)   indy3627 (78)

> ((quotes previous post in which TuffTodd94 quotes and criticizes indy3627))

((4 sentences elided))
1 You can be ugly towards me all you want. I don't care honestly. People think for
2 themselves and won't agree with you no matter how much you bully them. ☺

Here indy3627 recontextualizes and characterizes TuffTodd6's previous post as "be[ing] ugly" and identifies it as the speech activity of "bully[ing]," though she ends her post with a smiley face emoji. Her use of the smiley face patterns with various scholars' observations that women tend to use more emojis, and positively valanced emoticons and emojis such as the smiley face, in online and social media contexts (e.g., Al Rashdi 2018; Witmer and Katzman 1997), as well as research noting that emojis also have a "good-bye" function (Danesi 2017). In response, another man, ed_ab61 (post 79) quotes indy3627 and responds that TuffTodd6's post did not constitute bullying, and he characterizes indy3627's post as accusatory: "Accusations of bullying, when their was none" (thus there is some "ganging up" on indy3627, similar to what happened in responses to Marianne_J). The produced metadiscourse contests indy3627's. Then (in post 81) TuffTodd6 quotes indy3627's response to his previous post and states, "You keep bringing in up staw-men arguments . . . you did the same in the other thread. (. . .) And I ain't being ugly. I am pointing out facts . . . " He thus describes his own discourse as accomplishing the speech activity of "pointing out facts" (not "being ugly") and characterizes indy3627's discourse as illogical (she uses "staw-men" [straw-man] arguments, i.e., arguments that refute something the other person never actually claimed). Again in parallel with Sun_ofaBeach_22's treatment of Marianne_J, TuffTodd6 indicates his evaluation of indy3627's posts as not productive in this thread as well as elsewhere in the community's discourse. (Note that both of these sets of exchanges seem blatantly to violate the boards' guidelines, but there is no evidence of moderator presence.)

The exchange between indy3627 and TuffTodd6 continues across several more posts, which I briefly describe before showing the OP's response to all of this metadiscourse. In post 86, indy3627 contests TuffTodd6's use of "staw-men" [straw-man] and problematizes his tone, another metadiscursive move: "If you feel my conclusions are 'Straw' as you say then give me some real science that disproves what I've said. I welcome a lively discussion as long as it is supported by evidence and not presented in anger." In post 89, TuffTodd6 explains that he is "Not angry and not mad" and reiterates that she brings up "straw-men arguments." In post 102, indy3627 notes that TuffTodd6 does not provide scientific evidence and suggests that this argument is also "straw," and TuffTodd6 quotes a part of her post that argues that he is unfairly indicating that overweight people are lazy; he responds, "OMG Please stop," and amps up the drama with "Get off the cross, someone else needs the wood." This intertextual recontextualization of a known saying implies that indy3627 is acting as a victim (i.e., as someone who has been metaphorically crucified); in contrast, he explains that he has to "work" to become "ripped/cut/defined" (i.e., muscled and toned), and this includes "turning down a lot of food [he] wanted to eat . . ." In this interaction between two active posters, each poster questions the appropriateness of the other's posts, as well as the tone of the posts, using intertextual linking strategies, in particular the board's quotation function, to do so.

In the next post (post 107), CuddleSmash quotes post 106 (the ongoing exchange between indy3627 and TuffTodd6) and adds her own comment.

(17)   CuddleSmash (107)

   ((*quotes post by TuffTodd6, which includes parts of the exchange with indy3627, as just described*))

   1   Hey, no need to be rude over a difference of opinion. Also, you're way off subject at this
   2   point. Let's talk about cleaning eating studies or GTFO . . . . ☹

CuddleSmash addresses the tone of TuffTodd6's post (it is "rude") and indicates that it is topically inappropriate ("off subject" and not dealing with "clean eating studies"). She thus recommends he GTFO (get the fuck out, i.e., leave the thread), also using an angry face emoji to close her post. This opens a new exchange of posts wherein CuddleSmash and TuffTodd6 accuse each other of being rude and being off topic; then TuffTodd6 leaves the thread, announcing in his last post "Outta of your thread" (post 112).

My analysis of this set of posts demonstrates how posters use intertextual resources—the quotation function in particular—to reinvoke and problematize others' posts. In general, posts are problematized because they do not meet the thread's particular focus and/or break the general guidelines for participation on the discussion boards (i.e., they bully or constitute an "attack"). However, as mentioned, there are indications that this thread was in fact highly functional overall: it is long (283 posts) and unfolded quickly (all posts but two occurred in the 48 hours after the original post). It did not get shut down by a moderator, which either means the discourse was civil enough to not be perceived as breaking forum guidelines, or that no moderator kept up with the thread. Further, posters themselves evaluated the thread positively. As shown Trugeri in post 191 evaluated the thread as being "relatively on topic" and as including "a decent amount of friendly debate" and "one of the most neutral discussions" she has seen on the topic (extract 2); multiple posters positively evaluate, and thus communicate about, others' contributions, typically by thanking them for, or complimenting, what they posted.

In summary, posters to this thread on "clean eating" negotiate not only the concept of "clean" (which is required if they are to discuss studies comparing "clean" and "unclean" diets, which was the OP's request), but also what constitutes a productive post to such a thread, in terms of relevant and high-quality content, as well as tone. While "tone" is specifically addressed in the forum guidelines in prohibitions against bullying and personal attacks (for example), which are typically enforced by moderators, users themselves also use intertextual resources to engage in metadiscourse regarding their own, and especially others', posts. They thus co-construct the thread as not only an unfolding of meanings and guidelines, but also an unfolding set of relationships: users' posts, in intertextually linking to and commenting on others' posts, shape not only what is valued in the thread and influence who participates, but also how participants should treat one another more generally.

CONCLUSION

In conclusion, the analysis presented in this chapter demonstrated how intertextual strategies are used to create metadiscourse in this online discussion thread; this metadiscourse addresses words, aspects of posts, whole posts, and the entire thread. Participants engage in two primary metadiscursive activities or frames: they define terms that are important to the community of dieters and others interested in health ("clean" and "unclean" eating and food), and they negotiate what constitutes appropriate participation in the thread, given its purpose and focus on "scientific studies"; related, they simultaneously negotiate what counts more generally as appropriate participation in the community of practice (e.g., "bullying" as unacceptable). In addition, they use intertextual linking strategies that create humorous metadiscourse, which intermittently occurs (though sometimes it is not recognized as funny or is not appreciated).

I identified multiple intertextual strategies that are used to accomplish metadiscourse in this thread: quotation marks, the board's quotation function, exact repetition of parts of others posts as well as paraphrase, deictics (pronouns but also the "^" caret), and uses of visual material in the form of GIFs, images, and emoji. These serve to tie discourse to previous discourse, and to facilitate evaluation of and response to that discourse, which occur through the uses of adjectives, speech act and activity labels and characterizations, and speech acts. Some of the intertextual linking strategies are available offline as well as online—for example repetition or paraphrase of another person's words is a common feature of conversation, it is easy to produce gestural air quotes and use voice quality to indicate quotation, and deictic pronouns are as convenient in spoken interaction as in online text—but I have also shown how these online participants take advantage of the affordances of the medium to facilitate intertextual linking and engage in metadiscursive activities. The posters take advantage of the persistence of posts, the quotation function of the boards, the "^" symbol, and the easy (re)production of emojis, memes, images, and hyperlinks. Thus online intertextual linking, and the facilitated metadiscourse, may differ from forms offline.

Overall then, this chapter's findings advocate for an understanding of intertextuality and metadiscourse as fundamentally interconnected: to engage in (and understand) metadiscourse, posters (and other language users) must make (and recognize) intertextual links. These findings also reinforce previous research suggesting that understandings of food (in this case, as "clean" and "unclean") are negotiated moment by moment in interaction, including among members of online communities of practice centered around communicating about food and health, as well as studies highlighting how participation norms are negotiated among members of online groups. They extend existing research by highlighting metadiscourse as a fundamental component of such interactions, and delving into the specifics of online intertextuality that make it possible.

CHAPTER 3

"I fixed it for you"

Intertextuality and metadiscourse in a digital trope

Intertextuality is mobilized not only to engage in the metadiscursive activities of defining word meanings and appropriate forms of participation. In this chapter I examine how participants accomplish another consequential metadiscursive social action on the discussion boards: "fixing." This refers to instances where one poster, by way of intertextual linking strategies, adjusts some element of another person's prior post and uses metadiscourse to indicate explicitly that the post has been "fixed." This is widely recognized as an Internet trope or meme known as "fixed it for you" or "fixed that for you" (commonly abbreviated as FIFY, fify, FTFY, or ftfy). According to knowyourmeme.com (https://knowyourmeme.com/memes/fixed-that-for-you-ftfy), in contemporary use it tends to be used in a sarcastic way "to disparage the opinion or work of another," though the site notes that it seems to have initially emerged among computer programmers working together cooperatively (e.g., one person experiences difficulty making an image visible, and a second solves the problem and notes, "fify") (see https://www.cyber definitions.com/definitions/FIFY.html for a similar hypothesized history of the meme).

My analysis of examples of "fixing" reveals three functions in the context of the FriendInFitness (FIF) discussion boards: (1) It is used in a fairly literal or sincere sense, where a poster solves some "trouble" or "problem" in another's prior post, thereby providing assistance (similar to the initial use of the trope described by knowyourmeme.com); (2) "fixed" is used in a sarcastic sense, and the meme accomplishes disagreement (this is the most common usage, and probably the most widely recognized online, in line with the current knowyourmeme.com definition); and (3) the trope is used playfully, to joke and

Intertextuality 2.0. Cynthia Gordon, Oxford University Press. © Oxford University Press 2023.
DOI: 10.1093/oso/9780197642689.003.0003

construct humor. While the "fixed it for you" formula has wide use across many online websites and social media platforms and has been discussed in popular online discourse such as on knowyourmeme.com and urbandictionary.com, to my knowledge this chapter represents the first linguistic study of the "fixed it for you" trope, including a more formal identification of three basic functions, one of which (the joking function) seems to be to date undocumented.

In highlighting the functions of "fixed it for you," my analysis also shows how "fixing" another person's post is a highly structured online action that is characterized by a pattern that I summarize as *reproduce—replace—refer—remark*. Each part of this pattern is intrinsically intertextual: to *reproduce*, a poster who is "fixing" uses the quotation function of the discussion boards to reproduce some prior post; to *replace*, the poster adjusts some aspect of the prior post via font manipulations (using strikethrough, bold, or underlining) and/or via adding or deleting text or a visual element such as a GIF; *refer* is accomplished by use of deictics—the caret symbol (^) and/or the pronoun "it" (or, less commonly on these boards, "that")—which connect, via pointing, the fixer's discourse to the post being fixed; and *remark* is accomplished by the production of metadiscourse that names what has taken place, typically "fixed it," "I fixed it for you" or its abbreviation ("FIFY" or "fify"), or just "fixed." These features of the "fixing" pattern link online posts to prior posts, and text to prior text.

"Fixing" is not just a means of adjusting post content; it simultaneously accomplishes relational work among members of the community of practice. To explore this, I follow Tannen's (1994) conceptualization of the interconnected dimensions of power and solidarity in interaction, and her outlining of the polysemous and ambiguous nature of linguistic strategies in regard to these dimensions. Specifically, I suggest that the meme functions simultaneously as what Tannen (2003, 2007a) terms a "power maneuver" and a "connection maneuver." "Fixing" another's post, especially in a way that implies disagreement, is a power maneuver in the sense that it threatens face (as this concept was introduced by Goffman [1967] and extended by Brown and Levinson [1987]). It evaluates another person's discourse as inadequate or problematic, which leads me to draw some links between "fixing" and the phenomenon of conversational repair (e.g., as described by Schegloff 1992; Schegloff, Jefferson, and Sacks 1977) and to explain its potential as a threat to solidarity and to the positive face of the person whose post is being "fixed." "Fixing" implies that the person doing the fixing is more knowledgeable or competent, and the action is also viewable as an imposition on the person whose discourse is "fixed" (thus threatening negative face). The fact that "fixing," in particular its uses to construct disagreement, is an on-record and persistent form of what might be termed "correction" (e.g., Goodwin 1983; Jefferson 1974) or "corrective repair" (e.g., Dings 2012; Woude and Barton 2001) tends to support a hierarchy-based interpretation of the strategy. However, "correcting" or "helping out" with another person's discourse production can also be viewed through a more solidarity-based lens, especially in contexts where people are engaged in learning and asymmetries in knowledge are known to be present (such as in parent–child interactions and in classrooms; see, e.g., Dippold 2014 and Yang 2009). An online discussion board, where participants exchange information and seek advice and support, and use a shared set of affordances (of language and of the medium) to do so, is arguably one such context. In fact, in some cases (i.e., in the context of the "assisting" function), participants thank others who "fixed" their post, which demonstrates a solidarity-oriented interpretation. In cases where "fixed it for you" is used to joke, multiple participants often demonstrate appreciation. Even when the face-threatening action of "correcting" is taking place, such as in the examples where disagreement is constructed and the term "fixed" is used in a sarcastic sense, there is a metamessage of connection (in that the post is being acknowledged), following Tannen's (2007b) theorizing on repetition and intertextuality. In other words, each use of the trope (re)affirms in-group membership by reanimating a shared practice (a practice that is also used more widely on the Internet). Further, as examples in this chapter will show, the "fixed it for you" trope is used to animate regularly occurring debates on the boards, such as the debate examined in the last chapter of whether "clean" eating is a real and legitimate practice.

In what follows, I first briefly review relevant research on repair in interaction (including online), as my understanding of the "fixed it for you" trope is broadly grounded in the idea that pointing out and addressing a "trouble" or "problem" in another person's already-produced discourse tends to be a relatively face-threatening move that is accomplished in patterned ways. I then turn to analysis of nine "fixed it for you" examples drawn from the discussion boards across various threads, illustrating how fixing is a metadiscursive activity that features both power and solidarity across the three functions of assisting, disagreeing, and joking. In the Conclusion, I discuss how the intertexuality of fixing as a form and a metadiscursive activity—both within specific instances and across the practice more generally—serves as a binding function among users on the discussion boards.

REPAIRING (OTHERS') CONTRIBUTIONS TO (ONLINE) INTERACTIONS

In this section, I briefly review studies on repair, especially those focused on repairs initiated on other participants' discourse and repair in online contexts, which thus have links to "fixing." As research has shown, repair is fundamentally tied to discourse sequence and structure, and it is related to the management of face concerns and the negotiation of relationships. Existing research also indicates that metadiscourse is sometimes used vis-à-vis repair-related activities (such as when a participant labels an utterance as "correction"), and that repair is dependent on intertextuality (by way of repetition), though the terms "metadiscourse" and "intertextuality," and theorizing associated with these terms, do not surface in this body of research. These concepts figure prominently in my analysis of the "fixed it for you" trope, however, along with select findings about forms and functions of repair in discourse.

According to Schegloff (2000:207), the term "repair," as developed and used by conversation analysts, refers to "practices for dealing with problems or troubles in speaking, hearing, and understanding the talk in conversation (and in other forms of talk-in-interaction, for that matter)." In other words, repair is initiated (and often completed) when something is oriented to as problematic by at least one of the participants, momentarily making repair the interaction's main activity. Repairs can be initiated by the speaker of the trouble source (e.g., by self-interrupting) or by another participant (e.g., by expressing confusion through uttering "huh?"). Likewise, they can be completed by the speaker or another participant (e.g., by replacing a troublesome word with another). According to Meredith and Stokoe (2014:184), who examine self-repair in Facebook chat interactions, "[a]ny aspect of talk can become the target of repair," and repair is "an omnirelevant feature of interaction," including online.

"Correction" has been identified as a subtype of repair, and it is a subtype, I suggest, that is especially closely related to uses of "fixing" that construct disagreement. As Meredith and Stokoe (2014:186) explain, "correction is a class of repair which occurs when there has been an 'actual' error" (although as indicated by the authors' use of quotation marks, what constitutes an "actual" error is not necessarily clear). More broadly, "correction" occurs when "an utterance is deemed inadequate" in some way (Dippold 2014:403).

Identifying and fixing a problem in another person's talk constitutes a face-threatening act (e.g., Lerner 1996; Svennevig 2008). It can function to "challenge either an element in prior speaker's talk or the action put forward by prior speaker," as M. H. Goodwin (1983:670) points out; thus, correcting another person can serve as a means of disagreeing. Robinson (2006:139) demonstrates that repairing another person's talk is fundamentally intertwined with relationship management, since it serves as a means of displaying "disbelief in, disagreement with, challenge to, or rejection of" some action being produced by the speaker. A number of studies have thus explored how different means of initiating and accomplishing repair variously affect face and create assorted degrees of (dis)alignment among participants (see, e.g., Egbert 1997; Kasper and Prior 2015; Svennevig 2008; Waring 2005).

Other research highlights how the perceived face threat of repairing some other speaker's talk, and thus the form of such repairs, is shaped by context; some contexts where other-correction tends to occur more commonly and in less mitigated forms include parent–child conversations (Schegloff et al. 1977), classroom interactions of various types (e.g., Dippold 2014; Kasper 1985; Mackey, Park, and Tagarelli 2016), as well as other contexts where competence differences may be highlighted, such as in conversations between native and nonnative speakers of a language (e.g., Hosoda 2000, 2001). As Yang (2009:318) summarizes, repair in the form of correction "may well be more generally relevant to the not-yet-competent in some domain without respect to age." It is important to note that within such encounters, other-repair does not occur uniformly but, rather, varies depending on what activity is unfolding at a given moment. In general, though, in such contexts, a "helping" interpretation is often highlighted.

Intertextuality is inherently part of any type of repair or correction, as repair involves some "original" text or utterance, along with a text or utterance that comments on or recasts (some aspect of) that original. Repetition, be it full or partial, is an oft-identified strategy for accomplishing repair (e.g., Kim and Kim 2014; Schegloff 1992; Schegloff et al. 1977). For example, in their analysis of conversations among friends and family members, Robinson and Kevoe-Feldman (2010) find that full repeats are used to initiate repair on another's discourse, specifically to problematize the entire action. Examining spoken interaction among young children, Goodwin (1983) identifies what Halliday and Hasan (1976) call "substitution" as a strategy for accomplishing correction; this refers to "the replacement of one item in a sentence by another having a similar structural function" (Halliday and Hasan 1976:145, as cited in Goodwin 1983:663). As Goodwin explains, in such cases, the utterance doing the correcting "frequently maintains a shape similar to that of the prior utterance with the exception of the item being replaced, produced with emphatic stress, and thus marking it as an alternative to a similar item in the preceding utterance" (p. 663). Chui (1996) also identifies repetition as a key strategy (among others, such as replacement and addition) for accomplishing repair in Chinese conversations among friends.

In online discourse too, intertextuality (in the form of repetition) and face concerns are both parts of repair, and insights from research in this area are relevant to my discussion of the "fixed it for you" trope. Yang's (2009) examination of repair in Chinese online discussions that are part of teacher education courses in Hong Kong uncovered a preponderance of other-repair (owing to cultural factors as well as the learning context), but in her data only self-repair manifested patterns that can most clearly be related to intertextuality—"rephrasing," "reformatting," and (especially) "repeating." Yang found that other-repair was commonly used in the processes of knowledge-seeking and "cooperating with the speaker of the trouble source to continue the conversation" (p. 339). Schönfeldt and Golato's (2003) analysis of repair in multiparty German online chat discourse shows that partial repeats are often used to initiate repair on others' discourse, though those others are often left to complete the repair, and that identified trouble sources are similar to those in everyday conversation, such as lack of understanding of who exactly a pronoun refers to, and occasionally to factual or grammatical errors. The authors also address trouble sources that are shaped by the chat medium. For example, when a first pair part is not responded to in an appropriate amount of time, a participant might complain (e.g., "hey, no time for me?") or describe a nonverbal action (e.g., *looks around*).

Collister (2011) examines a repair strategy used among members of a community of online gamers, which she labels "*-repair," since the repair involves using an asterisk "as a repair morpheme to mark the corrected version of a previously incorrect discourse item" (p. 918). She discovered this pattern of repair while conducting an ethnography among players of the fantasy adventure game *World of Warcraft*, which is a massively multiplayer online role-playing game (MMORPG). The morpheme is used to repair a typo in a prior line of chat, or a production error (such as when a player forgets to include a piece of needed information in a message); "correction" aptly describes these instances of repair. The following example, adapted from Collister (p. 919), shows how this works when a player named Aniko mistypes "out" as "ot":

1   Aniko: when I run ot
2   Aniko: out*

As Collister explains, Aniko uses the asterisk after the corrected version of the word, but in other cases, it appears before. Further, the caret (^) is occasionally used instead by some users; Collister thus suggests it is an "allomorph" of the asterisk in *-repair (p. 919). She also finds that *-repair is used for other-initiated, other-completed repair as well, and this is often perceived as teasing (though she does not provide specific examples). The caret or asterisk is used as a means of tying the original to the repaired version, creating intertextuality (though Collister does not use the term).

In Gordon (2019), I examine user comments on expert-written blogs that appear on the FIF website (these appear in an area separate from the discussion boards), showing how posters collaboratively initiate, accomplish, and show appreciation for repair activities, i.e., when commenters initiate or complete "correction" on some aspect of a blog post. While the "fixed it for you" formula did not emerge in my examination of ten such blog posts, these blog corrections, which involve identifying some aspect of the blog as troublesome, are mitigated through various linguistic strategies (such as complimenting a blogger before identifying the misuse of a lexical item in the blog post). Corrections are aimed at various aspects of blog text, including vocabulary and amount of information provided, as well as the choice of accompanying images, such as when readers of the blog identify an accompanying image as not making sense. Similarly, in the "fixed it for you" examples I examine in this chapter, both text and images are repaired.

The aforementioned studies highlight various forms and functions of repair online. A number of repair-focused studies, both on and offline, also highlight some level of participant awareness that some kind of "repair" or "correction" is taking place, such as when commenters to a blog collaboratively accomplish repair, though without explicitly naming the activity (Gordon 2019), or when online gamers routinely use a symbol that functions as a morpheme for repair or correction (Collister 2011). Dippold's (20145) study of classroom discourse also shows participant awareness of repair or correction as an activity: in the classroom, one instructor explicitly indicates to students that "correction" is occurring or has taken place, such as by saying "Don't take corrections personal" (p. 407), and another tells the researcher in a post-recording interview how in class he prefers to wait until a student has finished speaking "and then do the corrections after" (p. 411). Earlier, Jefferson (1987:97) highlighted that corrections are sometimes "exposed"; i.e., correction becomes "an interactional business in its own right." The examples of "fixing" that I consider are of this type in the sense that they are explicitly marked with the metadiscursive term "fixed" (or its abbreviation, "F" or "f"), along with other routine, intertextual structural elements that accomplish fixing and mark it as a particular type of "interactional business." In the context of this "business," posters accomplish different functions as they negotiate power and solidarity. I now turn to my analysis.

"FIXING" ON THE FIF DISCUSSION BOARDS

This analysis shows that the metadiscursive activity of "fixing" is both highly structured and multifunctional, being used to assist, construct disagreement, and joke and play. While one instance of "fixing" may accomplish multiple functions at once, for presentation purposes I organize examples into what I identified as their primary function. Following the sampling technique Herring (2004) describes as "by phenomenon," I have drawn these examples from across the website's discussion boards and threads; all involve use of the term "fixed" (or "fify," "FIFY," "ftfy," or "FTFY," abbreviations in which the first "f" stands in for "fixed"). Examples were identified by using the boards' search function. I stopped collecting examples when I reached "inductive theoretical saturation" (Saunders et al. 2018), that is, when additional examples did not lead to the identification of new categories (i.e., new examples fit into my existing categories based on the overall functions of helping, disagreeing, or joking).

Examining these multiple occurrences of cases where one participant "fixes" some aspect of another's post, I identified a pattern for accomplishing this action, which I refer to as *reproduce—replace—refer—remark*. In what follows I highlight the fundamental role of intertextuality in creating the meta-discursive "fixed it for you" trope.

"Fixing" as assisting

In this section, I consider examples that demonstrate how "fixing" can be used to assist or help other posters manage technical aspects of the discussion boards. As mentioned, this is thought perhaps to be the "original" use of "FIFY"/"fixed it for you"—one person sincerely helps another person post something online. In addition to demonstrating the *reproduce—replace—refer—remark* pattern, this use of fixing highlights relations of both hierarchy and solidarity among posters: providing assistance shows solidarity but also highlights differences in terms of knowledge and expertise.

The first example is drawn from the Chit-Chat discussion board, a board characterized primarily by self-introductions, playful interactions, and discussions that extend beyond health and weight loss to other areas of life such as hobbies. The thread name was "Tell me . . .," and the original post read "How you feel today . . . in Gif!! Go!" This thread's purpose is for each poster to share a GIF that captures their current mood. This type of thread constitutes a "game," and it is quite common on the Chit-Chat board as well as the Games board (similar threads ask users to share a favorite GIF, or to share a photo of a puppy, or to list the name of the last film they saw). This particular thread opening resulted in participants posting a range of GIFs, including of a cat riding a robotic vacuum, a man dancing, a giraffe chewing, comedian John Stewart eating popcorn, characters from the TV show *Scrubs* dancing, a bearded man shaking his head, and a duckling falling asleep. Some of the GIFs featured text, and some did not. In the midst of the unfolding thread, Theo183 posts a contribution, but the GIF does not upload correctly, as shown in Figure 3.1 (it's the only content for extract 1a):

(1a) Theo183

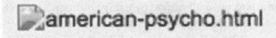

Figure 3.1. Theo183's failed GIF.

Here Theo183 has attempted to upload a GIF from the movie *American Psycho* wherein actor Christian Bale does a funny dance while wearing a raincoat just before his character gruesomely murders the other man in the room with an axe. In the next post, baynesofwolves makes the fix (I use one still shot below to represent the GIF she posts, shown in Figure 3.2).

(1b) <u>baynesofwolves</u>

    fixed it for you ^^^

Figure 3.2. Fixed GIF.

User baynesofwolves posts directly after the "troublesome" post, *reproducing* the GIF in the correct format, which also serves to *replace* the faulty GIF—it is "repeated" but in the correct format. The "it" in baynesofwolves' "fixed it for you^^^" *refers* to Theo183's post, as do the three pointing carets. In using this format, she accomplishes "fixing" in a way that does a favor for Theo183: he made a posting error that prevented his message from coming across, so she assists. One intervening post occurs by another poster, but then Theo183 acknowledges and shows gratitude for the help, posting, "Thanks! 😊 I'll get the hang of it eventually." (Interestingly, I observed in August 2018 that baynesofwolves' correct posting of the GIF changed back to the way Theo183's originally appeared—as an html link, but not a GIF; while I do not know for sure, it is possible this change occurred for copyright or technological reasons.)

Across the discussion boards, it is common to use "fixed it for you" to provide sincere assistance to other posters regarding posting images, videos, and GIFs. There are many examples; I will describe a few more here. In one, a poster tries but fails to post a GIF in a discussion thread called "RESPECT YOURSELF IN YOUR PROFILE PICS" on the Chit-Chat discussion board. The intended GIF, which does not post (as Theo183's did not), shows a character from the television cartoon *South Park* dressed as a police officer and racing forward on a motorcycle, and the text captures the character's catchphrase ("RESPECT MY AUTHORITAY [authority]"). The fixing poster quotes the previous poster's failed post and then posts the GIF in the correct format, adding

"FIFY" and an animated smiley face emoji offering a flower, which looks something like this when still-captured:

(2)   Still shot of animated emoji used in "FIFY" post

This animated emoji, colloquially known as "a flower for you," can be interpreted as emphasizing that the "fixed it for you" is sincerely offered in this case to assist the poster whose GIF failed to post.

An example similar to this one is when a poster attempts to post before-and-after weight loss photos to a thread called "I think Im seeing progress" on the Success Stories discussion board and fails to do so. Another poster reposts the photos, this time correctly, and adds "Fixed it for ya! Way to go!" In another thread on the Success Stories board called "my results so far," a poster tries to post her before-and-after photos but the photos do not show properly; another poster posts "Fixed 'em for ya. 'IMG' has to be lower case. Way to go! Keep up the great work!" and underneath that posts the images correctly. The comment that "'IMG' has to be lower case" provides some technical information for why the images initially failed to load correctly, and we see evidence of generosity not only in the fixing, but also in the compliment and encouragement. This example also highlights hierarchical aspects of using the trope: one poster has more knowledge than the other, and here the "fixing" poster takes up somewhat of a "teacher" alignment not only by assisting, but also by explaining how to post correctly. The casual use of "'em" for "them" and "ya" for "you" helps mitigate this, however, and can be viewed as evoking solidarity.

There seems to be a widespread understanding that posting image-related content to the discussion boards can be challenging; for example, a poster attempts to post an image on a thread on the Success Stories board to show his weight loss success and comments, "Let's see if this works." It initially does not, and another poster makes the image viewable and adds, "^^^ FIFY ^^^." This involves using the abbreviated form of "fixed it for you," as well as multiple uses of the caret to *refer*, and thereby intertextually connect, to what has been fixed. There are also numerous threads focused specifically on how to post image-related content, including "How to attach a picture into my post," "HOW TO POST PICTURE," "How to post a Gif," "How to post a video," and "Quick Refresher on How to Post Pics/GIFs."

In addition, worth noting is that there is metadiscourse on the boards demonstrating posters' recognition that "fixing" is a way of helping and that it is a discernible activity that can be referred to. For instance, one poster tried to post a GIF to a thread called "Flaunt It" on the Chit-Chat discussion board, but it didn't work, and the poster added the following text to the post: "Y U NO WORK GIF??!!!?!?" Another poster quoted the post and added "Jus put the link and let someone else FIFY" (i.e., just post the link and someone else will fix it for you; in other words, someone else will help you by posting the GIF correctly).

In summary, "fixing" is a metadiscursive activity or practice, grounded in intertextual linking, that is widely used on the FIF discussion boards to assist other posters with using the online platform, specifically to post image-related content. These posts aim at helping and are taken up as helpful by others. While, following theorizing by Tannen (1994), helping another person entails both power and solidarity, "fixing" as assisting is typically oriented to through the lens of solidarity, as participants show appreciation. With a "fixed" posted image or GIF, people who initially failed to post correctly are able to have their content understood and acknowledged. The hierarchy aspect becomes more visible when expert posters provide explicit instructions on how to post image-related content in threads with titles such as "How to post a gif." However, it may be that on such threads, which might be viewable as contexts of learning (following Yang 2009), hierarchy is relatively backgrounded to shared pursuit of knowledge (in this case, technical knowledge about how to post to the boards). The metadiscursive activity of "fixing" as helping focuses on solidarity.

"Fixing" to construct disagreement

Before showing examples of how the "fixed it for you" trope is used to disagree with or contradict another poster, it is important to point out that "fixing" is only one way of doing this. Chapter 2 showed numerous examples of one poster disagreeing with another poster's post in terms of content appropriateness, thereby suggesting their post was a "trouble source," such as by quoting their post and adding "That's not really helpful"; definitions of "clean eating" were contradicted by offering alternatives. Posters across the boards sometimes quote others' posts and then use words and phrases that make their disagreement apparent (e.g., "No . . . just no."; "Uhh . . . wait what the what?? No."; and "Wrong.") or use language to contradict an immediately preceding post without quoting it.

In the landscape of ways of constructing disagreement, "fixed it for you" stands out for its structural predictability and its status as a metadiscursive meme or trope. Its function to disagree is related to, but different from, its use to assist: "fixing" here offers (sarcastic) "assistance" that the other person likely does not want, as the "fix" is actually a contradiction. As mentioned, this use seems to be the most common use of the trope online, and it is prominent on these boards as well.

An example of "fixing" being used to accomplish disagreement is drawn from the just-mentioned thread on the topic of the importance of diet versus exercise for weight loss. A poster had indicated that she had lost weight by keeping track of her calorie intake and expenditure, using the term "CICO" (calories in, calories out). In other words, by monitoring both her diet and exercise, she had successfully lost weight. A participant called ColdBen responds to this by disagreeing (and correcting), suggesting that reducing carbohydrates (carbs), not calories in general, causes weight loss; it is ColdBen's post that will be "fixed."

(3a)   ColdBen
    1   If you've lost weight via CICO it's because you reduced your carbs in
    2   the process.

ColdBen is suggesting that weight loss is about cutting carbohydrates specifically, not calories (which contradicts the previous poster and can be conceptualized as an instance of corrective repair in that it addresses some kind of "error"). After six intervening posts by other posters, VinoSorbet quotes ColdBen's comment and "fixes" it, manipulating font and adding words to do so, and comments on what she has done ("Fixed it for you"). (As in the previous chapter, material that is reproduced using the quotation function of the discussion boards is shaded gray.)

(3b)   VinoSorbet

> ColdBen
> If you've lost weight via **low carb** ~~CICO~~ it's because you reduced your ~~carbs~~ **calories** in the process.

    1   Fixed it for you

VinoSorbet uses the boards' quotation function to *reproduce* the entirety of ColdBen's comment, exploiting the affordances of the medium to create intertextuality (between ColdBen's "original" and her reproduction of it) and facilitate the fix. This differs somewhat from the examples examined in the previous section in that faultily posted GIFs are typically not reproduced in their faulty forms with an accompanying correct form (and instead only the correct GIF is produced). In contrast, "faulty" text-based posts are (partially or fully) reproduced, as occurs in this example. VinoSorbet also *replaces* some of ColdBen's text; specifically, she uses strikethrough to cross out "CICO" and bold font to add the phrase "low carb" in its place, and strikethrough to cross out "carbs" and bold font to replace it with "calories." The bold font on the terms calls further attention to them. She thus changes the meaning of ColdBen's post: she suggests that weight loss is all about calorie deficit and is not about carbohydrate intake specifically (i.e., if you have tried a low-carb diet and believe you lost weight specifically from reducing carbs, you are wrong; in fact, by reducing carbs, you inadvertently reduced calories, and calories are what matter). VinoSorbet also adds her own comment after quoting and adjusting ColdBen's post: "Fixed it for you" (line 1). The "it" *refers* to ColdBen's post and treats it as separate from her current discourse, and "fixed it for you" *remarks* what she has done: it calls attention to and names her discursive move. Her "fixing" is used to advance a perspective that contrasts and disagrees with ColdBen's.

The next example is drawn from a thread called "understanding my own body type"; the thread was posted on the Goal: Gaining Weight and Body Building discussion board (which tends to be populated by posters, often but not exclusively men, interested in bodybuilding). The OP, lewispaul111, indicated that in his experience, whenever he started working with an online fitness coach, the coach would design a workout and make nutritional recommendations for him based on his body type. The OP thus wanted to know how he could determine his own body type, so that he could design his own diet and workout. Rock_IAO is the first poster to respond; he suggests that lewispaul111 "Just follow FIF recommendations for steady, safe and lasting weight loss" since this "works perfectly for all body types." In response, lewispaul111 clarifies his goal, "I wanna gain muscle." Rock _IAO replies to this clarification in a five-paragraph message in which he makes recommendations regarding eating, working out, and resting; he describes his own workout (in terms of doing a warm-up using high-intensity interval training, or HIIT, lifting weights for three hours a day, taking rest days, and getting cardiovascular exercise); he suggests that genetics determine different body types (and boasts about his own body type); he suggests a website to help lewispaul111 determine his own body type; and he offers encouragement. Rock_IAO's post appears below; it is the one that is later "fixed."

(4a)   Rock_IAO

> lewispaul111
> I wanna gain muscle.

1   My bad; this is good though.

2

3   Eat clean and with a slight surplus. Go slow. And remember to rest those muscles

4   as that is key to weight gain. So many guys don't get that.

5   When I hit the weights, I need a solid 4 days to recover. On that strength training day,

6   I begin with HIIT as a morning warm up, then hit lower body and again after lunch,

7   targeting upper body. It's a three hour routine.

8

9 My muscles are dead the following day, and I take a whole day off from any training.

10 On the 3 following days I do various cardio routines with differing intensities.

11 Of course, you might not want to do all that cardio given our goals are different.

12

13 As for body type, your gains will be determined by genetics, and just focus on

14 becoming the best version of yourself whatever. It could very well be that some

15 training routines are better for different body types.

16 I am pure **MESOMORPH** with gifted athleticism which makes everything so much

17 easier.

18 Here is a test to see where you fit there. It's hardly an exact science.

19 ((*link elided*))

20

21 Good luck . . . and keep lifting brother!

22 🙂

Rock_IAO suggests in line 3 that lewispaul111 eat "clean" (as shown in the previous chapter, this concept is controversial on the discussion boards), eat slightly more calories than is recommended for weight maintenance ("a slight surplus"), and take his time with developing an exercise/weightlifting program ("Go slow. And remember to rest those muscles.") (line 3). He signs off in a friendly way, offering "Good luck," as well as encouragement to "keep lifting brother!" (line 21), and a smiley face emoji (line 22). After one intervening message, in the eighth message of the thread, djm1978 "fixes" Rock_IAO's message. He uses the boards' quotation function to *reproduce* the entirety of Rock_IAO's lengthy post and uses strikethrough to *replace* two words with nothing (i.e., he deletes the words "clean" and "and"). I have reproduced the full quotation of Rock_IAO's post, adding an arrow at the left to make the change easier to spot. User djm1978 also adds his own comment (in the comment, "macors" is a misspelling of "macros," or macronutrients).

(4b) djm1978

> lewispaul111
> I wanna gain muscle.

> Rock_IAO
> My bad; this is good though.

→ Eat ~~clean and~~ with a slight surplus. Go slow. And remember to rest those muscles as that is key to weight gain. So many guys don't get that.

> When I hit the weights, I need a solid 4 days to recover. On that strength training day, I begin with HIIT as a morning warm up, then hit lower body and again after lunch, targeting upper body. It's a three hour routine.
>
> My muscles are dead the following day, and I take a whole day off from any training. On the 3 following days I do various cardio routines with differing intensities. Of course, you might not want to do all that cardio given our goals are different.
>
> As for body type, your gains will be determined by genetics, and just focus on becoming the best version of yourself whatever. It could very well be that some training routines are better for different body types.
>
> I am pure **MESOMORPH** with gifted athleticism which makes everything so much 1 easier.
>
> Here is a test to see where you fit there. It's hardly an exact science. ((*link elided*))
>
> Good luck . . . and keep lifting brother!
>

1 fixed it for you man . . .
2 just eat and lift, and hit micros/macors . . .

Poster djm1978 uses strikethrough in the first sentence that ROCK_IAO wrote in his own post (after quoting lewispaul111's "I wanna build muscle"); with this, the sentence transforms from "Eat clean and with a slight surplus" to "Eat with a slight surplus." With the term "clean" removed via strikethrough (along with a now unnecessary "and"), djm1978 *refers* to the post and *remarks* what he has done (line 1, "fixed it for you man . . ."). He also indicates that the OP should "hit micros/macors [macros]," which makes his disagreement clearer: this seems to suggest that the practice of eating "clean" foods (which, as seen in the previous chapter, is a troublesome thing to define) is not relevant here—instead of avoiding certain categories of foods, perhaps entirely (e.g., processed foods), lewispaul111 should focus on making sure that the foods he eats allow him to meet his body's needs for vitamins, proteins, and so on. This serves as a way of negating the value (and perhaps existence) of clean eating. However, the concept of clean eating is not removed entirely; the strikethrough makes the "clean eating" controversy, and djm1978's correction, readily apparent. Thus djm1978 "corrects" Rock_IAO: this part of his message is wrong. Use of the term "man" (line 1: "fixed it for you man . . .") may serve to mitigate the face threat; as seen in (2b), Rock_IAO previously used "brother" to address the OP lewispaul111. While beyond the scope of this chapter, it appears that these kinds of address terms are fairly common among men interested in bodybuilding who post on FIF's boards.

This "fixing" is taken up as disagreement by Rock_IAO. In his next post, he quotes djm1978's entire post and adds "lol" along with an image. The image features a photo (which appears to be a stock photo) of a muscled man with a confused look on his face; there is a lightbulb drawn over his head, which is crossed out in red; and "HUH???" appears in large text in red. This demonstrates Rock_IAO's rejection of djm1978's "fixing" ("huh" has been identified as a means of initiating repair; see, e.g., Drew 1997). This is the last post to the thread.

A similar example occurs in a thread posted on the General Diet and Weight Loss Help board, though this time one poster first indicates that something is wrong in the post before another poster makes the "fix." The thread is titled "46% body fat—Ugh!," and the original poster explained that she would like to lose weight and had just become aware that she is in need of losing not only inches, but also body fat (as she indicates in the thread's title and in more detail in her post, her body fat percentage is 46%; her aim is to reduce it to about 22%). Other participants chime in to share their body fat percentages, to wish her luck, and to ask how to figure out their own body fat percentages. Robbie_Cafaro (after quoting an exchange between himself and the OP wherein he suggests that body fat is more important than weight, and she agrees) gives his advice on how to lose body fat. Part of this post will subsequently be "fixed."

(5a)   Robbie_Cafaro

((quoted material, an exchange between Robbie_Cafaro and the OP, not shown))

1 Lowering body fat is a function of clean eating coupled with proper resistance and
2 cardio exercise.
3 Clean food intake is key.
4 And that's lean meats, low fat dairy, nuts, whole grains, fresh fruits and veggies.
5 If man makes it, don't eat it. Processed foods have been demineralized and loaded
6 with salt, sugar and fat.
7
8 As for protein, I do not use shakes; we can't trust that the product is really what the
9 label claims.
10 Supplements are a huge scam.
11 Stick with lean meats for protein and whole foods mostly for general nutrition.
12 That's it . . . simple
13
14 Check and track body for free here:
15 ((link elided))

LennyBrown, in the next post, uses the boards' quotation function to *reproduce* one sentence from Robbie_Cafaro's post: "Clean food intake is key" (line 3, above). He adds to it, "Stop making things up." In this way, LennyBrown disagrees (again the concept of "clean eating" is at issue here) but doesn't offer a specific "fix." Another poster, IronNoggin, quotes two of Robbie_Cafaro's sentences and, in conjunction with deletion, bold font, and underlining, accomplishes "fixing."

(5b)   <u>IronNoggin</u>

> <u>Robbie Cafaro</u>
>
> Lowering body fat is a function of **eating at a caloric deficit <u>with adequate protein intake</u>**, coupled with proper resistance exercise.
>
> Clean food intake **(i.e., macronutrient manipulation) becomes increasingly important when trying to reach extreme (i.e. single-digit) bodyfat levels.**

   1   Fixed it for you.

IronNoggin *reproduces* part of Robbie_Cafaro's post and quite heavily revises those sentences. To make his changes more apparent, below I reproduce the quoted extract from Robbie_Cafaro's original post just above IronNoggin's adjustments to that post (which, because it was quoted by IronNoggin, is shown in gray).

(5c)

a Robbie_Cafaro: Lowering body fat is a function of clean eating

aa IronNoggin: Lowering body fat is a function of **eating at a caloric deficit <u>with adequate protein intake</u>**,

b Robbie_Cafaro: coupled with proper resistance and cardio exercise.

bb IronNoggin: coupled with proper resistance exercise.

c Robbie_Cafaro: Clean food intake is key.

cc IronNoggin: Clean food intake **(i.e., macronutrient manipulation) becomes increasingly important when trying to reach extreme (i.e. single-digit) bodyfat levels.**

IronNoggin has made several substantive changes. In line aa (IronNoggin's reproduction of Robbie_Cafaro's "Lowering body fat is a function of clean eating"), he uses bold font to replace "clean eating" with "eating at a caloric deficit with adequate protein intake"; his underlining of the last four words emphasizes the importance (to him) of protein. In bb, he deletes "and cardio" from Robbie_Cafaro's "coupled with proper resistance and cardio exercise," which suggests that cardiovascular exercise is not relevant for lowering body fat. Robbie_Cafaro's "Clean food intake is key" (line c) is modified even more: IronNoggin replaces "is key" with the following: "(i.e., macronutrient manipulation) becomes increasingly important when trying to reach extreme (i.e. single-digit) bodyfat levels." IronNoggin thus explicitly defines "clean food intake" as relating to manipulating the intake of macronutrients (and thus may avoid the interpretation of "clean eating" as referring specifically to avoiding processed foods, for example). This change also suggests that Robbie_Cafaro's recommendation to eat clean is not relevant for the OP, a woman who aims to reduce her very high body fat percentage roughly by half to reach 22; IronNoggin's "fix" indicates that clean eating is primarily for those seeking extreme results (i.e., having body fat in the single digits), and thus it does not apply here.

After making these adjustments to the quoted part of Robbie_Cafaro's post, IronNoggin adds "Fixed it for you" (extract 5b, line 1). He thus *refers* to the discourse he has quoted and *remarks* the action he has completed. Neither of the posters participates again in the thread, though another poster, Carayyy, quotes IronNoggin's fixing post (5b) and adds, "Adequate protein intake is imperative but won't help you that much if your still eating a shedload of fast carbs" (i.e., if you are still eating a lot of simple, fast-burning carbohydrates), thus offering an alternative perspective that disagrees (though without using the "fixing" formula).

A final example of the metadiscursive "fixed it for you" trope being used to disagree is drawn from the Food and Nutrition discussion board. The thread was called "Mother shamed for sending her child to school with Oreos." This original post included a link to a news story called "Preschooler gets note about cookies in her lunch: No Oreos for you." The story described how a four-year-old child in Colorado came home from preschool with a note from the teacher scolding the child's mother for having packed Oreo cookies as part of her child's lunch (and the teacher did not allow the child to eat the cookies). Posters to the discussion thread respond by addressing the issue of whether schools (or perhaps society as a whole) versus parents bear responsibility for what a child eats, what constitutes good parenting, anecdotes about their own parenting experiences, descriptions of the school policies they have dealt with, the amount of sugar in processed foods, chemicals in processed foods, and related issues.

The post that is later "fixed" was posted by a user named lizfrank7707. She advocates for the idea that all schools should ban sugary foods, with the hopes that parents would follow the rules, and children will ultimately benefit. She thus seems to be suggesting that schools and parents should work together (and that parents who break school rules are in the wrong).

(6a) lizfrank7707

   1 Whilst no one should shame a parent we should as a society start to see

   2 the growing problem of children's health.

3 For me an Oreo or cake or chocolate bar should be a treat for a child not an everyday
4 normal part of lunch.
5 If all schools agreed to the same there should be no issues. Children will do what the
6 grown ups tell them to. If the teacher says no sweet things and all the parents abide by
7 it children will eat the sandwich or whatever they are given.
8 I actually wish only water was drunk at school not fruit juices.
9 We have to get tougher for the sake of our children.
10 As a parent we should not run out of a piece of fruit or a carrot.
11 The parents who put Oreos etc into their children's lunch packs are making it hard for
12 every other parent to try and make healthy lunches as children will always complain
13 they haven't got it. That's why I wish schools would ban sugary foods completely.

About three hours later (with over 50 intervening posts), Jonesybuilt22 makes a repair to this post. She uses the boards' quotation function to quote (i.e., *reproduce*) the entirety of lizfrank7707's post but makes only one minor change: she *replaces* only two words, using bold font to call attention to them (I have added an arrow to make the changes easier to spot below) Specifically, she changes the word "our" to "my," and the word "We" to "I"; these minor changes adjust the meaning of the sentence in which they are embedded, as well as lizfrank7707's post: "We have to get tougher for the sake of our children" becomes "I have to get tougher for the sake of my children." Jonseybuilt22 also adds her own text after the quoted text, *remarking* that she has "fixed" the post.

(6b)   Jonseybuilt22

> lizfrank7707
> Whilst no one should shame a parent we should as a society start to see
> the growing problem of children's health.
> For me an Oreo or cake or chocolate bar should be a treat for a child not an everyday
> normal part of lunch.
> If all schools agreed to the same there should be no issues. Children will do what the
> grown ups tell them to. If the teacher says no sweet things and all the parents abide by
> it children will eat the sandwich or whatever they are given.
> I actually wish only water was drunk at school not fruit juices.
> → **I** have to get tougher for the sake of **my** children.
> As a parent we should not run out of a piece of fruit or a carrot.
> The parents who put Oreos etc into their children's lunch packs are making it hard for
> every other parent to try and make healthy lunches as children will always complain
> they haven't got it. That's why I wish schools would ban sugary foods completely.

1 ^fixed
2 and what is your definition of healthy?

The small change of two words suggests that people are responsible for their own children; what a child eats is an individual parent's choice (and is not the responsibility of schools or wider society). This issue is brought out explicitly elsewhere on this thread. It is also a theme on the boards, as well as in public discourse more broadly: there is some debate about whether healthy eating is an individual or collective responsibility, or both (Gordon and Cheng [2017] consider how, on one FIF thread, participants negotiate accountability for obesity by using various discursive strategies to assign blame to both cultural trends such as large restaurant portions, as well as to individuals' lack of self-discipline). As scholars have noted, that parents (and especially mothers) are responsible (and should be held accountable) for their children's poor eating habits is a common ideology (e.g., Gordon 2011), and this ideology is part of neoliberalism and capitalism (e.g., Weber 2009; Guthman 2011; Gailey 2021). Jonseybuilt22 uses "^fixed" to metacommunicate about the change she has made advancing the perspective that each parent is responsible for their own child's eating habits. Instead of using the deictic pronoun "it" to *refer* to the quoted post, she uses the caret (^). As the thread unfolds, lizfrank7707's post is also quoted by others who also disagree with her, and she in turn clarifies her position. "Fixing" thus serves as a metadiscursive activity that plays a part in the larger activity of constructing disagreement and sharing contrasting perspectives.

In conclusion, the examples discussed in this section demonstrate the routinized and intertextual nature of "fixing" as a practice, while also demonstrating how it is a strategy used to animate issues of controversy on these boards, such as what "clean eating" means, whether calories or carbohydrates matter for weight loss, and whether eating practices are an individual or collective responsibility. In other words, the "fixed it for you" trope is used to display disagreement, which helps illuminate differences in perspective, opinion, and experience among posters. Examples 5a–c hinted at how "fixing" might not always be intended and/or interpreted seriously, as Rock_IAO responded to having his post "fixed" with "lol" and a silly image. We saw in Chapter 2 how "clean" eating also became a topic for humor (when an over-the-top alcoholic beverage was called "clean"). In the next section, I turn to how fixing can be a metadiscursive activity that is humorous and playful.

"Fixing" to joke and play

The first example of the "fixed it for you" pattern being used to engage in humor and play is drawn from the Chit-Chat message board, a board that, as mentioned, tends to be focused on casual, non-serious, non-health-related interactions as well as games. The thread where this example appears was started by 183hues, who titled it "Is it okay if I just don't eat for a few days?"

(7a)   183hues

    1 I mean, like if I don't eat for the next 4 days but I eat a ton on this weekends . . . .

    2 can I save up all my calories and drink a bottle of tequila and eat pizza and

    3 cheese fries all weekend?

The poster asks if it is acceptable to fast or starve oneself with the purpose of "saving" all the calories for unhealthy weekend eating and drinking, such that the starvation will balance the binging and not cause weight gain. Although the poster's intent is unclear, the post is treated as a joke by most of the posters, perhaps because of the extreme unhealthiness of "tequila" and "pizza and cheese fries," the fact that alcohol is often treated with humor on the boards, and that the post appeared on the Chit-Chat board (rather than, for instance, on the General Health, Fitness and Diet board). Apparently, if any moderators saw the post, they did not interpret it seriously at first either; if they had seen it and interpreted it as a serious post, they would likely have determined that it breaks the discussion boards' prohibition of promoting unsafe eating behaviors—here, fasting for four days, then binging—and it would be a thread that could be shut down, or "locked." (In fact, in August 2018, when I went to look back at the thread, I found it was no longer present on the FIF discussion boards, so it is likely that it was locked and deleted.)

Several posters to the thread speculate that 183hues is a troll, meaning the poster just wants to start trouble on the boards, while many others express appreciation for the humor and respond in kind. One such response in the thread is one that gets "fixed"; it is shown below. The post ends with an animated emoji of crying with tears at the end of line 2 (a still shot of the animated emoji looks something like this: ●).

(7b)   rattracker

1   I've heard of people who fast for religious purposes but I'm not sure tequila

2   is going to get you closer to God. *((animated crying emoji not shown))*

This post demonstrates the non-serious uptake of 183hues' post. The idea that tequila might bring someone closer to God is an absurd one. The animated crying emoji seems to reflect a mock overemotional reaction (if tequila likely does not bring people closer to God, that is a tragedy). Emojis help "to convey an important aspect of the linguistic utterance they are attached to: What the user intends by what he or she types" (Dresner and Herring 2010:256); they are what Gumperz (1982) calls contextualization cues. The use of the overemotional crying face here arguably functions to reinforce the humorous tone of the exchange, while also closing out the post.

Twenty-six messages later, Canwesnuggle *reproduces* the post, using the boards' quotation function, and "fixes" it, continuing the humorous key.

(7c) Canwesnuggle

> rattracker
> I've heard of people who fast for religious purposes but I'm **POSITIVE** tequila
> is going to get you closer to God. ((*animated crying emoji not shown*))

1 There, I fixed it for you.

Canwesnuggle *replaces* "not sure" with "POSITIVE" (in all caps and bold font). This alters the meaning of rattracker's post, but it is not a serious disagreement or difference in perspective: it functions as joking, working to create play collaboratively through a metadiscursive activity. While rattracker expresses mock misery that tequila will not bring a person closer to the divine, Canwesnuggle asserts, with extreme certainty, that tequila definitely has that power. In addition to making this change, Canwesnuggle also *refers* to and *remarks* what she has done in line 1 ("There, I fixed it for you."). This joking "fixing" post fits in with other joking posts that do not follow the "fixing" format, such as those suggesting the OP use cocaine, heroin, or crack instead of drinking tequila, or those who kid around about their own experiences with drinking, such as luaufish, who quotes the same message that Canwesnuggle did but instead of using the "fixed" formula simply describes his or her own experiences. The poster also uses an animated laughing emoji, as noted below.

(7d) luaufish

> rattracker
> I've heard of people who fast for religious purposes but I'm not sure tequila
> is going to get you closer to God. ((*animated crying emoji not shown*))

1 last time I had half a bottle of Tequila on an empty tummy, I'm pretty sure I saw God
2 ((*animated laughing emoji not shown*)) I may have been praying to a porcelain God,
3 but meh. Cinco de May 2009 . . . ahh . . . good times. Definitely a religious
4 experience!

Here luaufish uses the quotation function to *reproduce* rattracker's post and jokes by indicating that he or she "saw God" when "praying to a porcelain God" (which is slang for vomiting into a toilet bowl), and describing this as "a religious experience." Luaufish's use of the animated laughing emoji also contributes to the playful, lighthearted tone of this post and matches rattracker's use of an animated emoji. The earlier post (extract 7c) by Canwesnuggle that "fixed" rattracker's post accomplished something similar to this one—joking and creating solidarity—though luaufish does not use the fixing format. As "fixing" is not the only way to disagree, it is also not the only way to joke and play.

Another example of the fixing trope occurs in a thread called "The Singles Hangout" on the Chit-Chat discussion board. This thread is an unusually long, continuous thread, with over 2400 pages of posts as of August 2018. In a section of the thread where posters were greeting each other with good mornings (on the 740th page of the thread), WizeGuy7 had posted, "Thumping headache today, it is yet to leave me in peace!" and Marta3331 quotes this and adds a comment to it, as shown below. Her post is later "fixed" by another poster.

(8a)   Marta3331

> WizeGuy7
> Thumping headache today, it is yet to leave me in peace!

   1   *hands painkiller and glass of water*

Marta3331's comment on WizeGuy7's quote uses asterisks to frame her contribution as an action: she symbolically (and playfully) offers the man with a headache a painkiller and some water to take it with. AskTania quotes this exchange and "fixes" Marta3331's post, which continues the play, and makes it even more ridiculous (in so doing, she actually reproduces the exchange between WizeGuy7 and Marta3331 twice, "fixing" the second iteration).

(8b)   AskTania

> WizeGuy7
> Thumping headache today, it is yet to leave me in peace!
>
> Marta331
> *hands painkiller and glass of water*
>
>
> Thumping headache today, it is yet to leave me in peace!
>
>
> *hands painkiller and glass of **wine***

   1   fixed it for you . . .

AskTania *reproduces* Marta3331's post (which itself quotes WizeGuy7's), *replaces* "water" with "wine" (using bold font to call attention to the change), and *refers* to the post and *remarks* what she has done (line 1, "fixed it for you . . ."). While the structural formula matches the serious, disagreement-oriented "fixing" posts, given the ridiculous change from offering water to offering an alcoholic beverage (exactly what one does not need when one has a headache, and something that one should not mix with painkillers), her post functions to extend and intensify the joke and does not function as a serious "correction." Like the Bloody Mary example in Chapter 2 and examples 7a–d in this chapter, which involve tequila, it also uses a reference to alcohol as a source of humor.

The next example again shows "fixing" being used for the creation of a meta-discursive play or joking activity. While it follows the *reproduce—replace—refer—remark* pattern, it uses the "FIFY" acronym for "fixed it for you." The example is drawn from a thread called "Skim Milk or Whole Milk for weight loss?"; the thread was posted on the General Health, Fitness and Diet discussion board. In the thread, posters discuss the pros and cons of drinking skim versus whole milk. A user named subsawa wrote a post that explains, in three very short paragraphs, how she discovered that because it takes a smaller amount of whole milk than skim to make her coffee to her preferred "whiteness," she ultimately consumes fewer calories by using whole. She begins her post with the following sentence, which is the one that is "fixed."

(9a) subsawa (extract)
1 I've discovered, to my utter surprise, that just referring to the milk in my coffee,
2 I consume fewer calories if I use the whole milk that we have in the fridge for the
3 kids.

Subsawa's post contributes to the ongoing discussion by noting that people may consume different amounts of milk, depending on the milk's fat percentage and what you are doing with the milk, which may affect calorie intake. Several messages later, saturnjai quotes this sentence from subsawa's post and "fixes" it in a way that is humorous.

(9b) saturnjai

> subsawa
>
> **I've discovered, to my utter udder surprise**, that just referring to the milk in my coffee, I consume fewer calories if I use the whole milk that we have in the fridge for the kids.

1 FIFY 😇

Here saturnjai reproduces part of subsawa's post and uses strikethrough to cross out "utter," and replace the word with "udder," in order to construct a pun. The bold font also calls attention to the change. The comment he adds to *refer* to and *remark* what he has done appears as the FIFY acronym, and to this he adds an emoji that can be described as "smiling face with halo." This contributes to the light tone of the message and may indicate that creating the pun is equivalent to being a good person or doing a good deed. (Note that before saturnjai's quoting of subsawa's post, another had quoted it and treated it seriously, saying she preferred cream in her coffee; subsawa does not reply to either of these posts, and no other posters quote either of them, as the thread soon ends.)

In summary, the analysis presented in this section demonstrates how "fixing" serves as a means of engaging in a metadiscursive activity in a joking and playful way on the FIF discussion boards. In this usage, the overall activity is treated as non-serious. Sometimes, the "fixing" post extends a post that is itself joking, while in other cases it "fixes" a relatively serious post as a means of creating play. Emojis are sometimes used as contextualization cues that reinforce the playful nature of the "fix."

CONCLUSION

This chapter identified the functions of a prominent trope, illuminating the pattern of *reproduce—replace—refer—remark* that characterizes a metadiscursive activity (or frame) that posters explicitly label as "fixing." The "fixed it for you" trope is used to assist via providing technical help to another poster who attempts but fails to post a photo, GIF, or video; to assert that a previous poster's opinion/understanding as expressed in a previous post is wrong and that the correcting poster's is correct (i.e., to construct disagreement); and to play while metacommenting on another's post (to introduce play and joking into an interaction, or to continue ongoing play and joking).

This analysis contributes to understanding how one recognizable online metadiscursive activity functions by identifying, structurally unpacking, and explaining how "fixed it for you" is created by way of intertextual linking strategies and is used on a website's discussion boards. The persistence of online discourse facilitates these multiple uses of the "fixed it for you" formula—and opens up many possibilities to do what Becker (1995:9) calls "reshaping" old texts "into present contexts"—in that words and other content from previous posts can be easily brought up to the current moment, and "fixed." This may explain the ease with which I found examples, as well as why, when presenting these data publicly, audience members tended right away to recognize what "fixed it for you" or "^fixed" refers to.

Intertextuality is a fundamental aspect of "fixing," facilitating the accomplishment of this metadiscursive activity and shaping the form that it takes. Posts that contain some kind of "error" or element that merits change (or parts of such posts) are *reproduced* using the boards' built-in quotation function, putting it into juxtaposition with the content of the current poster's post. Textual manipulations are used to *replace* parts of the post with new words or with nothing (i.e., deletion), and these changes are *referred* to using deictics (the caret, or the pronouns "it" or "that") and *remarked* upon with mention of the post being "fixed" (or fify/FIFY in the abbreviated form). These strategies are facilitated by affordances of the medium and of the platform; for example, the quotation function is fundamental, and the ability to use strikethrough in typed discourse allows fixers to leave evidence of the target "problem," and to create intertextual links between the "original" and "fixed" versions. In addition, intertextuality is the basis for play: the humor that arises in the cases where "fixed it for you" is used for joking emerges because posts are changed in clever and unexpected ways.

"Fixing," in its uses for all three primary functions discussed in this chapter—assisting, disagreeing, and playing—is a social action that addresses not only discourse but also relationships between participants. It highlights hierarchy (especially when a knowledgeable poster assists another, or when one claims power by correcting and disagreeing with another), but it also evidences solidarity (especially in uses for assisting and joking). But power is also part of joking: it reveals one's cleverness (see Norrick [1989] for more on this perspective) and may be used to "one-up" the humor offered by another poster. Likewise, solidarity is part of disagreeing in that it shows acknowledgment of another's post, identifying it as worthy of attention. Repetition likewise demonstrates attention and thereby speaks to solidarity on some level (following Tannen 2007a). Further, the routinized pattern of fixing, no matter the intended or perceived purpose, can be understood as sending a metamessage of rapport in that routinized interactional patterns serve to bind members of a group together (e.g., Gordon 2009; Tannen 2007b), which may include members of an online community of practice. On these boards, "fixing" is a metadiscursive activity, facilitated by intertextuality, that links participants together into helping exchanges, arguments and debates about health-related ideas and practices, and collaborative playful discussions.

CHAPTER 4

"I wanted to offer a brief explanation for the locking of this thread"

A moderator's use of GIFs and text to cut off communication

The previous two chapters addressed how posters to the FriendInFitness (FIF) online discussion boards regulated their own interactions by using intertextual strategies to engage in the metadiscursive activities of defining terms and guidelines for discussion and of "fixing." In this chapter, my analysis turns to the discourse of moderators to demonstrate how moderators in general, and one in particular whose discourse is my analytic focus, use intertextuality, in both linguistic and visual forms, in interesting and creative ways to accomplish the metadiscursive action of "locking" those discussion threads that they identify as breaking the guidelines of the boards. While the bulk of the discourse on the discussion boards consists of text, as is evidenced in my analyses presented in the previous two chapters, the phenomenon I examine in this chapter fits with Herring's (2013:15) pointing out that in the context of discourse 2.0, "semiotic systems other than verbal language" are frequently used to communicate (often but not always in conjunction with language). Though discussion boards do not represent the cutting edge of discourse 2.0, they nonetheless are a context in which text and image-related content together create meanings and, as I show, work together in the accomplishment of metadiscourse.

The FIF moderators are easily identifiable as such on the boards in that under each moderator's profile picture and username, the designation "FIF Moderator" appears (instead of "FIF Member"). While they sometimes post as

Intertextuality 2.0. Cynthia Gordon, Oxford University Press. © Oxford University Press 2023.
DOI: 10.1093/oso/9780197642689.003.0004

regular participants in the community of practice, such as by sharing their exercise routines or congratulating other posters for weight loss success, they act in the moderator role by keeping an eye on discussion threads for violations of the boards' guidelines for civil, productive, and safe discussion. These guidelines are available to all users on a page called "Community Guidelines" (and indeed, any poster can flag a post as a violation of these guidelines, for moderator review). Moderators (privately) can warn individual posters that they need to modify how they are posting to the boards or they will face consequences, such as eventually being suspended from the boards. (As I only had access to the public areas of the site, I have not seen this take place, but it is mentioned on the Community Guidelines page that moderators do this). However, the moderators publicly enact their role too: when an entire thread has "gone off the rails"—which some posters capture using a meme such as the derailing train shown in Chapter 1 (Figure 1.2, example c), and others refer to as a "dumpster fire," as in "I'm not reading this dumpster fire" or "Wow, this thread turned into a dumpster fire really quickly"—moderators may choose to "lock" the thread, meaning that no more posts can be added (and in some cases, the thread is also deleted entirely). Locking is necessarily metadiscursive in that its occurrence is marked by a post wherein the locking moderator explains what aspects of the thread justify the locking action. Moderators explain, for example, that threads are locked due to posters exchanging personal attacks, or due to posters advocating starvation and other unsafe weight loss methods, or when the topic has become inappropriate, such as threads that become overtly religious or sexual, or those that are clearly a sales pitch for some product.

As might be expected, the action of thread locking is sometimes appreciated by posters and sometimes not. Stopping offensive interaction arguably protects posters and helps keep the boards focused on relevant and civil content (something that was sought, for instance, by many participants in the "clean eating" thread examined in Chapter 2). However, the action is also face threatening to posters' autonomy: the discussion is silenced, so anyone interested in the discussion, or just enjoying watching the "dumpster fire" blow up, can no longer post to the thread or watch it unfold. Sometimes posters actually appreciate the thread-locking action itself, specifically the humor of some of the thread-locking posts. In this chapter, I show how intertextuality facilitates, especially for one popular moderator called tspring, the completion of the administrative and metadiscursive task of locking in a way that exerts power while also building solidarity with posters. In how this moderator locks threads by way of intertextuality—using the standard locking text, adjusting the text (through strikethrough and adding new text), and especially by using GIFs that link to some aspect of the thread—she constructs not only metadiscourse that informs and entertains many posters, but also an identity for herself as someone who is friendly, creative, clever, and knowledgeable about popular culture.

In what follows, I first review previous research on the discourse of moderators. Because GIFs play an important role in the thread-locking messages that are my focus, I also discuss GIFs, memes, and text–image relationships and work that recognizes GIFs as a prominent resource for online creativity. After introducing some background on the discourse of moderators on FIF, I show a typical thread-locking message by a moderator that uses only the standard locking template and then analyze several examples of creative thread locking by tspring, including one where she shows awareness of her thread-locking strategies (i.e., she produces metadiscourse about her own metadiscourse). I also analyze extracts from a thread wherein posters praise tspring for her thread-locking skills, which reinforces and co-constructs tspring's identity as a creative moderator. In the conclusion, I discuss how intertextuality—both textual and visual—is mobilized to create the metadiscourse that is inherently part of the administrative task of thread locking on these boards, while also constructing humor and play.

DISCOURSE OF MODERATORS

The discourse of discussion board moderators is relatively understudied. When researched, moderators' participation is usually considered at a more macro level, such as Wright's (2009) examination of the multiple "roles" moderators play in two government-run online discussion forums in Britain aimed at facilitating and increasing civic participation. Wright observes that moderators may serve as greeters, conversation stimulators, conflict resolvers, censors (who delete inappropriate posts), and cleaners (who close or remove "dead" or "stale" threads), among others. A couple of these roles—notably, censors and cleaners—bring up issues that are problematic in the context of democratic and civic exchange, as individuals' voices are silenced by moderators (and sometimes, why this happens is not clear to users). Wright suggests that democratic online exchange can be improved with clear guidelines, transparency, and the involvement of an independent (outside) moderator.

As part of his essay exploring what he calls "the theory and practice of computer conferencing," Feenberg (1989) identified various functions moderators of such conferences serve: contextualizing functions (opening the discussion, setting the norms of behavior, and setting the agenda); monitoring functions (recognizing and evaluating participants' contributions, and soliciting comments from participants); and meta functions ("meta-commenting," which Feenberg uses to refer to communicating about discourse to remedy problems in norms, clarity, relevance, and so on; and "weaving," or summarizing the discussion and finding unifying themes in posts). Durrington and Yu (2004) draw on Feenberg's framework of moderator roles to investigate discussions in online undergraduate and graduate technology education courses that were moderated either by students (with the instructor as a regular partici-pant) or by the instructor. The student moderators were expected to and did perform the contextualizing and monitoring functions, which means they performed actions such as opening the discussion and encouraging ongoing participation among their peers. The authors also found that students par-ticipated significantly more in the student-moderated, as compared with the instructor-moderated, discussions. The meta-commenting function identified by Feenberg—which most closely relates to the kind of moderating that takes place in the FIF data, since it involves remedying problems such as interac-tional norm violation—was not examined.

Stommel and Koole (2010), in their study of the discourse of an online sup-port group for people with eating disorders, note that the site has numerous rules and regulations that the moderators, often ex-sufferers of an eating dis-order themselves, enforce. While their analysis does not focus specifically on moderators' discourse, they observe that moderators edit posts when rules have been violated. For example, users are not allowed to use certain terms, such as "pro-ana" (pro-anorexia), or to name exact numbers (such as a waist measurement, or the number of times a poster steps on a scale per day), as these behaviors may encourage other participants to increase their disor-dered behaviors. When users communicate about such activities, moderators edit out these words and numbers and replace them with material in square brackets. For example, a user's post of "I am pro-ana" would be modified to "I am [glamorizing illness]," and a sentence wherein a poster indicates the number of times she weighs herself per day would appear as "I weigh myself [*] times a day." As Stommel (2008:12), observes, the moderator contributes to "setting the limits of, and thereby constructing" the community, an activity that is accomplished collaboratively on the forum in interactions among post-ers and moderators. Similarly, Mudry and Strong's (2013) study of a support forum for self-identified problem gamblers finds that "senior members" of the community and moderators both play roles in socializing novice members into the community, and working to establish behavioral norms by modeling appropriate behavior and policing the behaviors of other (especially newer) posters. For instance, senior members and moderators encouraged members to tell "their story (with sufficient detail) to the group," which is seen as essen-tial in the gambling addiction recovery process, and participated in celebrat-ing users' recoveries (p. 322). Smithson et al. (2011a), in their examination of the discourse of an online support forum for young adults who self-harm (by cutting), likewise observe that moderators and participants both actively enforce community norms.

In summary, the relatively limited research on the discourse of online dis-cussion moderators identifies a range of roles that they can hold or enact. The (interrelated) activities they accomplish include socializing (new) members; (co-)constructing community norms of interaction; policing, editing, and deleting users' posts; they also participate in ways more typical of "regular" community members. There is much to be learned, however, about the specific linguistic—not to mention visual—strategies moderators use to fulfill such inherently metadiscursive functions, locking threads that violate guidelines being one of them.

RELATIONSHIPS BETWEEN TEXT AND IMAGE-BASED CONTENT

Because not only language, but also image-based content (mainly in the form of GIFs but also memes), plays an important role in how the moderator whose discourse is the focus of this chapter locks discussion threads, in this section I briefly discuss theorizing on text–image relationships and how image-related online content functions, especially involving GIFs and memes.

As Bourlai and Herring (2014) note in their study of GIFs, or short looped video animations that sometimes include text, "images and text work together to create meaning" (n.p.). In Adami and Jewitt's (2016:65) words, "GIFs involve the selection of screenshots of media TV products, assembled with overlaid writing and made available" to members of a community "to be re-signified for specific communicative uses (such as commenting), and are often disentangled from the meaning that the selected images had in their original media context." The idea that text and image are interwoven to create meaning is emblematic of a large body of research that illuminates how communication occurs not only via language, but also via multiple multimodal means. For example, research has considered how gestures, gaze behavior, facial expressions, and objects are mobilized along with language in face-to-face interaction (e.g., Al Zidjaly 2015; Erickson 2004; Goodwin 2018; İkizoğlu 2021; Streeck 2021). Photographs, figures, and illustrations accompany text; together visual and textual elements convey meanings on magazine covers, and in children's books, comic strips, print advertisements, educational materials, and public signage (e.g., Bateman 2014; Kress and van Leeuwen 2006; Ledin and Machin 2018; Scollon and Scollon 2003). Machin (2004) highlights the growing role image banks play in corporate media: Getty Images, for instance, "is an ideologically pre-structured world," and their images advance specific marketing categories and clichés (pp. 334–335). In computer-mediated contexts, scholars have investigated the multimodal features of VoiceThread (which uses text, video- and voice-recordings, and images) (e.g., Herring 2013); how semiotic resources such as images, text, video, and music are intertwined to communicate in PowerPoint presentations (e.g., Al Zidjaly 2011, 2015), on YouTube (e.g., Tovares 2020a), and on interactive livestreams of eating known as *mukbang* (e.g., Choe 2019); how emoticons and emojis are coupled with text in email (e.g., Georgakopoulou 2011; Skovholt, Grønning, and Kankaanranta 2014), in text messages (e.g., Tagg 2012; Tannen 2013), in

WhatsApp messages (e.g., Al Rashdi 2018; Al Zidjaly 2017; Sampietro 2016), in online gaming (Graham 2019), and on the Korean instant messaging platform KakaoTalk (Choe 2020); how image-based content in conjunction with text creates meaning on Twitter (e.g., Al Zidjaly, Al Moqbali, and Al Hinai 2020; Vásquez 2019), Flickr (Thurlow and Jaworski 2011), and Instagram (e.g., Mapes 2020); how words, photos, emojis, and stickers interplay in instant messages exchanged among family members (e.g., Choe 2020); on how memes (or "image macros") interweave image and caption (e.g., Dynel 2016); and as mentioned, how video loops are combined with text to make GIFs (e.g., Adami and Jewett 2016; Bourlai and Herring 2014; Gürsimsek 2016).

Gürsimsek (2016) analyzes GIFs used on the microblogging platform Tumblr in communication among fans of the television show *Lost*; she suggests that both creating and using (i.e., posting) GIFs are usefully understood as examples of design and creativity, and that their use involves transmedia literacy and facilitates engagement in online participatory culture. Drawing on Lemke's (2002, 2009) model of semiotic functions, Gürsimsek (2016:336) highlights the following graphic design elements that play into the design and meaning of a GIF: *figure/ground* (the relationship between the foregrounded figure and backgrounded elements), *layering* (overlapping, simultaneous components of an image or sequence), *time and motion* (the depictions of temporal or spatial change), *color and transparency* (parameters that are used by designers to create contrast, harmony, or other relations between graphical elements), and *framing* (borders that provide the frame for graphics). She shows, for example, how an animation that centers a confused character's facial expression is overlaid with text ("NOT SURE IF TROLLING") to create a reaction GIF that conveys that the poster of the GIF is confused; the character's facial expression becomes an embodied action, the reaction to another's post, which might or might not be characterizable as trolling. Tolins and Samermit (2016) make a similar point in their analysis of reaction GIFs used in text messaging exchanges.

The image-related elements of computer-mediated communication are not new; Herring and Androutsopoulos (2015:141–142) point out that emoticons have long existed and "have evolved over time from text to cartoonish icons to emoji (animated icons) to animated gifs (short video clips that loop endlessly)," and all of these work in dialogue with text when it is present. The meanings of older and seemingly simpler visual design elements in computer-mediated communication are also complex. Dresner and Herring (2010:50) point out that emoticons and emojis can be understood not only as emotion indicators that "are mapped directly onto facial expressions" (as when a smiley face indicates happiness), but also as conveyors of non-emotional meanings that are "mapped conventionally onto facial expressions" (as when a winking face indicates the intention of joking), and indicators of illocutionary force that "do not map conventionally onto a facial expression" (as when a smiley face is used to downgrade a complaint). Indeed, it is now commonly understood that emoticons and emojis function as what Gumperz (1982) calls "contextualization cues," indicating how some message should be interpreted in online and digital contexts, including on email (Georgakopoulou 2011; Skovholt, Grønning, and Kankaanranta 2014), Facebook (Theodoropoulou 2015), KaKaoTalk (Choe 2020), and WhatsApp (Al Rashdi 2018; Al Zidjaly 2017). For example, Al Zidjaly (2017:580), who examines how people engage in social protest on WhatsApp in the Middle Eastern country of Oman by creating and posting what she calls "lament-narratives," includes in her analysis an initiating WhatsApp message that outlines a range of complaints of Omani citizens. This post consists of a meme that "utilizes a repetitive interaction between textual facts and complementing emojis," which helps to "create a catchy rhythm, emphasize the point, create the sense of a never-ending problem, and add an element of playfulness" (p. 580). For instance, typed information indicating that water services are inconsistent (i.e., are commonly cut off) is followed by a drop-of-water emoji and a pair-of-scissors emoji; a statement of the fact that Omanis were no longer allowed to buy used cars in Oman was followed by a car emoji followed by the pair-of-scissors emoji. Language, emojis, and repetition of both text and image functioned together to create meaning in this case, and specifically for Omanis to register their complaints about government policies and services in a reasonable way.

More broadly, emojis (and arguably other image-related content items), as contextualization cues, also function in regard to politeness; in other words, they accomplish work related to face and relationships. For example, they can help ease the closings of synchronous text message exchanges (e.g., Sampietro 2016; Tannen 2013), mitigate requests by adding a note of humor (e.g., Darics 2010), and often co-occur with speech acts oriented to others' positive face, such as thanking (e.g., Darics 2010; Skovholt, Grønning, and Kankaanranta 2014). In Chapter 3, analyzed examples included several uses of emojis that seemed to function in this way (such as the animated laughing with tears emoji), and in Chapter 2, the original poster asking about "clean" eating used a GIF from a science fiction television show that I suggested helped to create a friendly tone for her thread.

In addition to meaning being created through text combined with some type of image-based content, images also create meaning when juxtaposed with one another to create a kind of repetition of similarity, or construction of contrast. Decades ago, Berger (1972:30) observed that in their rooms, both adults and children would often artfully display multiple photographs, postcards, and other materials (such as newspaper clippings and notes) on a corkboard or taped to a wall; he suggests that the materials and the relationships between them convey something about the identity of the person who curated the collection. Berger also notes how producing reproductions of artworks affects the meaning of original artwork; interpreted as a kind of repetition, this can be connected to theorizing in linguistics that suggests that as something is repeated, it takes on new meanings (e.g., Johnstone et al. 1994; Tannen 2007b). Further, having a reproduction changes the meaning of the original: it becomes something it was not before, "the original of a reproduction" (Berger 1972:21).

In line with theorizing by Bakhtin (1981, 1984, 1986), existing research shows how reproductions could serve to honor the original in some way, as in a poster of a fine art piece (e.g., Berger 1972), or to parody it, as in puppets of politicians that appeared on the 1980s British TV show *Spitting Image* (Meinhof and Smith 2000). The most important part of this for the purposes of this chapter, however, is that two iterations of the "same" thing become linked, and this serves to create connection and meaning. An example of this is discussed by Kress and van Leeuwen (2006) in their description of compositionality as part of their "grammar of visual design." They note the phenomenon of what they call the "visual rhyme," when repetition of color or form "provides a strong sense of unity and cohesion" among parts of a multipage text (p. 204). Such "rhymes" also "form another key connection device," such as when a product is known for being a particular color, and various print advertisements are themed in that color (p. 204).

Recent research on online memes also highlights how repetition of features creates connections between iterations. While some memes consist of circulating phrases (e.g., "Winter is coming," the motto of one of the families featured on the TV drama *Game of Thrones*), many memes "braid text and image—and even audio and video—in their expression and commentary" (Milner 2013:2363). These are known as "image macros"; image macros "superimpose verbiage on an image as form of caption" and are typically humorous (Zappavigna 2012:103). They can be considered as "units of popular culture that are circulated, imitated, and transformed by individual Internet users, creating a shared cultural experience in the process" (Shifman 2013:367). The GIF involving the *Firefly* character animating toy dinosaurs that was examined in Chapter 2 is a GIF that includes looped video and text; it also meets this definition of "meme." In Chapter 1, I gave an example of the ways an iteration of a meme, in this case of the I LOVE THIS THREAD meme featuring a cat hugging a ball of yarn (see Chapter 1, Figure 1.1), connects to other cat memes, as well as to other memes that evaluate online discourse (I LOVE THIS POST, I LIKE WHERE THIS THREAD IS GOING) (see Chapter 1, Figure 1.2). As mentioned in Chapter 1, Segev et al. (2015) explain that memes can be organized into "families" that are made up of "family members" who share aspects of content and form; individual memes are thus interconnected by specific recurring features (though, as for human families, some meme families are more cohesive than others). Whether a meme consists of only words, or a still image (with or without words), and/or a GIF, it has similarities between iterations of the meme—i.e., repetition—that connect them together into groups.

In his analysis of memes and public participation in the Occupy Wall Street movement, Milner (2013) remarks that memes involve intertextual references, including to pop culture, current and historical events, and so on; "vernacular creativity" describes how these references are multimodally interwoven to articulate various perspectives (p. 2365). Miltner and Highfield (2017) emphasize that GIFs are inherently intertextual in that they remix existing material to create new meanings: GIFs have the capacity "for interpretive flexibility; the separation of GIFs from their original texts imbues them with multiple layers of meaning that are not universally accessible to all audiences" (p. 2). This means that to appreciate a meme or GIF and its meaning, it is helpful to be able to recognize what family or families it belongs to, as well as to recognize the source and history of its elements (such as of a phrase or short video loop). This holds for other types of video-related content as well. For example, Tovares (2020a) analyzes a YouTube video in which Ukrainian soldiers re-enact a famous painting that depicts the writing of a defiant letter to an enemy, thereby intertextually linking to the painting; the soldiers "mobilize multimodal resources to engage in creative insurgency," specifically to insult Russian President Vladimir Putin and his country's antagonistic policies toward Ukraine (p. 214). Without recognizing this connection, the video would be difficult to interpret (see Gordon [2009] for how lack of access to what Becker [1995] calls "prior text" in everyday family interaction leads to layers of meaning being unrecognized).

Wiggins and Bowers (2015:1891) describe memes as "artifacts of *participatory digital culture*" (italics in the original) that are "produced, reproduced, and transformed to reconstitute the social system" of a group. Similarly, Shifman (2013:365) notes that a meme passes cultural information from "*person to person, yet gradually scales into a shared social phenomenon*" (italics in the original). As many GIFs circulate widely and become memes, it is not surprising that similar arguments have been put forth regarding GIFs themselves (e.g., by Miltner and Highfield 2017). My analysis will show how one discussion board moderator creatively puts GIFs into juxtaposition with each other and uses GIFs in conjunction with recontextualized text, in announcing that she is locking a discussion thread.

MODERATING DISCUSSIONS ON FIF

On FIF, I was able to identify six volunteer moderators who were active during the course of my collection of instances of the thread-locking phenomenon (in 2015). The primary role of moderators, as mentioned, is to enforce the rules and guidelines for use of the discussion boards, and this necessarily involves metadiscourse. The set of "Community Guidelines" the discussion boards featured during my data collection (which have evolved over time but cover the same basic areas) aimed at facilitating civil engagement; for instance, it was indicated that "attacks" and "insults" are prohibited: it is expected that participants will "show respect to all groups and individuals," not post "intentionally hurtful posts," and not post vulgar or sexually explicit material. (While moderators are responsible for policing vulgar material, posters mentioned that the platform had an automatic way of identifying some common vulgar words and changing them to *kitten*. This is similar to how inappropriate words and phrases were identified and replaced in a forum for disordered eaters—as seen in Stommel (2008)—though on FIF, moderators themselves did not do this.) On the FIF boards, participants are also prohibited from posting from multiple accounts, posting the same topics on multiple boards, "protesting a moderator or admin action" (posters are advised to discuss these grievances privately), and posting private messages publicly. "Political topics" and "divisive topics" (such as those that are only aimed at a select group of users) should be kept off the main forums and communicated about in groups (which have another designated area on the website). The guidelines also caution against promoting unhealthy weight loss methods, such as those that encourage "anorexia, bulimia, or very low calorie diets of any kind" or promote "non-medically prescribed supplements." In addition, there is a prohibition against posting advertisements, fundraising posts, and spam. Several examples from the list of guidelines include, verbatim: "No Attacks or Insults and No Reciprocation"; "No Profane, Vulgar, Sexually Explicit or Illegal Images"; "No Profane, Vulgar, or Sexually Explicit Language"; "Do Not Troll or Harass Groups"; "No Advertising, Self-Promotion, or Fund-Raising"; and "Please Post in English On the Main Forums" (as mentioned in Chapter 1, there are other boards on the site for communication in other languages, such as Spanish and Korean).

These kinds of guidelines or rules to follow are typical of many online communities, as seen in the previous discussion of prohibition of advocating unhealthy behaviors on a discussion forum for disordered eating (Stommel 2008; Stommel and Koole 2010). On FIF, according to the board guidelines, people who act in violation of the guidelines may receive "warning, suspension of posting privileges, or, in extreme cases, removal of a user from the site," and after a moderator has had to deal with such violations three times, the user will be permanently banned, as described in the "Three Strikes and You Are Out" guideline.

Part of moderators' enforcing of the discussion board guidelines is determining when a particular thread has degenerated into a state where multiple users are repeatedly breaking the boards' guidelines, for instance when a thread topic has turned political or to promoting disordered eating, or when a discussion has degenerated into personal attacks, or when trolls have taken over. Such threads are "locked"; a locked thread will accept no additional posts. Sometimes these locked threads are deleted entirely from the boards, but it is not clear how often this occurs or exactly how or why this decision is made, though posters are informed that moderators have the power to do this. On several occasions, I collected a thread (by downloading it), and then went back to look for it online, finding no evidence that it ever existed. (As seen in Chapter 3, a thread that could be viewed as advocating starvation and binge eating was removed from the site, but not before I downloaded it.)

Sampling "by phenomenon" (Herring 2004), in September 2015, I collected the one hundred most recently locked threads on the FIF discussion boards. Note that because some locked threads are deleted, as mentioned, these one hundred very likely do not represent all locked threads, though they do seem to give a good cross section. Because these threads are locked, they take no new posts, but they can change in their appearance (e.g., when users change their profile pictures; sometimes a GIF that originally loaded correctly later fails to load; and sometimes individual posts are deleted).

The website provides moderators with a template to be used to announce to posters that a thread is being locked (a segment of which will be shown in excerpt 1). However, looking across the one hundred locked threads, I found that moderators sometimes adjusted this template by adding or replacing wording (including using the typographical modification of strikethrough), and/or by adding a GIF or image, which is the focus of this chapter. My analysis focuses on the ways in which one particularly creative moderator creates intertextual connections to facilitate the metadiscursive activity of thread locking while also maintaining solidarity with posters and displaying a positive self-identity. While there is ample research suggesting that making and using GIFs is a means of engaging creatively in digital discourse contexts (e.g., Vásquez 2019), I am not aware of any studies that examine GIFs as part of metadiscursive activity undertaken in discussion board moderating.

INTERTEXTUALITY AND "LOCKING" THREADS

In this section, I briefly show how moderators draw on three primary intertextual strategies to lock threads (though not all draw on all of them, and not to the same degree). All six moderators recontextualize the thread-locking announcement template; this textual template assesses the discourse of the thread, announcing and explaining and justifying the thread locking. They all sometimes add text to this standard text (either before, after, or in the middle of it), and this discourse comments in some way on the discourse of the thread. (The first example will show use of the standard template.) Some of the moderators use images or GIFs as well: of the 100 locked threads, 33 included a GIF or image. Tspring, the moderator whose posts I focus on, locked 33 threads (i.e., she was a very active moderator, locking nearly one-third of the locked threads that I was able to locate). In 20 of those 33, she included a GIF or image. In other words, most of her thread-locking posts included a GIF or image, and she used more GIFs and images than did any other moderator (another one used 11; a third used 2; the remaining three moderators did not use GIFs or images in the locked threads I identified).

I demonstrate how using these thread-locking strategies, including just using the standard template (a practice used by all moderators), is intertextual and allows moderators to appeal to the boards' guidelines and accomplish evaluation, and thereby justify their decision as they produce discourse about discourse. Tspring goes beyond this to infuse the situation with humor and play. Another way of looking at this is that in locking threads, moderators have opportunities to do facework and to construct their identities. Tspring seems especially adept at mitigating the thread locking, building solidarity, and constructing for herself a positive identity, and this is acknowledged by posters, especially in one thread that was started to praise her as an effective thread locker. I begin, however, by showing a thread that is locked in the most typical manner.

Locking using the standardized text template

This example involves a moderator called CyberJoe7. A thread was started where the original poster reported that she was afflicted with anorexia and was seeking strategies to hide food so others in her family did not know she was starving herself. This kind of discourse is not allowed on the boards (as generating strategies to hide food and secretly engage in starvation clearly advocates unsafe eating practices and promotes disordered eating), and the thread does not get very far—CyberJoe7's thread-locking post is the thread's fourth post. To lock the thread, he uses the standardized template of text used by all moderators, as shown below. (In this and other excerpts presented in this chapter, I do not add line numbers to the standardized template because it includes reference to numbered guidelines for participation in the discussion boards. In this excerpt, "MLM" is short for "multilevel marketing," a pyramid sales business model; "ana" is short for anorexia and "mia" for bulimia.

(1)   CyberJoe7 FriendInFitness Moderator
       Dear Posters,

       I wanted to offer a brief explanation for the locking of this thread.

The forum guidelines include this item:

3. No Promotion of Unsafe Weight-Loss Techniques or Eating Disorders
   a) Posts intended to promote potentially unsafe or controversial weight loss products or procedures, including non-medically prescribed supplements or MLM products will be removed without warning.
   b) Profiles, groups, messages, posts or wall comments that encourage anorexia, bulimia, or very low calorie diets of any kind will be removed, and may be grounds for account deletion. This includes positive references to ana/mia, purging, or self-starving. Our goal is to provide users with the tools to achieve their weight management goals at a steady, sustainable rate. Use of the site to promote, glamorize, or achieve dangerously low levels of eating is not permitted.
   c) Photos intended to glamorize extreme thinness will be deleted.
   d) Those seeking support in their recovery from eating disorders are welcome at FriendInFitness.

   ((material directing those struggling with eating disorders to outside resources elided))

   If you would like to review the forum guidelines, please visit the following link:

   ((link elided))

   At our discretion, this locked thread may be deleted entirely in the near future.

   Thank you for your understanding.

   CyberJoe7

   FriendInFitness Moderator

This post, in announcing the thread locking, mobilizes intertextuality as a resource in a number of ways. In terms of genre, it intertextually references traditional formal letters, with its salutation "Dear Posters," its layout, and the sign-off (here, "Thank you for your understanding"; "With respect" is also often used by moderators). This instance of interdiscursivity (to use Fairclough's 1992 term) plays to posters' negative face in that it reflects a certain degree of formality and politeness. The "I wanted to offer a brief explanation for the locking of this thread" and "The forum guidelines include this item" are both standard across all thread-locking messages. These also accomplish facework by addressing concerns the posters might have (and perhaps to avoid what Wright [2009] found in his analysis of online discussion—people being confused about exactly why their posts were marked as violating the site's guidelines). The middle part of the message is material that has been imported from the FIF Community Guidelines; moderators import those that they see as relevant for each particular case. At the end of the post, CyberJoe7 adds "FriendInFitness Moderator" after his name, which explicitly names his role; he is also (automatically) identified as "FIF Moderator" underneath his user profile picture and username. This moderator's post thus recontextualizes the standardized template form ("Dear Posters, I want to offer you a brief explanation for the locking of this thread.") along with the specific guidelines violated. This produces metadiscourse that calls attention to and evaluates the discourse of the thread. In this case, the moderator indicates that the thread is problematic because it involves "Posts intended to promote potentially unsafe or controversial weight loss products or procedures"—specifically, behaviors associated with "ana" (and use of this word—short for "anorexia"—echoes its use in the original post). In other words, the thread violates guideline 3 of the boards ("No Promotion of Unsafe Weight-Loss Techniques or Eating Disorders"). This thread-locking message, thus, via recontextualizing (and making particular) a standardized message, creates metadiscourse while evoking the politeness of traditional formal letters through use of a greeting and sign-off, and emphasizing the moderator's institutional authority through the identification of him as an official moderator as well as his use of the thread-locking template. It serves as an example of the most typical locking post, as this plain format is used by all moderators on occasion, even by those who sometimes add creative touches to it, and by tspring, who often does.

Locking using a GIF related to the thread's title

I now turn to a post by the moderator whose discourse is my focus—tspring. In this example, she uses the standardized template along with a GIF. Her GIF has intertextual links to something previous in the thread—the thread title—which creates humor, orients to solidarity, and demonstrates her creativity while also accomplishing the metadiscursive activity of announcing that the thread will be locked.

The title of the thread is "Bread??" The original post reads, "Whats people's views on bread and weightloss. Some people say stay clear etc. Any thoughts?" (As became evident in previous chapters, the role of foods high in carbohydrates, such as bread, in weight gain and loss is highly contentious on these boards.) The thread involved 327 posts, with some people indicating they lost weight while eating bread in moderate or reduced portions and a few indicating that bread slows weight loss due to some effect

Figure 4.1. GIF related to the thread's title (still shot).

it has on the metabolism. As the thread unfolded, one poster started to become very active and also criticized those who didn't understand his perspective. For example, he indicated to a poster, "you are quite a piece of work" and "quite delusional"; he accused another of taking things out of context and making "an unrelated self serving point" in his post; he attacked another as "toying" and "baiting" him. Some of those he attacked responded, and other posters started to criticize him as well. This degenerated into back-and-forth accusations of "cherry picking" facts, posters claiming others were using pseudoscience to support their arguments, and accusations of "childish" behavior. In other words, posts to the thread increasingly came to break the FIF discussion forum guidelines, especially the one against personal attacks. (Simultaneously, the thread came to feature a good deal of metadiscourse produced by posters, as is evident in the quotations above.)

To cut off this communication, ahead of the usual template letter about locking the thread, tspring posted a GIF. I show the GIF below as a still shot (as the movement is not especially important here) in Figure 4.1; this appeared at the beginning of tspring's post, and it is followed by the text of tspring's locking message, presented in (2). The cartoon character shown in the GIF is standing atop a city wall, and the movement shows him looking over the wall to the long way down, and then back up again.

(2)   tspring (text accompanying locking with a GIF related to the thread's title)

Dear Posters

I wanted to offer a brief explanation for the locking of this thread. Earnest and respectful debate on any message in the forums is acceptable. Attacking the messenger is not.

The forum guidelines include this item:

1. No Attacks or Insults and No Reciprocation
a) Do not attack, mock, or otherwise insult others.
((post continues with text from guideline 1 and the link to the guidelines, elided))

Thanks for your understanding,

tspring

The GIF that tspring inserts ahead of the template text is created from a moment that occurred in the Disney children's movie *Aladdin* (1992). The titular character—who, having been hungry, had stolen a loaf of bread and had been pursued by guards throughout the city—was standing at the edge of the (very high) wall surrounding it, about to jump to escape. He utters the words "All this for a loaf of bread?," which appear in text on the GIF. (As Deborah Tannen pointed out to me, this film moment itself, and hence the GIF, serves as an intertextual reference to Victor Hugo's [1862] novel *Les Misérables* by way of the character Jean Valjean, who was imprisoned for 19 years after being caught stealing a loaf of bread.)

The moderator uses this GIF to draw intertextual connections between the thread—a thread focused on the seemingly mundane topic of bread, yet which devolves into a series of personal attacks—and Aladdin's seemingly never-ending attempt to lose the guards (including having to jump off a high wall), given the relatively small reward (a single loaf of bread). The word "bread" itself and the image provide the intertextual links to make this GIF a particularly clever one in this context, a way of humorously topically linking it to the thread while simultaneously negatively commenting on the thread's content and development. In this way, it may serve to mitigate the locking message. The moderator's use of the GIF also reveals her pop culture knowledge and skill in deploying it—every time I have presented this example publicly, be it at a conference or in a classroom, the audience laughs, appreciating what tspring has done. To communicate about the discourse of this thread, tspring uses not only the recontextualized language and formatting of the discussion board guidelines, but also a GIF that evaluates the thread negatively ("all this") and creates humor, mitigating the face-threatening act of locking, while also appealing to solidarity (as she presumably does this to entertain and connect with posters).

Locking using a GIF relating to a GIF in a just-prior post

The next example again shows tspring's use of a GIF in a thread-locking post, but this time the GIF relates not to the thread's title, but rather to a just-prior post. The example is drawn from a thread titled "People on FriendInFitness-Vent." In her original post, the OP complained that some people who post on the site do not provide positive support. The thread quickly degenerated into an exchange of insults between the original poster and others in the thread, with one poster calling such posters "mean girls." This could serve as a reference to the 2004 movie *Mean Girls* (which involves a clique of popular high school girls ganging up against a new girl), or to cliquish young people more generally, or both. Another poster, seemingly recognizing the reference, jokes about use of this term: "Why do people keep trying to turn this into some kind of high school made-for-TV movie? Mean girls LOL," which indicated that this was overly dramatic (as "made-for-TV movies" often are). In the 108th post of the thread (the second to last), a poster called Sallie87 quotes that post (shown in gray highlighting), and to this she adds her own text, as well as a GIF. The GIF is shown in a series of still shots in Figure 4.2 (to be read from left to right one row at a time; I have eliminated the last few stills, which show the young men who appear in the GIF making a vulgar gesture, as it is not relevant to my analysis). The GIF is included in Sallie87's post, the text of which is shown in (3a). This is the post to which tspring will indirectly link her locking post.

(3a)   Sallie87 (post providing intertextual anchor for the thread-locking post)

   Why do people keep trying to turn this into some kind of high school made-for-TV movie? Mean girls LOL

1   Fair warning: If you burst into song and a choreographed dance routine imma gonna
2   slap you upside the head ((*winking emoji not shown*)).

The text of Sallie87's post can be interpreted as teasing the poster whose discourse she quotes. The movie *Mean Girls* includes an oft-parodied scene wherein the main character and her popular high school friends perform an over-the-top and hypersexualized choreographed dance routine in front of their school, and Sallie87's mention of "song and a choreographed dance routine" indexes that. She also jokingly threatens that she's going to "slap upside the head" anyone who feels the need to start dancing; the use of a winking emoji at the end of her post (☺) supports a joking interpretation here. The GIF that Sallie87 adds is of three men dancing who look ridiculous (and at times vulgar); it loops a clip of a scene from a rap video parody called "The Dance Routine" (2011), made by the British comedy group The Midnight Beast. One man is dressed in blue, one in green, and the other in red, but their outfits are otherwise similar: all three wear sweatsuits and bright white sneakers. The primary background color of the GIF (provided by the wall graffiti) is blue.

Figure 4.2. Screen shots from "choreographed dance routine" GIF.

The men play to the camera, as is common in music videos. While this poster creates some humor simply by posting a GIF that is playful by definition (it is a parody) along with the winking face emoji, I now turn to how it is intertextually referenced by tspring.

In the 109th (and last) post of the degenerating thread, tspring indicates that she is locking it. She begins her post with a GIF that links intertextually to this just-prior post by Sallie87. This is shown in Figure 4.3. The beginning of the text that follows the GIF in tspring's thread-locking message is shown in (3b).

Figure 4.3. Screen shots from another choreographed dance routine GIF.

(3b) <u>Locking using GIF related to immediately prior GIF (tspring)</u>

> Dear Posters,
>
> I wanted to offer a brief explanation for the locking of this thread.
>
> The forum guidelines include this item:
>
> 2. No Hi-Jacking, Trolling, or Flame-baiting
> ((*remainder of post elided*))

The GIF used by tspring is from an aerobics competition from the 1980s (identified online as the 1988 Crystal Light National Aerobic Championship); video of the competition resurfaced on the Internet in 2014 set to "Shake It Off," a pop song by Taylor Swift. The three men dancing, their orientation to the camera, and some of their gesticulations in particular, as well as the blue color schemes (they are wearing blue, and part of the background of their set is blue), their similar distance from the camera, their gleaming white sneakers, and the fact that they all wear the same outfit link these GIFS together to the GIF posted by Sallie87 as a sort of "visual rhyme," to use Kress and van Leeuwen's (2006) term (see also Ledin and Machin 2018). For example, notice the similarities between the pairs of still images shown in Figure 4.4.

	Stills from Sallie87's GIF	Stills from tspring's GIF
Dancing men bending forward		
Dancing men with arms up		

Figure 4.4. Pairs of still shots from the two GIFs.

In the first pair of still shots (shown in the first row), the men bend forward; in the second they stand straight with their arms up. The broad similarities in these dance routine moves, along the other aforementioned commonalities, link the GIFs together. The GIFs are far from identical, of course; for example, while each trio is wearing period-specific clothing, the outfits are from different periods (arguably 1990s for the first GIF, 1980s for the second), and in the first GIF each dancer wears a different color (one green, one red, one blue) whereas in the second, the men are dressed identically. Further, the GIFs differ in another important way: the video loop was drawn from a music video parody for the first GIF; for the second, the loop was drawn from a competition (and in its longer video form had recently been set to music from a contemporary pop song; the GIF is not musical). Arguably, the second GIF is even funnier than the first in that it depicts a "serious" activity that has been reframed; the men depicted in the frame are not aware that the actions they are undertaking have been recontextualized as laughable.

In summary, tspring's GIF is humorous, and the intertextual connection between Sallie87's GIF and tspring's is funny: tspring offers another "choreographed dance routine." This adds humor and play to the thread-locking post. Both GIFs also show different time periods of dance performance in pop culture, creating a humorous juxtaposition between the two while making "cross-references to everyday popular culture events," which, as Bourlai and Herring (2014:n.p.) point out, helps makes GIFs into successful memes. In this case, the juxtaposition is between two GIFs instead of encapsulating a juxtaposition in one. In creating this juxtaposition, tspring shows creativity and playfulness as she locks the thread. This is another example that has elicited laughter from the audience every time I have publicly presented it. Tspring thus enacts her administrative role, negatively evaluating the thread's discourse and announcing the thread's locking, in a friendly and playful way.

Locking by using a GIF related to one used by the OP, and adjusting the standardized text

The next example of a thread locking occurred in a thread titled "I lost 10 pounds in a week and I'm doing every thing right . . or so I thought! smh" (smh stands for "shaking my head"). The thread consisted of 98 posts. The OP, Nadia, starts her post with metadiscourse, labeling her post ("Ugh. This is a rant"). She goes on to explain that she is frustrated because she wants to lose weight but has problems eating in moderation, feeling like she either overeats or completely starves herself. Early on in the thread, another poster remarked, "OP . . . don't I remember a previous thread where this was discussed with you?" This serves as an indication that the thread might be problematic (as posting the same thing on multiple boards breaks the forum guidelines).

The OP was very active on the thread and substantially contributed to its undoing. When one poster suggested she should "eat more calorie dense foods," Nadia criticized her for not telling her what that meant, and when the user responded she should "google it," she indicated that this was an inappropriate response—she did not appreciate being told to do an online search herself. As the thread developed, Nadia responds positively to some posters' contributions, such as by thanking them, but she also interprets and labels others' participation as inappropriate, along with directing personal attacks to other posters (note that all of these actions are metadiscursive—she evaluates others' discourse). For example, in one post, she ridicules what she identifies as the "fat shaming comments" of other posters and also criticizes one specific poster who noted that she (Nadia) also posted fat shaming comments. In addition, Nadia taunts this poster by suggesting that she is illiterate and by calling her "passive aggressive." She ends this post with two GIFs. First, she types "Shocking" (sarcastically evaluating the other poster's behavior) and adds a GIF of a character from the 2003–2019 TV sitcom *Arrested Development* (still shot shown in Figure 4.5).

The GIF is an image of the matriarch of the sitcom family, Lucille Bluth, an often-GIF'ed character (Yahr 2021) due to actor Jessica Walter's expressive face and the character's usual habit of saying haughty things and often holding an alcoholic beverage. In this GIF, Lucille looks up and down at another of the show's characters (who is not shown).

Nadia, the OP, produces more text after this GIF—"You won't derail my thread. Not on my watch. Goodbye."—and adds a second GIF, this one from the reunion show of the VH1 reality TV show *Basketball Wives LA* (Season 4, in 2015), which focuses on the lives of wives and ex-wives of professional basketball players in California. A still shot from this GIF is shown in Figure 4.6; the GIF shows one of the show's stars, Evelyn Lozada, flipping her hair back as she mouths the word "And?"

Nadia negatively evaluates another poster's behavior, using "Shocking" sarcastically, meaning it indicates that the other poster's posts (which she deems offensive) are not shocking, but rather typical and expected, and by using the Lucille Bluth GIF of her looking someone up and down

Figure 4.5. Still shot from Lucille Bluth "eyeing up" GIF.

Figure 4.6. Still shot from Evelyn Lozada "hairflip" GIF.

judgmentally. After the text indicating that the poster "won't derail my thread. Not on my watch. Goodbye," the GIF of the basketball wife doing what is recognizably a hairflip appears. According to urbandictionary.com, "hairflip" is a term used when "a member of an online community leaves a group or forum because they just can't take the heat." It is not clear if the poster Nadia addresses actually stops reading the thread, but she doesn't post again before the thread gets locked. It's possible that the GIF and "goodbye" might also indicate that Nadia will henceforth ignore the poster who offended her, or perhaps that she will report the poster to the moderators. Either interpretation fits in with the fact that the act of hair flipping is generally understood as dismissive. Both GIFs can be described as conveying emotional processes (following Ledin and Machin 2018), and the emotions are negative.

Despite this post, the thread continues, with the OP's participation. One poster observes, "Wow, this thread is a total dumpster fire," producing metadiscourse that foreshadows the thread locking that is to come. In the 98th post, tspring posts her thread-locking message. She uses a different GIF of Lucille Bluth along with one of the character Fozzie Bear from The Muppets. Between these, she inserts her own text, "I . . is the following a guideline yet?" A still shot from each of the two GIFs appears in Figures 4.7 and 4.8., standing in for each GIF.

Moderator tspring's post constructs her overall negative evaluative stance toward what has transpired, while also echoing elements of Nadia's post in interesting ways, working to tie the posts together. They are structurally alike: each involves two GIFs, with text in between. Each uses a Lucille Bluth GIF first. While Nadia, the OP, used the GIF showing Lucille looking another person up and down in a critical way to dismiss another poster, tspring uses a GIF of Lucille closing the door as part of a message that critiques the discourse of the thread (it's time to "close the door" on the thread) and helps announce the thread's locking. The second GIFs are less closely matched but still are related in some way: both can be interpreted as GIFs that may serve to

Figure 4.7. Still shot from Lucille Bluth "closing door" GIF.

Figure 4.8. Still shot from Fozzie Bear "facepalm" GIF.

depict emotional processes (Ledin and Machin 2018) and as an "embodied enactment" of what the poster is feeling (following Tolins and Samermit 2016; Gürsimsek 2016 also discusses this GIF function). The hairflip GIF used by Nadia could be interpreted as embodying Nadia as she dismisses the poster who has offended her, while the Fozzie Bear GIF also may embody tspring's reaction to the thread (she is frustrated, making a facepalm gesture—a gesture that itself has become an online meme as well as an emoji; see https://knowyourmeme.com/memes/facepalm). Tspring's "I . . . is the following a guideline yet?," which is placed between the two GIFs, seems to indicate confusion; she begins a sentence with "I" but then pauses (ellipses are used) and restarts her thought, referencing the board guidelines. This reinforces that this thread is perplexing and frustrating. The use of these GIFs in juxtaposition with Nadia's use of GIFs is creative and humorous, which orients to entertaining and building solidarity with posters (but probably not with Nadia). The content of the GIFs also relates to justifying the locking of the thread (i.e, by demonstrating moderator frustration) and indexes the locking itself (a metaphorical "closing the door" on the thread).

In addition to using GIFs that creatively echo a post by the OP, the moderator, tspring, also does something interesting with the intertextually imported standardized text, shown below. She uses strikethrough to delete text, while also adding words to the message, as can be seen in the arrowed lines. (The text shown in this excerpt appeared right under the GIF shown in Figure 4.8.)

(4) <u>Main text of thread-locking message (tspring)</u>

> Dear Posters,
> I wanted to offer a brief explanation for the locking of this thread.
>
> The forum guidelines include this item:
>
> 2. No Hi-Jacking, Trolling, or Flame-baiting.
>
> Please stay on-topic within a forum topic. Off-topic or derogatory remarks are disrespectful. ((*standardized text continues, but is elided here*))
>
> In many cases we are able to edit out the posts that violate this guideline, but
> → ~~unfortunately this particular thread has become too volatile to moderate efficiently.~~
> → I can't even.
>
> If you would like to review the forum guidelines, please visit the following link: ((*link elided*))
>
> With respect,
> tspring
> FIF Moderator

As shown here, in addition to using the GIFs, tspring crosses out the professional-sounding text that is part of the standardized message, "unfortunately this particular thread has become too volatile to moderate efficiently," indicating its deletion but leaving it visible. She replaces this with the more emotional and personal "I can't even," which can be described as an Internet meme in the sense that it is widely circulated; according to urbandictionary.com, its meaning is "an expression that denotes so many emotional responses that the user can't even comprehend what has been said or seen." This echoes the GIFs: something about the thread is so ridiculous that there is nothing that can be said. This alteration of the standard locking template, which includes intertextual reference to the widely circulating phrase "I can't even," reinforces tspring's affective response to the thread and adds to the humor of the thread-locking message.

Overall then, in this locking post, the moderator uses GIFs that intertextually link to those used by the OP and uses the standard text with modification (text marked with strikethrough, and text added), to create humor and display herself as an atypical moderator who is able to recontextualize meaningful material—both words and images—in performing the administrative and metadiscursive task of announcing a thread's locking.

Locking by using a GIF and commenting on the moderator's own thread-locking practices

This final example of a locking post shows tspring using additional text along with the standardized locking messaging, and a GIF. In the example, she also produces metadiscursive comments about her own practices; i.e., she produces metadiscourse that points to the fact that she apparently consciously chooses GIFs that connect in some (creative) way to the thread. This could be described as a kind of "second-order metadiscourse" in that it is "metapragmatic discourse about the pragmatics" of some other "metapragmatic discourse" (Silverstein 1993:43).

The thread the moderator locks was 47 messages long. It started as an interaction about a "lemon cleanse" diet, which is a "dangerous" topic that goes against the boards' guidelines in the sense that it advocates the unhealthy eating practices of fasting and only drinking lemon water (and in fact a poster notes this early on in the thread). The thread addresses cleanses, mainly how they do not work, and also involves posts that playfully offer productive uses for lemons (such as cleaning copper and seasoning potatoes). The thread becomes completely derailed when one poster claims that while he has used cleanses to try to counterbalance the fact that modern foods are genetically modified and full of pesticides, it was prayer to Jesus that cured him of hepatitis B, an intestinal blockage, and the hiccups. At this point other posters produce metadiscourse that evaluates his post and its claims as inappropriate, nonsensical, and/or non-serious. For example, various posters remark that it is off topic (e.g., "this has what to do with a lemon cleanse?"). One quotes the Jesus-focused post and describes it with "^That. That is some comedy gold. It's got everything, woo, conspiracy theories and Jesus. Bravo!"; another quotes the post and evaluates it with "HAHAHAHAHAHAHAHAHAHAHAHAHAHA." Note that these are all

Figure 4.9. Still shot from Flash Gordon GIF.

intertextual linking strategies explored in previous chapters. Several posters post reaction GIFs and images that also take the thread in a more playful direction (e.g., a GIF of someone laughing while eating popcorn; an image of a dog wearing a tinfoil hat; a cat image with the text "OMG it's a miracle!" superimposed onto it); these seem to relish the oddness of the post. A few posters continue to discuss the topic seriously, such as when one poster asks another if their cleanse experience worked, but the joking discussion of Jesus and Christianity as sources of healing for physical ailments and of food-related conspiracy theories (with the poster's mention of genetically modified foods and pesticides) comes to dominate.

In the 47th post to the thread, tspring announces that she is locking it. She begins her post with a GIF from the 1980 movie *Flash Gordon* that shows the titular superhero zooming toward the viewer on some sort of flying machine (a still from the GIF is shown in Figure 4.9). She then adds text ahead of the standard template (noted with arrows in excerpt 5) that reflects on her practice of strategically choosing GIFs for thread-locking posts. In the standard template, tspring indicates that the thread is being locked because it violates the community's guideline that divisive topics (and religion specifically) should not be discussed on the main boards, but elsewhere on the site (in the "Groups" section).

(5) Text of locking message with comments on GIF choice (tspring)
  →   This thread seems as good as any for a Flash Gordon gif, it's not like we're running
  →   the risk of having it not make sense in context. And as with all threads that end up
  →   with religious references, I give you:

    Dear Posters,

    I wanted to offer a brief explanation for the locking of this thread. The discussion is
    welcome to continue in groups.

The forum guidelines include this item:

15. Divisive Topics Are Better Suited For Groups, Not the Main Forums

Divisive topics and posts, particularly those that seek input from or are relevant to only a select group of users, are better placed within an appropriate Group rather than the Main Forums. For example, topics relevant to only one religion should not be placed on the main forum but rather within a group related to that religion.

If you would like to review the forum guidelines, please visit the following link: ((*link elided*))

At our discretion, this locked thread may be deleted entirely in the near future.

With respect,

tspring

Here tspring, in the arrowed lines, explains her choice of the Flash Gordon GIF: this thread is so nonsensical that there is no especially coherent or sensible GIF to choose ("This thread seems as good as any for a Flash Gordon gif, it's not like we're running the risk of having it not make sense in context."). According to Wikipedia, Flash Gordon was created and originally drawn by Alex Raymond as an adventure comic strip character (first published in 1934), and while the 1980 movie version (from whence the GIF is drawn) was a flop, it later gained a cult status, so it is possible that the GIF is recognizable to FIF posters. Further, tspring names the character and source text ("Flash Gordon"), in case posters do not recognize it (as I did not, despite being a Gordon myself).

Most interesting to me, however, is how in both choosing a nonsensical GIF and explaining that she is doing so because the thread is nonsensical, the moderator constructs metadiscourse that highlights her frequent and recognizable practice of including a GIF that is in some way coherent in the context of the thread, having intertextual links to some aspect of it, be it the title or topic, or the content of some prior post. In other words, she produces metadiscourse about her own metadiscursive thread-locking practices: even for a thread that does not make sense, tspring can identify the right GIF to use in the thread-locking post (which implies that her usual thread-locking GIFs make sense).

Posters' metadiscourse about the moderator's locking posts

Examples 1–5 demonstrated how one discussion board moderator creatively uses GIFs as part of her thread-locking posts in ways that, I have argued, portray her as creative and knowledgeable. While locking a thread is necessarily a show of power on the boards (and, indeed, shows tspring acting in her institutional role), she locks in ways that also orient to power on another level (i.e., she could be seen as "showing off") and, arguably seemingly more important, to solidarity. I am not the only reader of the boards who has noticed and enjoyed tspring's thread-locking practices: as mentioned, discussion board participants themselves show they appreciate tspring's thread-locking posts and identify her as having a unique moderator identity by addressing her as an individual. An OP started a thread called "Dear tspring," which generically frames it as a "response letter" to all the "Dear Poster" posts, creating interdiscursivity. The content of the post read, "You are the best thread closer . . . EVAH" (ever). The message also included a GIF, which alternates a moving image of a smiling young man (Zayn Malik, then a member of the pop boyband One Direction) who is dancing, juxtaposed with a still image indicating (in the spirit of somewhat vulgar humor) where the viewer should place their finger on their computer screen (GIF link: https://weheartit.com/entry/28198190). These two juxtaposed elements are shown in still shots in Figure 4.10.

The joke is that the viewer puts their finger on the blue dot, but then the image changes so their finger is on the young man's dancing/thrusting groin area.

This post on the one hand intertextually references tspring's repeated use of GIFs in her thread-locking messages. On the other, it sets the stage for the playful and humorous GIFs and memes that follow; it sets the tone. The thread is 53 messages long, and it unfolds as a playful celebration of words of appreciation and praise, along with image-related content (notably, GIFs) in response to a recent thread-locking post by tspring that was especially impressive. (Despite

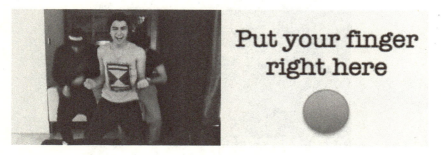

Figure 4.10. Screen shots from the first GIF in the "Dear tspring" thread.

repeated searches, I was unable to identify which particular thread locking this was, or if the thread is even still available online.) Through multimodal means and mobilizing intertextuality, the posters reinforce tspring as a uniquely talented moderator, acknowledging her as a master of intertextual connections and metadiscourse (though of course they do not use those terms).

The second post to the thread is the meme shown in Figure 4.11. It is followed by text in the post that indicates, "Agree!"

This meme features Fry, the main character from the cartoon TV show *Futurama*. This still shot of the character is often seen in memes, usually just altered by adding different text (e.g., NOT SURE IF HUNGRY OR JUST BORED; NOT SURE IF TROLLING OR JUST STUPID). The content of this meme could perhaps be interpreted as indexing the fact that tspring, like all posters, always has the choice to use image-based content, or just text. Whether or not this meaning is intended or interpreted, some other posters comment with GIFs, some with memes that involve text and image, and others just with typed comments.

For example, other posters comment "+1" (which signals agreement), "Yup," "Too funny!!!!," and "I do agree that was the. Best. Threadclose. Ever." Another posts the following—"In for the end GIF Waiting for hours to see how it closed."—followed by a smiley face; in other words, she indicates that she was watching the thread to see how it was locked by the moderator and was glad she did.

Yet another poster adds, "That was the perfect finish. Like finding a big puddle of hot fudge down at the bottom of an ice cream sundae," thereby using language to create a mental image. Another user follows that post with the meme shown in Figure 4.12.

Using an "I SUPPORT THIS POST" meme (part of the broad meme family of memes praising posts and threads which was discussed in Chapter 1), this

Figure 4.11. Meme in the second post in the "Dear tspring" thread.

Figure 4.12. "I SUPPORT THIS POST" meme.

user co-signs onto the previous post praising tspring's thread closing with a visual pun: the metal support for the post, which looks like a face, appears to be indicating that it is supporting the wooden post; the poster to the thread is in favor of a previous contribution to the thread.

A user quotes another who had posted that the "thread close was phenomenal!" and added, "celebration time!" along with a GIF of a cat standing at a record turntable and acting as an DJ at a party, with other cats dancing in the glow of yellow, green, red, and blue laser lights in the background. A still shot of the GIF is shown in Figure 4.13.
This is a common type of meme (cats) and contributes to the celebratory feel of this thread.

Another example of a GIF posted to this thread that praises tspring is one that was taken from the 1992 movie *Wayne's World*. This GIF shows the two main characters, Wayne (played by Mike Myers) and Garth (played by Dana Carvey), repeatedly bowing down; one of their catchphrases, "we're not worthy" appears in text at the top. A series of stills is shown in Figure 4.14.

This GIF shows the comedic characters Wayne and Garth bowing down to tspring (something the characters usually do in the movie for their music idols and attractive women), suggesting interpretation of this GIF as a form of embodied or symbolic action. A post that functions similarly consists of an image of the two main characters from the 1989 movie *Bill and Ted's Excellent Adventure*. This image shows the two titular characters (played by Alex Winter and Keanu Reeves, respectively) with fists raised in victory, and it includes text capturing one of their catchphrases, as seen in Figure 4.15.

In certain ways, this meme echoes the Wayne and Garth meme—two comedic (and not especially bright) best friends who are completely ridiculous, and who are marked by the time period represented in their movies (the

Figure 4.13. Still image of cat dance party GIF.

Figure 4.14. Stills from "we're not worthy" GIF.

Figure 4.15. "Most excellent" meme.

early 1990s for *Wayne's World*, and the late 1980s for Bill and Ted's *Excellent Adventure*). This may represent an effort by posters to honor tspring not only by posting GIFs and memes, but by posting those that could be viewed as an echo or intertextual repetition of another post on the thread.

In addition to these and other images and GIFs being posted, it is also remarked by posters that, "tspring is cool" and "I like it when mods [moderators] close a thread with gifs. Even though a thread is locked, I still read to the very end." Two posters also comment that other moderators might be jealous of the attention tspring is receiving in the thread (pointing to acknowledgment that tspring's GIF use might be interpreted through the lens of power more so than solidarity).

As further evidence that tspring's unique identity, created through her use of GIFs in the metadiscursive task of thread locking, is recognized (and co-constructed), in the 44th post to the thread, a participant posts, "The lack of tspring in this thread is pathetic." This seems to mean that the thread is deficient because tspring herself has not posted (and perhaps she has not even noticed this thread praising her).

At the time data were collected, the profile picture tspring was using was the one, shown in Figure 4.16, below.

This image is a drawing of Cthulhu, a creature created by writer H. P. Lovecraft in the 1928 story "The Call of Cthulhu," which has since appeared widely in popular culture, including online. This particular iteration shows a cute Cthulhu sleeping. In response to the observation that tspring has yet to participate in the thread, users, perhaps attempting to draw her attention, post their own GIFs and images of Cthulhu; these are shown in Figures 4.17, 4.18, and 4.19. The first is a still from a GIF of Cthulhu dancing under the

Figure 4.16. tspring's profile picture.

Figure 4.17. Still from dancing Cthulhu GIF.

Figure 4.18. Still from happy-Cthulhu-eating-a-person GIF.

stars; the second is a still from a GIF of a simply drawn Cthulhu eating a humanoid while others look on joyfully; and the third is a playful thumbs-up given by a scarier-looking Cthulhu.

These posts playfully and metaphorically "call out" to tspring—they visually represent the character of her profile picture, with one (Figure 4.19) even including the name "Cthulhu"—to notice and acknowledge a thread created to celebrate her skills as a GIF-using thread locker.

Figure 4.19. "Cthulhu approved" image.

In the 52nd post, tspring joins the discussion, posting, "I just found about this because no one Betelguesed me in here. Thanks for the love, although I am annoyed that I forgot to include a twinkie gif." "Betelguesed" is a reference to the 1988 movie *Beetlejuice*, which involves a main character who is conjured by uttering his name three times (the character's name is spelled out as "Betelguese," rather than "Beetlejuice," in the movie when the character's headstone is shown, though the movie title is spelled "Beetlejuice"). Tspring shows appreciation for those praising her ("Thanks for the love"), while also continuing the intertextual play through the movie reference—posters called out to her at least three times, and she has thus arrived. (I am uncertain what specifically "a twinkie gif" refers to, or why it is relevant here, but it seems to denote something she meant to also include in the thread-locking post that is being celebrated here, and which I could not locate.) Tspring also includes a GIF in her post, an animated loop from the 2011 comedy movie *Bridesmaids* that responds to the posters and creates additional humorous intertextuality. In it, the bride in the movie (played by Maya Rudolph), is toasting her unusual and outrageous group of bridesmaids. A still from this GIF is appears in Figure 4.20; it expresses gratitude and also creates connection among posters to the thread.

In posting this GIF, tspring demonstrates appreciation of the posters who enjoyed one specific thread-locking post and/or enjoy her thread-locking in

Figure 4.20. Still from *Bridesmaids* GIF posted by tspring.

general, while also expressing her own appreciation for their uses of GIFs, images, and funny posts in the thread: just as the bride from *Bridesmaids* is a "weirdo" in the "pack of weirdos" that are her bridesmaids, so tspring is a GIF user in a pack of GIF users. This could be viewed as contributing to solidarity between the moderator and posters, while also reinforcing tspring's identity as especially creative in how she mobilizes intertextuality to accomplish the metadiscursive activity of thread locking.

CONCLUSION

This chapter has considered how moderators use intertextuality as a resource for announcing the locking of threads on the FIF discussion boards, with a focus on one moderator's practices that are highly multimodal and especially creative. All six active moderators at the time of data collection used the standard template: "Dear Posters, I wanted to offer a brief explanation for the locking of this thread"; reference to the specific violated guideline(s), along with possible outcomes; a link to the forum guidelines; and some kind of sign-off (e.g., "Thank you for your understanding"). In using this template, the moderators created metadiscourse—they communicated about the thread (or a specific post on the thread), providing evaluation and justifying the locking of the thread. They also highlighted their institutional authority (as mentioned, all moderators' usernames are followed by "FIF Moderator"; sometimes this designation was also added to the sign-off).

My main analytic focus was on the locking posts of a popular moderator called tspring; I demonstrated how the standard text could be modified to create a more personalized assessment of the quality of the content of, and/ or forms of participation in, the thread, as in the "I can't even" example, which involved the use of strikethrough and the addition of replacement text (somewhat reminiscent of the "fixes" examined in the last chapter, though it is not labeled here as a fix). Most notable about tspring, however, and what she seems to be most recognized for by others in the community of practice, was her use of GIFs in thread-locking messages. While three of the six moderators sometimes included GIFs or images in the one hundred posts I examined, she used the most, and I immediately noted her especially clever GIF choices, which had intertextual links to various aspects of the thread to be locked: the title given to the thread by the OP, a GIF in a prior post by the OP, or a GIF in the immediately prior post in the thread. The Flash Gordon GIF was linked to the overall shape or tone of a thread that began as a discussion of a lemon cleanse diet: humorous nonsense. The moderator's GIFs are thus intertextually linked to a thread's prior text (specific words), its overall topic and/or tone, or previously posted GIFs. This use of GIFs created fun and humor, an interpretation that is supported by the existence of a thread on the boards that praised how tspring had locked one specific thread, while also revealing that multiple users attend to thread-locking posts because sometimes they are done very well (especially by tspring).

The analysis suggests that moderators, at their discretion, may take advantage of the affordances of the medium, using GIFs, images, and words and typographical manipulation to perform their institutional roles, and specifically a metadiscursive task, in atypical ways. I have focused on illuminating the practices of one moderator who maximally took advantage of these affordances—that the discussion boards allow GIFs, that GIFs are readily available online, and that they are relatively easily recontextualized—to accomplish individual identity work while she locked discussion threads that had degenerated to some point of no return. She produced intertextual links between her own post and the problematic discourse of the thread (sometimes in a specific post) by using the standard text template (sometimes with adjustments), which demonstrated institutional authority. She thus not only created metadiscourse but also constructed humor by pulling material from popular culture and making it relevant to a specific instance of thread locking, creating connection and solidarity on the discussion boards.

Worth noting is that while any user could enjoy any given GIF as a GIF, not all users would be able to recognize the GIFs' sources. I—a white, highly educated American woman in her mid-forties who spends some time online—recognized many (but not all of them). I believe this is because many were dated to a time period when I was a watcher of popular television shows and movies. Recognizing the sources of GIFs brings layers of meaning to which not all users have immediate access (though the ability to do a reverse image search and to search for GIFs using descriptors and the word "GIF" made all of the GIFs sources findable when I searched for them). In this way, some users might not recognize or appreciate tspring's thread locking to the same extent as others, which might have the effect of excluding some posters who are not "in" on the joke.

CHAPTER 5

"I would suggest you tell this ∧∧∧ to your doctor"

Online collaborative problem-solving about offline doctor–patient communication

The last three chapters examined intertextual linking strategies as part of metadiscursive activities that consisted primarily of discourse about online discourse. Specifically, posters negotiated definitions of a term that was central to their unfolding discussion thread and what constituted appropriate participation in that context; they "fixed" the posts of others who had posted earlier in the same thread that they did; and a moderator produced discourse about the discourse of unfolding threads in her posts that announced the threads' locking. With acknowledgment that online and offline social worlds are not dichotomous but rather are intertwined, as has been argued by Jones (2004) and Bolander and Locher (2020), among others, in the next two chapters I focus on discussion board discourse that addresses "offline" discourse: previous conversations that occurred face to face (i.e., discourse that did not occur on the boards). Each chapter focuses on one thread that was started by an original poster seeking support and advice regarding how to handle an offline communicative event that happened in the past (a doctor–patient encounter; an argument between partners). In this chapter, I consider a discussion thread started by a woman who tells a brief narrative describing a doctor–patient encounter she had, specifically how her doctor told her she needed to lose more weight than she expected or believes she needs to lose; she indicates her displeasure with this interaction and seeks guidance regarding how to understand what happened and what to do next.

Intertextuality 2.0. Cynthia Gordon, Oxford University Press. © Oxford University Press 2023.
DOI: 10.1093/oso/9780197642689.003.0005

What results is a collaborative, metadiscursive activity that can be described as "problem-solving."

The thread I examine in this chapter is but one example of how offline and online communication are interconnected in everyday life. Aarsand (2008), for example, considers how students working on classroom computers alternate between, and integrate, online and offline interactions with their peers, and thereby construct their relationships and identities; DiDomenico and Boase (2013) explore how young women friends intermittently orient to their cell phones in a casual conversation together, dynamically shifting their attention and involvement; Gordon and İkizoğlu (2017) examine how an original poster of a thread to a weight loss discussion board (on FriendInFitness [FIF]) constructs her boyfriend's identity as a "picky eater" in part by describing his offline eating practices in detail and the general types of interactions she has with him as she attempts to encourage him to adapt healthier eating and exercise habits. Posters to the FIF boards—and many other online communities of practice focused on the exchange of information and support—share, ask for advice about, and discuss offline communication, such as regarding interactions they have had with physicians and other healthcare providers, partners, parents, friends, and coworkers. For example, on the boards, sample threads that begin with, and/or lead to, this type of metadiscourse are titled "How did your doctor tell you you're fat??"; "Doc wants me to do 1100 calories a day—I think she's cray cray" (crazy); "When someone comments on your weight"; "Is your family/relatives supportive of your weight loss?"; and "Unsupportive friends and family, 1200 Calorie diet." In analyzing a single discussion thread that focuses on unpacking an offline doctor–patient interaction, I thus highlight a common struggle depicted on the boards: dieting or watching one's weight may affect everyday communication and relationships, including between doctors and patients, since doctors at times comment on patients' body weight.

A feature that stands out in this thread (as was the case for the "clean eating" thread examined in Chapter 2) is that the original poster is extremely active. In the next chapter I examine a thread where a different original poster begins by telling about her past experience and problem but then does not participate again, and there is not really a resolution to the OP's specific situation. In contrast, the thread I analyze here features posters generally working together to explore and try to assist with the OP's problem effectively, collaboratively engaging in discourse about the discourse of the OP's offline interaction (as well as others), in addition to the discourse of the unfolding thread. In this case, the OP's active participation contributes to the construction of back-and-forth exchanges between posters, and to a quite productive discussion overall (as the OP herself assesses it near the end of the thread). In this sense, the thread represents what Ochs, Smith, and Taylor (1989) refer to as an instance of "problem-solving." Examining family conversations during dinnertime, they suggest that dinner conversation can be viewed as an "opportunity space" where co-participants can collaboratively make sense of prior experiences. In line with this, in my examination of one discussion thread in which a doctor–patient interaction is described, evaluated, and worked through by participants on FIF, I view these online discussion boards as an "opportunity space" to make sense of prior offline interactions. This extends previous research exploring how people introduce problems in online support contexts regarding various issues related to health and illness—such as metabolic problems (Andersen 2017), self-harming behaviors (Smithson et al. 2011b), and picky eating (İkizoğlu and Gordon 2020)—and how others respond to such instances of what Smithson et al. (2011b) call "problem presentation," or to what Morrow (2006) terms "problem messages."

My analysis identifies and explicates intertextual linking strategies through which participants tie their posts together, thereby co-constructing an activity that aims to contribute to solving the dilemma presented by the OP: how to interpret and understand an unwelcome comment that her doctor made about her weight during a face-to-face medical encounter. The thread is metadiscursive from the beginning: the topic is a prior face-to-face encounter. Others' reported communicative experiences with healthcare providers also emerge as the thread unfolds, a common phenomenon in the discourse of support groups of various types that can be understood as "reciprocity" (as in Smithson et al.'s [2011b] study of online self-harm support) and as instantiation of Sacks' (1992) notion of "second stories" (as in Arminen's [2004] study of the discourse of Alcoholics Anonymous). In addition to this metadiscourse focused on offline discourse, and as seen in prior chapters, metadiscourse appears in the form of discourse about the discourse of the thread itself. I identify seven intertextual linking strategies that construct the metadiscourse that facilitates the problem-solving activity on the thread: posing information-seeking questions, paraphrasing and reframing, telling matching stories, creating constructed dialogue, using the boards' quotation function, pointing through symbols or words, and advice giving. Several of these strategies also emerged in previous chapters (notably, uses of the quotation function and deictic pronouns and symbols). The interweaving of these strategies realizes the shared "opportunity space" for communicating about communication in order to solve a problem and perhaps improve future communication. The thread also serves as an example representing a general "cultural preoccupation with communication," including its "problems, breakdowns, and remedies" (Craig 2005:661), and a demonstration of how metadiscourse is fundamental to the construction of ideologies (as argued by, e.g., Coupland and Jaworski [2004] and Thurlow and Mroczek [2011], among others), in this case regarding doctor–patient communication.

Given the thread's focus on practical communication-related problem-solving, considering the content of the posts also reveals thread participants' expectations about doctors' versus patients' interactional responsibilities, or what Sarangi (2016) calls a "role responsibility framework" for doctor–patient communication and care. Thus, in examining the thread, I demonstrate how participants exploit the intertextual possibilities of language and medium not only to collaboratively accomplish meaning-making about a specific instance of offline communication, but also to communicate about responsibilities of doctors and patients regarding weight loss communication more generally— to create shared perspectives and ideologies. Given this focus on collaborative meaning-making over the course of a single thread, this chapter again harks back to the "clean eating" chapter (though in this thread, there are fewer antagonistic exchanges, perhaps because the thread is shorter, or the topic not as controversial).

In what follows, I first briefly review previous research on problem-solving, as well as studies that highlight storytelling as a prominent part of online support discourse, in particular as a part of initial posts that outline problems that are then taken up by others as the topic of discussion, as happens in the thread I analyze. I also discuss work that reveals that scrutinizing discourse about discourse reveals expectations and ideologies about appropriate communication, since the OP's description of a troublesome doctor–patient interaction leads to broader claims about how such instances of communication should work. Second, I introduce the thread that is my focus in more detail and explain why I chose it. I then turn to the analysis, demonstrating how the aforementioned intertextual linking strategies work toward constructing a problem-solving episode that stretches across the thread's posts. In the discussion, I address how this metadiscursive thread not only attends to the original poster's problematic doctor–patient encounter, thus providing her with the kind of support one might hope to get in an online forum, but also a larger "problem" regarding the distribution of responsibilities in medical encounters wherein the sensitive topic of body weight is addressed: the difficult task of achieving effective (and pleasant) doctor–patient communication. The posts by thread participants construct both patients and doctors as responsible for successful weight-related communication, a theme that also emerges in other threads, as well as more broadly in various health-related contexts.

PROBLEM-SOLVING IN (ONLINE SUPPORT) DISCOURSE

As reviewed in previous chapters, existing research on the discourse of online support forums identifies such forums as a context for numerous activities, including soliciting and providing advice and information, seeking and giving encouragement, telling stories, and socializing. My focus in this chapter is problem-solving, a collaborative activity that potentially includes all of these. Original posters often present their problem—in other words, their reason for posting—by using narrative or narrative-like discourse, as does the OP of the thread I analyze, and how this is done shapes the thread's unfolding. In this section, I review research on the activity of (face-to-face conversational) problem-solving. As this work centralizes narrative discourse as a fundamental part of this activity, in particular in terms of problem presentation, I next discuss research on the role of narrative in online support contexts. Narrative is one of many strategies used to accomplish what can be broadly understood as "problem-solving" online, as the analysis will show.

As mentioned, my understanding of problem-solving stems from work by Elinor Ochs and her colleagues on family dinner table conversations. Ochs, Smith, and Taylor (1989) examine family dinner talk and explicate how what they identify as "a problem-solving discourse activity" unfolds through a process of co-narration. They demonstrate how this is a "socially-accomplished cognitive activity" (p. 238) that links past, present, and future; helps create family relationships; and socializes younger family members into ways of solving social puzzles and working through dilemmas. In these narrative occasions, there is no "single knowing teller" vested with the "authority to define a narrative problem," and this propels the activity forward (p. 242). Taken-for-granted elements in prototypical stories—such as the setting and relevant background information—may be elaborated and revised as the telling unfolds, and different perspectives are offered by participants. The authors thus refer to these as "detective stories." (Later, Ochs, Taylor, Rudolph, and Smith [1992] describe this type of joint storytelling as "a theory-building activity.") In collaboratively told family stories, "missing" information may be recognized, provided, and reworked into the story. Experiences may be reinterpreted, and participants' understandings—and ideas about what to do next—may change over the course of the interaction. In this way, entire problem-solving episodes can be conceptualized as the collaborative construction of a non-prototypical narrative, or what some scholars call a "small story" (e.g., Bamberg and Georgakopoulou 2008; Georgakopoulou 2007; Page 2010; Tovares 2010), a perspective I take in an analysis of this thread published elsewhere (Gordon 2015a).

One problem-solving activity that Ochs, Smith and Taylor (1989) analyze was initiated by a school-aged daughter during a family dinner. The girl's telling about what happened focused on her school principal's unfairness: he gave one of her classmates a fairly lenient punishment (a one-day detention) for lifting a classmate's dress on the playground. The mother, father, and younger brother actively contribute to the telling; for example, the mother highlights the daughter's emotional reactions to the other girl's action of lifting the dress. As the telling unfolds, however, it becomes apparent (through the brother's offering of information) that the daughter had received a one-day detention earlier in the year for a lesser offense, which shifts the narrative perspective: the principal's identified "unfairness" traces back to his previous punishment of the daughter, which was the same as the punishment of the dress-lifting girl, despite the less serious nature of the daughter's infraction. While this does not seem to be the telling the daughter wanted to bring out (in the video, it can be seen that she glared at her brother), the participants together constructed it in this way, offering different understandings of the initial event and the daughter's reaction to it. There is also some projection of possible future actions stemming from this problem-solving activity, as the brother asks his sister about whether she will be "out" (i.e., thrown out of school) if she gets another detention (the parents reassure him that detentions set to zero each new year, so there is no need to worry).

Ochs, Smith, and Taylor's (1989) study is in line with broader observations among researchers that collaborative narrative co-tellings (rather than more monologic tellings) are commonplace in some communities and contexts (e.g., Blum-Kulka 1997; Goodwin 1986; Mandelbaum 1987; Norrick 2019); for example, story recipients may add details to an unfolding narrative, ask for more information, and offer alternative interpretations. This study also captures the important idea that narratives do not only recapitulate the past (the focus of the traditional Labovian [e.g., Labov 1972] model) but also project into the future such as by invoking hypothetical scenarios or providing guidance (e.g., Beach and Japp 1983; Goodwin 1990; Gordon 2005). These are all phenomena that emerge in the discussion thread I analyze.

Vehviläinen's (2009) examination of in-person meetings between Finnish master's-level students and their thesis supervisors also links the telling of past problem-oriented narratives (in this case, by students) to future actions (which here are specified in the advice supervisors provide). The author analyzes advice as a "problem-solving activity" (though Ochs et al.'s [1989] use of the term is not mentioned) and highlights various strategies that contribute to it, notably asking questions using one of two formats—either by "Invoking Incompetence" or by "Proposing Potential Problems and Candidate Solutions." Especially relevant for my study, Vehviläinen observes that supervisors' advice not only provides the "remedy" to a problem but also involves establishing what she calls the problem's "relevance" (meaning if the problem is relevant to the students' work, or if indeed it even exists). In other words, "advice giving is, fundamentally, a problem-solving activity" and "advice sequences involve both problem-establishing and problem-solving work" (p. 185).

In a study that also explores supervisor–supervisee discourse, Gordon and Luke (2013) examine narratives told by student counselors-in-training in the context of internship supervision occurring over email. They connect advice giving to Bakhtin's (1981, 1986) discussion of authorship and utterance addressivity to explore the jointly constructed nature of expert–novice interaction, especially how professional socialization is accomplished. Specifically, this study demonstrates how narratives told by counselors-in-training, of which many revolve around problems and challenges that they have faced while completing their internships, are "re-authored" by the supervisors, with the purpose of either reinforcing the counselor-in-training's perspective, or invoking new understandings (or "reframing," in the sense of Tannen and Wallat [1993]). The authors also show how supervisors' advice attempts to "pre-author" the future. While not explicitly conceptualizing the data as an example of "problem-solving," the study demonstrates how online (in this case, email) exchanges can provide a context for collaboratively working through challenging situations by producing discourse about prior experiences and subsequently providing advice.

Existing research on narrative as well as on problem-solving and advice is relevant to the context of online problem-solving activities, which tend to be initiated by a post that tells a story about past events, and may unfold in ways that include interactive activities such as gathering more information, reformulating the narrative's point, telling of matching stories, expressing empathy, and providing advice (regarding both how to interpret what happened, and what future actions the original poster should take). There is a relatively large body of research on the role of narratives online, and in online support forums more specifically, and while such studies tend not to focus explicitly on "problem-solving," they provide helpful background for my analysis of a thread that was started with a personal experience narrative that outlines a problem. For example, Andersen (2017) examines a thread on the topic of metabolism that was posted on a Danish health website, focusing on how the original poster presents her problem by describing her medical history, symptoms, and candidate diagnoses, in part through depicting prior interactions she had with healthcare providers and a family member. In the ensuing thread, others tell about their own experiences, give advice to the OP, and offer challenges to healthcare providers' approaches to treatment. These activities all contribute to achieving a shared understanding among posters. Related, Armstrong, Koteyko, and Powell (2012) find that in an online diabetes community, participants used short personal stories (among other strategies) to prioritize the site's identity as a place for information exchange while also establishing solidarity, including emphasizing mutual exchange and help.

These findings echo the observation of many studies that telling a narrative may lead to others telling reciprocal or matching stories (e.g., Tannen 1990). They also have connections to Arminen's (2004) analysis of (face-to-face) Alcoholics Anonymous meetings that showed how what Sacks (1992) calls "second stories" play a key role in creating alignment and providing support. In online support contexts, such stories have been demonstrated be used to construct support among sufferers of arthritis (Harrison and Barlow 2009), people who engage in self-harming behaviors (Smithson et al. 2011b), and those living with celiac disease (Veen et al. 2010). Matching stories occur quite commonly on FIF in general, and in the thread I analyze in this chapter in particular. As in these previous studies, depictions of problems also tend to lead to other activities such as information gathering and advice giving.

Page's (2012) examination of one thread started by a woman who self-identifies as being a first-time poster to a bodybuilding forum is especially relevant to my analysis. Page observes that narrating a problem serves as a means of advice solicitation and self-introduction, and she shows how posters to one thread, in sharing their own stories and experiences related to the post of the OP (original poster), contribute to its unfolding. The author finds that posters create various degrees of (dis)alignment with the OP and participate in ways that accomplish identity work for her as well as for themselves. In addition, she observes that the second stories that are told to create alignment with the OP go beyond narrating "parallel situations," to "also provide additional contexts from which to interpret the OP's problem and provide her with suggested solutions" (p. 39). In this sense, I suggest that this bodybuilding support thread could be viewed as an online instantiation of what Ochs et al. (1989) described as collaborative problem-solving.

Hamilton's (1998) exploration of how participants in an electronic discussion list on bone marrow transplantation describe conflict-laden offline interactions they had with doctors, with a particular focus on reported speech (or "constructed dialogue" [Tannen 2007b]), is also particularly germane to my analysis. Hamilton finds that posters construct identities as survivors (rather than victims) in the stories they post, such as by depicting themselves in the patient role as having actively initiated communication sequences with doctors. In narratives that alternate between direct and indirect forms of reported speech, narrators tend to animate doctors using the direct form (which suggests an exact reproduction of their words); this may reflect doctors' higher status (in line with findings regarding direct reported speech and social status by Johnstone [1997]). In narratives that depict doctors unfavorably, this strategy allows doctors to "incriminate themselves" when they are unhelpful or rude to patients—the reader (seemingly) has direct access to the doctor's words (Hamilton 1998:63). In narratives that focus on positioning the patient-narrator favorably, doctors are attributed constructed dialogue in the form of direct reported speech that praises the patient, which avoids the face-threatening act of tellers engaging in direct self-praise. Overall, in the stories they shared, listserv participants portrayed themselves as having to overcome not only the disease and treatment, but also insensitive or unhelpful physicians. In addition to demonstrating how posters construct their offline identities as good patients in an online context, this study also highlights the theme that dominates the thread I examine in this chapter—depictions of and communication about doctor–patient interaction. It is also especially relevant to this chapter in that the original poster in the thread I examine tells a story of a difficult interaction she had with her doctor, and her story includes constructed dialogue.

Taken together, research reviewed in this section highlights how problem-solving is a collaborative activity that often involves various strategies, notably telling stories and giving advice, and that through problem-solving, participants accomplish multiple functions, including constructing (dis)alignments, displaying empathy, and adjusting perspective. Extant research demonstrates that online support forums are sites for exchange of not only information, support, and advice, but also stories about offline experiences. Stories told online about previous offline interactions constitute metadiscourse and may serve to create communication ideologies, which I discuss further in the next section.

METADISCOURSE AND COMMUNICATION EXPECTATIONS AND IDEOLOGIES

Building on Verschueren (1999), Craig (2005:659) observes that metadiscourse, which he describes as "talk about talk," is often used for utilitarian purposes, such as to overcome difficulties in communication; likewise van Leeuwen (2004) observes that what he calls "meta-communication" is used to address communicative problems. Both scholars emphasize that discourse produced about discourse is an ordinary and common phenomenon. As the previous chapters in this book have suggested, it also frequently occurs online (certainly in the FIF discussion threads). This omnipresence can be seen as reflecting contemporary "communication culture" (to use Cameron's [2000] term). Craig suggests that metacommunication highlights "popular beliefs that communication is important, faulty communication is to blame for many human problems, and better communication can make a better world" (p. 662). Indeed, these beliefs not only underlie laypersons' metadiscourse, including online, but also academic inquiry motivated by the idea that studying communication about communication can help improve it, in part by identifying communication patterns and expectations.

One such inquiry is Jaworski and Sachdev's (2004) analysis of 178 teachers' references for students who applied for a language/communication program as part of their undergraduate training. By examining the metapragmatic comments teachers produced as part of their assessments of the applicants' "communication skills" in the letters they wrote for them, Jaworski and Sachdev uncovered ideologies about students' talk and silence. Students' talk was commonly mentioned by teachers in their letters (over 60% included mention of talk), and further it is presented in positive terms and in terms of students' academic prowess (e.g., "her observations are perceptive and sagacious"; p. 233). Silence, in contrast, was mentioned in just over 20% of the letters, and references were found to be primarily negative, especially when associated with academic skills (as compared with cases where silence was presented as an aspect of personality, which also occurred). Some mentions of reticence came with disclaimers, such as "In group discussions she may appear rather reserved but on an individual basis she is highly articulate" (p. 236); this serves as further evidence that mention of students' silence cues negative meanings (that then are mitigated to some extent). Overall, students' talk (as compared with silence) is conceptualized positively: metapragmatic comments about it connect talk with academic success (even though no such links have been consistently shown in scholarly research, as the authors point out). Jaworski and Sachdev suggest that teachers, who are gatekeepers to advanced educational experiences for students, should be made aware of the importance of how they write about talk and silence in recommendation letters, as it not only affects portrayal of individual students and ultimately their educational opportunities but also continually reifies dominant ideologies about students' loquaciousness versus reticence.

A work even more closely related to the focus of the current chapter is Gordon et al.'s (2009) interview-based study of accounts of medical communication produced by bereaved parents (each of whom had a child who died in the Pediatric Intensive Care Unit). The data were collected as part of a larger study focused on improving communication in this difficult context. In interviews, parents told stories and described their experiences communicating with the care team, and the analysis highlights how parents use accounts to evaluate the communicative behaviors they report. Findings also show that parents have nuanced understandings of communicative responsibilities, not only for doctors, but also for themselves. For instance, they viewed doctors as responsible for providing medical information clearly but also held themselves responsible for gathering information. Ultimately, this study revealed patients' expectations about the distribution of responsibilities in the context of medical communication and suggested that addressing expectations could improve it; for instance, because parents often perceived themselves as part of the team of carers, medical teams could make more efforts to include them in appropriate ways. Examining metadiscourse in the form of accounts uncovered these expectations.

Puhl, Peterson, and Luedicke (2013) also take a metadiscursive approach in the sense that data were collected by asking patients to consider terms such as "unhealthy weight," "fat," and "morbidly obese" and evaluate them, using Likert scales, in terms of how desirable, stigmatizing, blaming, and motivating to lose weight these would be if used by their doctors. In other words, the study highlighted lexical choice as a potential site for communication discomfort or failure and asked patients to communicate about these. Findings indicate that "morbidly obese," "fat," and "obese" were rated as the most undesirable, stigmatizing, and blaming terms, while "unhealthy weight" and "overweight" were rated as most motivating. Related to the thread I examine in that the problematic encounter the OP describes with her doctor is interpreted by some posters as a communicative one relating to the doctor's "bedside manner," these authors also found that 19% of respondents reported that they would avoid future appointments, and 21% would seek a new doctor, if they felt their doctor stigmatized their weight. (In fact, in the thread I analyze, it is suggested that the OP find a new doctor.)

Gordon and Luke (2016) examine metacommunication in a group supervision meeting about the practice and training experiences that student counselors-in-training had at local high schools as part of their degree program. Focusing on talk about the talk that took place at the schools, and specifically talk about address terms (i.e., what they should have the students call them) and the speech act of requesting information by way of questioning (i.e., what questions they should ask and to whom), the analysis demonstrates how the counselors-in-training use words creating negative affect, the verb "feel," and constructed dialogue to display stances of uncertainty and discomfort that characterize their transitional professional identities. Talk about address terms and asking questions encapsulated their uneasy navigation of their new professional relationships with the school's students (should the trainee counselors be like their teachers, or like their friends?) and school staff members (should the trainee counselors ask a lot of questions to learn as much as they can, or does this make them look incompetent?). Examining metadiscourse thus lends insight into our understanding of professional identity development, as well as the linguistic features that emerge in talk about difficult prior interactions.

Metacommunication, despite its reputation, is not a cure-all for interactional difficulties. A study by Jager and Stommel (2017) finds that metadiscourse, when used in online counseling sessions by counselors to address trouble in the ongoing interaction, may not be a functional strategy. This is despite the fact that, as they observe (following Schiffrin [1980], and in line with other studies reviewed in this chapter), psychotherapeutic contexts are often rife with metatalk. The authors show that discourse about the currently unfolding encounter—which is a quite different type of metadiscourse than discourse about a past encounter, such as examined by Gordon and Luke (2016) and is the focus of this chapter—was rarely used in their data set of over five hundred Dutch chat help service exchanges online. When it did occur, counselors used it to criticize their own communication (such as by indicating they regretted not being able to give advice that the client found useful), to accuse clients (i.e., they questioned the client's openness to hearing and accepting advice), and to explain (i.e., they outlined the institutional responsibilities of the encounter and/or suggested that the client's expectations were unrealistic). These efforts by the counselor to address the discourse of an unfolding troublesome interaction were usually met with the client signing off, i.e., ending the session, which suggests that this use of metadiscourse was not an especially productive one. It did, however, perhaps indirectly reveal something about clients' expectations about online counseling communication: they didn't want communication strategies used in the ongoing encounter to be made the object of discussion. (Recall that in the analysis of the "clean eating" thread in Chapter 2, metadiscourse also sometimes resulted in bad feelings and participants' leaving the thread, even though in most cases, it was used productively, to help define the difficult term "clean" and to adjudicate appropriate thread participation).

In summary, metadiscourse has been identified as an often but not always useful resource for addressing problems in communication, and, most relevant for my analysis that follows, it reveals not only understandings of prior experiences but also expectations about how people should communicate in particular social contexts and professional roles, i.e., ideologies. For example, doctors are expected to communicate professionally but not coldly, and many patients would feel stigmatized if a doctor used the label "morbidly obese" to refer to them. Research that uncovers such expectations and preferences is undergirded by the culturally held belief that communication, including between doctors and patients, can be improved, and that communicating about it is a means of doing this.

INTERTEXTUALITY, METADISCOURSE, AND PROBLEM-SOLVING

The thread I analyze consists of 46 posts, produced by 24 participants, including the original poster, Alma_Michelle, over the course of 50 minutes. I chose it in line with Herring's (2004) identification of sampling "by theme" (i.e., by thread): it represents one sequential unfolding on the theme of problems in doctor–patient communication (both what is communicated and how), and one woman's (the OP's) experience in particular. In addition, because the OP was a very active poster, and others responded typically in helpful ways, the thread seemed to represent an especially earnest and collaborative one. (I noted no violations of the forum guidelines, though there are some somewhat direct criticisms between posters.) Alma_Michelle posts 14 times; 17 other women participate in the thread and six men do. The most frequent posters after Alma_Michelle are getgoinggogo (a man) and cbitts32 (a woman), with four posts each. Three other women each posted twice; the remaining participants each posted once. This thread offers an opportunity to examine a discussion about a common scene—doctor–patient interaction about body weight—which represents a potentially sensitive encounter. The active participation in this thread, including by the OP, makes it an ideal context in which to explore ways participants link posts to engage collaboratively in a metadiscursive problem-solving activity regarding communication that happened offline.

In her original post, Alma_Michelle describes a problematic interaction she had with a doctor in a thread she titles "Healthy BMI, Doc Says I Still Need to 'Drop a Few'" (i.e., lose a few pounds). BMI stands for body mass index. It is a height-to-weight ratio that, according to the Centers for Disease Control, is "a fairly reliable indicator of body fatness for most people." A "normal" BMI is between 18.5 and 24.9. In addition to the thread title, which highlights a communicative issue through her focus on what her doctor "says," Alma_Michelle's post consists of three paragraphs; the text of the first is shown in extract 1a.

(1a) <u>Alma_Michelle (OP)</u>

1 So I went to a new doctor today for a regular check-up/exam. After getting my
2 height/weight, the doctor told me I needed to lose weight even though my BMI is still in
3 the healthy range, under 25. Quote: "I'd like to see you drop a few pounds" . . .
4 SERIOUSLY?? There's a "range" for a reason!! So essentially, because I'm closer to
5 24.9 than 18.5, I need to lose weight? Whatever happened to having a range of healthy
6 weight?

Alma_Michelle describes her offline interaction, using constructed dialogue in the form of "direct reported speech" to quote what the doctor reportedly uttered to her word for word; this can be seen as allowing the doctor to self-incriminate (following Hamilton 1998). Alma_Michelle not only reports exactly what the doctor supposedly said ("Quote: 'I'd like to see you drop a few pounds'" [line 3]; "drop a few" was also quoted in the thread's title); she also immediately negatively assesses this quotation in all capital letters—"SERIOUSLY??" (line 4) —followed by two question marks for emphasis. In doing this, she produces metadiscourse, in this case, discourse that evaluates the doctor's discourse that she has just shared on the thread. This questions the doctor's judgment, while also demonstrating Alma_Michelle's own understanding that there is "a range of healthy weight" and that the "healthy" range for BMI is between 18.5 and 24.9 (which is generally accepted). Alma_Michelle's post continues:

(1b) <u>Alma_Michelle (OP) (continued)</u>

7   Granted, I am trying to lose a few pounds to get back to my personal ideal. But even with
8   those couple extra pounds, I still felt good about myself because I knew I still fell within
9   an average/healthy weight range and I knew I was working towards my goal. However,
10 now I just feel bad about myself and I am so discouraged . . . I've lost any and all good
11 self-esteem about my body image :(Encouragement welcome!

Here the OP provides more background information, including how the encounter adversely affected her emotional and psychological state. Alma_

Michelle's use of the frowning-face emoticon contributes to this construction. (Note that when I initially downloaded this thread, the frowning-face emoticon appeared as shown above in line 11; revisits show that it has since been transformed into the frowning face emoji.) She ends the paragraph by requesting encouragement from other FIF users ("Encouragement welcome!").

The final paragraph of the post begins with ETA—"edited to add"—which means that Alma_Michelle made her post, but then adjusted it to add what follows:

(1c)   Alma_Michelle (OP) (continued)
12   ETA: I normally look and feel my best between 140–145, but now I feel forced to lose
13   even more weight than that. . . . Hence my new goal of 125, according to the doc. So, still
14   upset!! :(

In this excerpt from her initial post, Alma_Michelle emphasizes that the physician's goal for her—125 pounds—is well below where she feels she looks and feels best (between 140 and 145 pounds). Her use of "according to the doc" in providing the 125 figure is metadiscursive in that "according to" points to the information source (Hyland 2005), which in this case is a previous offline conversation that Alma_Michelle has just described. "According to" also can be used "to indicate the content" of what was said, "without endorsing the content as true" (Sherman 2018:629). In this context, it seems to assist Alma_Michelle in questioning the credibility of the doctor, while also highlighting the contrast between her impression that she might be carrying "a couple extra pounds" (extract 1b) and her doctor's perspective (a "goal of 125" pounds). She thus reports feeling "forced to lose even more weight" than she planned and is "still upset" about the conversation (emphasized by a second frowny-face emoticon).

An underlying theme of the thread that unfolds following this post—that doctors and patients have communication problems—is not new; it is well documented that doctors struggle to approach sensitive topics (e.g., serious diseases; Linell and Bredmar 1996) or those that are morally loaded (e.g., failure to lose weight; Webb 2009). Doctors make efforts to approach such face-threatening topics with what Lutfey and Maynard (1998) call "interactive caution." However, this problem is far from being solved: for example, Kahan (2018), in a paper providing an overview of articles published on healthcare providers and obesity management for patients, finds that while it is widely recognized that the topic of patient body weight needs to be approached, and should be approached with care (such as by asking the patient permission to discuss weight and by being nonjudgmental), communication around the topic is "suboptimal" with many obese people never even being diagnosed as such by their doctors. While Jackson and Gray (2005) caution veterinarians to deliver news about fat pets with care, Stephens (2009) implores doctors to overcome the "zeal to be polite" regarding overweight and obese children, as it leads to lack of recognition of the problem by parents, lack of documentation by doctors, and a lack of action that can hurt children long-term. Thus, body weight (including of pets and children) remains a difficult topic of discussion for healthcare providers, with pitfalls ranging from potentially stigmatizing lexical choices (Puhl, Peterson, and Luedicke 2013); to choosing between various ways to initiate weight-related discussions, such as asking patients if they think they are overweight, telling them that they are, or deducing it with them from a BMI calculation (Speer and McPhillips 2018); to generally failing to display adequate empathy and attribute appropriate patient autonomy (Pollak et al. 2009).

Indeed, Alma_Michelle's original post makes clear that the doctor's comment about her weight upset her, although it seems to be the content of what she said, rather than how she said it, that is the problem (though both the content and form of the doctor's communication are problematized in the unfolding thread as multiple perspectives emerge about what happened). In what follows, I identify and explicate strategies that interconnect participants' posts to accomplish online problem-solving regarding offline communication; in other words, I demonstrate how intertextual resources construct metadiscourse about language and communication that occurred in a different context. These include asking information-seeking questions, paraphrasing and reframing, telling matching stories, constructing dialogue, using the discussion boards' quotation function, pointing to something posted before, and giving advice.

Asking information-seeking questions

A primary way that thread participants contribute to the unfolding metadiscursive problem-solving activity is by attempting to bring into Alma_Michelle's initial formulation other potentially relevant information. They do this by asking questions about various things, notably about the sequence of what happened in the situation (e.g., if the doctor contextualized her comments in any particular way), Alma_Michelle's relationship with the doctor (note that some of the participants incorrectly assume that the doctor is a man), and her body type and health practices. This strategy is used especially early on in the thread: instead of immediately giving advice or sharing their own experiences, many posters ask questions to learn more about the OP as well as the discourse that occurred between her and her doctor. Following Ochs, Smith, and Taylor (1989:242), it seems that "there is missing information" that is sought, typical of problem-solving episodes. The posts asking questions of the OP intertextually reference her original post.

For example, the first user to post after Alma_Michelle, garnetgal19, asks, "What is your height and body frame type? What about your body fat percentage?" One minute later in the third post to the thread, camclaine posts another question: "how tall are you?" Through questions such as these, thread contributors attempt to bring into the discussion additional information, in this case, about the OP's physical body, to help determine if the doctor was justified in suggesting that she should lose as much weight as she said. A question asked by smithsusan (in post 31)—"Do you strength train?"—similarly indicates a need to know more about Alma_Michelle's body composition in terms of muscle versus fat to understand the (un)helpfulness of the doctor's comment better.

While Alma_Michelle does not respond to each and every question posed to her, she is very responsive. For instance, she explains that she is five feet four inches tall and wears a size six, and that she has a "relatively flat" stomach but not "rock-hard abs." Her posted responses facilitate the collaborative problem-solving that unfolds: other forum participants—to use Ochs et al.'s (1989:241) words—"encourage" "continuation and elaboration" as they attempt to engage in "the joint working out" of the problem. In using information-seeking questions, participants tie their contributions back to Alma_Michelle's original formulation, both identifying missing information and creating intertextual connections that increase understanding of the doctor–patient encounter she described.

Questions asking more about Alma_Michelle's emotional state are largely absent; this may owe to the detailed way in which she described her emotions from the outset (including her use of emoticons). However, as the thread advances, Alma_Michelle's emotional response is evaluated in light of the new data, including information about her relationship with her doctor, how their encounter unfolded, and her body type and health-related activities.

Paraphrasing and reframing

A second way posters participate that is intertextual and facilitates the problem-solving activity is by paraphrasing and "reframing." My understanding of reframing stems from Tannen and Wallat's (1993:59) discussion of "frames of interpretation" that participants use to understand situations, events, utterances, and so on.

In the discussion thread, participants essentially restate or reinforce what the original poster expressed (paraphrasing, which can be thought of as a form of repetition), or they shift, offering a different understanding (reframing). I understand reframing to be similar to "formulations," a concept that can be traced back to Garfinkel and Sacks (1970). Formulations function to "propose or imply a reworking of events described or implied by a previous speaker" (Antaki, Barnes, and Leuder 2005:643) and play important parts of communication in contexts both educational (e.g., Vásquez 2010) and therapeutic (e.g., Antaki et al. 2005; Buttny 1996). It is thus not surprising that reframing is a strategy that appears in an online discussion thread that foregrounds seeking understanding about what an OP experienced, as well as her emotional response.

While paraphrasing and reframing are, conceptually, two different strategies, in practice the distinction is blurred. Reframings can be very dramatic or very subtle. Further, because paraphrase, like all forms of repetition, necessarily alters meaning (following Tannen 2007b), a reframing is always accomplished to some extent, whether intended or not. Finally, both work to shape another's understanding of a situation, whether reinforcing or adjusting it (see Gordon and Luke 2013).

A post by ashutchens, the sixth post in the thread, includes paraphrase and reframing together: she paraphrases one element of Alma_Michelle's post—her identification of the doctor's talk as worthy of negative evaluation—but also suggests that Alma_Michelle misinterpreted what the doctor said.

(2)　ashutchens (post 6)
1　It doesn't sound like the doctor was very professional (unless you've been seeing the
2　same doc for years and he/she is comfortable to speak with you that bluntly). However,
3　from what you shared, the doctor definitely wasn't encouraging you to get down to 125
4　pounds. You said you feel your best around 140–145 which is a few pounds away
5　. . . which is what the doc suggested.

The OP initially quoted and negatively assessed the doctor's comment (e.g., in commenting, "SERIOUSLY??"); here ashutchens paraphrases how she interprets the doctor's depicted communication—as not "being very professional" and being executed "bluntly" (lines 1–2). In addition, though, ashutchens formulates or reframes, explaining that Alma_Michelle seems to have misunderstood the doctor, who in fact was in agreement with Alma_Michelle's stated goal of 140–145. This presents a different take on what happened and is metadiscursive. Similar to Robles and Castor's (2019:145) finding that metadiscourse serves to (re)frame what others are "doing, what it means, and what moral issues are at stake" in a video-recorded confrontation between a county clerk in the US state of Kentucky and the same-sex couple whom she was denying a marriage license, the metadiscourse used by ashutchens offers a reframing of what the doctor did, what it means, and (more indirectly) its appropriateness or moral implications. The use of the discourse marker "however" (line 2)—which, according to Schiffrin (1987:164), indicates "referential contrast"—highlights the reframing and is also an instance of what Schiffrin (1980) calls meta-talk in that it serves to "bracket" what follows.

Another thread participant, cbitts32, suggests a less dramatic readjustment of Alma_Michelle's interpretation. In so doing she glosses over the details and focuses on what is shared between patient and doctor.

(4) cbitts32 (post 4)

1 Okay, so you are here to lose a couple pounds. Good for you! Your Dr. Essentially
2 agreed that it would be a good idea.

Cbitts32 uses "okay" to start her post in a way that Beach (1993) describes as "pivotally," meaning it responds to prior discourse but projects toward something new. Indeed, cbitts32 proposes that the doctor's goals for Alma_ Michelle and Alma_Michelle's own goals are in fact extremely similar (as she is posting on a weight loss discussion board, and her doctor wants her to lose weight), characterizing what took place in the interaction using the metadiscursive term "agreed" (though mitigating it with "Essentially"). She offers a different understanding of the encounter: it was a reasonable and even positive one, with doctor and patient sharing similar perspectives. In other words, this poster suggests that the doctor did nothing wrong.

Another user, getgoinggogo, offers a very different reframing in the thread's 18th post (which he also prefaces with "okay" in the form of "Ok"): he indirectly acknowledges that the doctor's and Alma_Michelle's perspectives differ, but he suggests she try to understand the explanation behind this difference. Specifically, he suggests that the doctor's assessment should not be interpreted in the context of the general BMI (body mass index) measure, but in consideration of the fact that she was able to examine Alma_Michelle as an individual patient. This implies that the doctor's assessment was valid. Getgoinggogo uses a series of rhetorical questions to achieve this reframing.

(5) getgoinggogo (post 18)

1 Ok, are you actually healthy though? I mean are your blood tests also in the middle of the
2 range, or veering close to or over the ends? Any chance of problems with lady parts? Do
3 diabetes, hypertension, coronary artery disease run in your family? Are any immediate
4 family members your doc's also treated suffering from obesity-related diseases?
5
6 I'm not expecting answers, my point is your doc has actually evaluated you, while the
7 BMI chart compares individuals to a population and doesn't give individualzed info, like
8 your doc can.

Getgoinggogo proposes that the doctor's examination of Alma_Michelle— which she reported taking place in her initial post—could have revealed a health concern that would suggest that she really should lose weight; the BMI measure would not be meaningful in this case. Thus, getgoinggogo creates metadiscourse: The message conveyed by the doctor was reasonable and well informed (since she had access to "individualzed info" [individualized information; line 7]).

Another poster, camclaine (very early in the thread, in the third post), after inquiring about Alma_Michelle's height, reframes the message of the doctor (whom she misidentifies as being a man) as an "opinion."

(6)   camclaine (post 3)
    1   how tall are you? and your doctor is one opinion . . if you disagree, then don't take
    2   pressure from him.

In contrast to getgoinggogo, camclaine does not suggest that Alma_Michelle should be thinking about the generalized BMI measure or consider that the doctor may have done an individualized exam. Instead, she suggests that she should assess the doctor's comment as "one opinion" among the many that different doctors might offer. Indicating that a message is an "opinion"—either through direct labeling or by using associated terms such as suggesting someone is speaking about their "feelings" (rather than facts)—is a metadiscursive strategy that can serve to undermine the speaker's credibility and mark an utterance as inappropriate, given the context (Robles and Castor 2019). In this case, it lessens the doctor's credibility—and thus devalues the discourse she reportedly produced in the interaction with Alma_Michelle—and sets the groundwork to offer the advice that follows ("don't take pressure from" the doctor). (I will discuss advice in a later section.)

In a similar pattern, cjd513 reframes Alma_Michelle's post as being about the doctor's interactional style—she in some sense offers "a change in what the discussion is about," to use Tannen's (2006:601) terms—and then offers advice: "You aren't liking the doctors bedside manner, find a new doctor" (post 20). In an extract from post 40 (which also includes advice, as will be discussed later), jcoffee3 expresses empathy in a way that provides a paraphrastic overview of the main issue: "I'm just sorry you had to hit one of the old fashioned believers in the steel clad height/weight chart that left no room for different body frame types!" This encapsulates Alma_Michelle's problem as being about the doctor's hyper-reliance on standard measures such as BMI, which serves as an echo of a concern explicitly expressed in the original post—that the doctor is relying too much on BMI measures instead of taking into account the range of variation for healthy individuals. However, it also offers a reframing in suggesting that this shortcoming of the doctor is due to her being "old fashioned," an understanding not expressed by Alma_Michelle.

Through paraphrasing and reframing—both extremely common on the thread, and sometimes shading into each other—participants recontextualize elements of the OP's initial narration, and at times parts of later posts by her and others. These strategies are fundamentally intertextual and metadiscursive in that they reformulate prior discourse and in so doing comment on it in some way. In the examples here, posters sometimes more or less reinforce the OP's perspective and other times offer new understandings. Both strategies advance the collaborative problem-solving activity.

Telling matching stories

A third intertextual strategy that constructs metadiscourse and contributes to the problem-solving activity is one that has been studied at great length in online support contexts: posters contribute a story to the thread that "matches" the story told by the OP. This is a way for posters to demonstrate empathy, reinforce the OP's initial understanding of what happened, normalize what happened, and offer examples of how they have managed similar situations. In so doing, they, like Alma_Michelle, construct metadiscourse in the form of online discourse about offline discourse. Their stories also comment on Alma_ Michelle's telling and are metadiscursive in that sense.

In the extract below, jcoffee3 describes her experience in a way that largely matches the OP's story by describing generalized doctors who "demand" that she lose weight because they don't understand her. Following this, she describes how she manages difficult doctors now.

(7)   jcoffee3 (post 40)
  1 It looks like you've stirred up a firestorme here, but I'm going to toss in my two cents.
  2
  3 I have a framework that is extremely dense and thick. And, when doctors look at me, they
  4 see someone who's much lighter than I actually am. So, when I step on the scale, they
  5 automatically demand that I lose weight. However, when I was at my stockeiest (can't
  6 say thinnest, because I've never been THIN) I actually weighed in around 250–260, but I
  7 looked like I was around 180.
  8
  9 Thankfully, I finally got a doctor that UNDERSTOOD the way I was put together, and
 10 told me never to go below that weight. So now when I have a doctor tell me to loose
 11 weight, I either ignore them, or tell them that I'm working on getting down to a healthy
 12 weight. If they don't like it, then when ever they start pressing the issue, I tune them out.

Jcoffee3 begins her post with metadiscourse about the thread (it's a "firestorme" [i.e., firestorm, line 1]; in other words, posters are passionate about the topic), and about her own post (it represents her giving her own perspective: "I'm going to toss in my two cents" [line 2]). In the post's second paragraph, she provides background information about her body, in a similar way to how Alma_Michelle provided information about hers. This serves to point back to Alma_Michelle's story. The problem she has is not an exact match with Alma_Michelle's, but it is similar: this poster indicates that she has "a framework" (i.e., "frame" as in "body frame" [line 3]) that is "extremely dense and thick," which leads doctors to underestimate how much she weighs, and then when she is weighed, they "demand" (line 5) that she lose weight. The word "demand" implies that these doctors' comments are not appropriate, creating intertextual links to Alma_Michelle's evaluation of her doctor's comment about her weight with "SERIOUSLY??" (extract 1a) and her comment about feeling "forced" to lose weight (extract 1c).

In the last paragraph of her post jcoffee3 provides a resolution to her own problem: after having one good doctor who "UNDERSTOOD" (which she emphasizes in all caps) her body's unique composition and therefore did not recommend that she lose weight, she responded differently to any doctor who started "pressing the issue," which by this word choice implies that jcoffee3 views this negatively and as inappropriate, again harking back to how Alma_Michelle questioned her doctor's behavior, such as through her use of "according to." The post by jcoffee3 ends by the poster indirectly offering advice to Alma_Michelle (which patterns with previous research linking storytelling and advice giving as activities) by providing what she did as an example: she subsequently has "ignored," chosen to "tune out," or given platitudes to such doctors (lines 11-12).

In the next example, Sparrow begins her post with a general observation about how doctors address the issue of body weight with patients and then turns to her own short narrative. While it is not about a doctor telling her to lose weight, it is thematically matched to Alma_Michelle's in that it provides an example of a doctor behaving in a way doctors are not supposed to (as Alma_Michelle's is implied to have done), suggesting that they are fallible.

(8)   Sparrow (post 41)

1   Funny how some doctors won't tell even their morbidly obese patients who have multiple

2   serious weight-related problems that they should lose weight; while other doctors will tell

3   every patient who walks through the door to lose weight.

4

5   I had one doctor actually start writing a prescription for high blood pressure medicine. I

6   asked her about it, and she told me it was for high blood pressure. To which I responded,

7   "but I don't have high blood pressure". She looked at my chart again, and put away the

8   prescription pad. Moral of the story . . . don't just "accept" everything your doctor says.

9   You said you"re a grad student, right? Put some of your learning skills in there . . . ask. If

10   she won't help you understand, find another doctor. She may have good reasons for what

11   she said . . . but sounds like you don't know.

This matching story is one where the teller, in the role of patient, observed a doctor making a mistake, and told the doctor. Like jcoffee3's story, this story is not a perfect match to Alma_Michelle's. For example, the doctor's mistake here was writing a prescription, not saying something wrong or insufficiently explaining something to the patient; furthermore, Sparrow spoke up in the interaction she depicts. Nevertheless, this story has parallels with Alma_Michelle's story (doctors are not perfect) and intertextually links to it, and it brings another offline encounter into the online thread. It also constructs a counter-narrative to the "doctor knows best" perspective on medical care (see Heritage 2021 for an analysis suggesting that, as compared with the 1960s, there has been a general decline in doctors' discursive expressions of epistemic authority and certainty as they diagnose patients in primary care encounters in the United Kingdom and the United States).

In this example too, we see providing a matching story shading into advice giving. Sparrow metacommunicates about this in using the phrase "moral of the story." This comments on the previous discourse (labeling it as a story) and also serves as an instance of generic intertextuality (following Bauman 2004; Briggs and Bauman 1992) in that this phrase is often used at the endings of certain types of stories and serves as a "generic framing device." Sparrow's advice is to be more active in talking to the doctor and making her explain herself, as she herself was—she is communicating to Alma_Michelle about communication in an effort to improve her communication. In addition, Sparrow animated herself in the story pushing back against the doctor's action of writing a prescription for blood pressure medication and explaining what she was doing: she indicates that she responded by saying, "but I don't have high blood pressure." This represents an example of constructed dialogue, the strategy considered in the next section, which often emerges as part of story-telling in this thread.

Constructed dialogue

Constructed dialogue is the fourth strategy I identified that, by way of intertextuality, creates metadiscourse aimed at advancing the problem-solving activity. In the initial formulation of the problem, Alma_Michelle claims to reproduce directly what the doctor said to her: "Quote: 'I'd like to see you drop a few pounds.'" Other posters, too, use constructed dialogue to provide different perspectives, as did jcoffee3 in the previous example, where she depicts herself as having acted agentively vis-à-vis the doctor (following Hamilton 1998). While some examples are constructed as if they are a direct report of previous speech, many of these examples highlight the inherently "constructed" nature of constructed dialogue (it is this nature that underlies Tannen's 2007b introduction of the term). In constructing dialogue, a speaker is not a "neutral conduit" (p. 110); instead, the speaker communicates something about the discourse purportedly being "reported." Thus, constructed dialogue is intertextual—it links current interactions to those prior. It is also metadiscursive—it says something about the prior discourse.

For example, deceasedsocks (in post 24) shares the following, voicing "normal" doctors, such as Alma_Michelle's:

(9)   deceasedsocks (post 24)
    1   My new doctor doesn't tell me I need to keep losing. She's so proud of how far I've
    2   come she doesn't rant like normal docs who are like "lose more/exercise more/eat less/
    3   sweat yer butt off!"

Deceasedsocks presents "normal docs" (line 2) speaking in unison—an instance of what Tannen (2007b) calls "choral dialogue"; they produce prototypical orders related to losing weight. This offers a different perspective on Alma_Michelle's situation: there are doctors out there (like desceasedsocks' own) who are "proud" (line 1) of their patients' weight loss progress and who therefore don't "rant" (like Alma_Michelle's is implied to have done through the use of this metadiscursive term).

The choral dialogue enforces Alma_Michelle's initial understanding of her doctor's behavior (it was inappropriate), while also linking to her original post in providing a kind of matching story (though in the form of a habitual narrative, and highlighting how "the same" experience—interacting with a doctor—played out differently). It simultaneously creates intertextual links to other posts in the thread that suggest the doctor's style of communication is part of the problem (e.g., posts about "bedside manner"). Posts such as these accomplish a kind of reframing as well—what Tannen (2006) refers to as a change in what an interaction is about—by shifting from Alma_Michelle's initial focus on the content and meaning of her doctor's talk to the message's form. In a similar spirit, Sparrow used constructed dialogue in the doctor–patient interaction story she told (as was shown in extract 8): "I had one doctor actually start writing a prescription for high blood pressure medicine. I asked her about it, and she told me it was for high blood pressure. To which I responded, 'but I don't have high blood pressure.'" She presents herself as having initiated talk with her doctor by using the term "asked," the doctor responding with constructed dialogue presented in the form of indirect reported speech ("she told me it was for high blood pressure"), and herself as having responded in turn using constructed dialogue in the form of direct reported speech ("I responded, 'but I don't have high blood pressure.'"). In these different ways, offline dialogue is brought into the online context.

Another poster, sayif067 (in post 19), constructs a different type of constructed dialogue by directly quoting select words that Alma_Michelle used in her initial post. She suggests a different interpretation of what the doctor said (i.e., she reframes) and argues that the words Alma_Michelle used to describe her feelings do not correspond with what happened. In other words, she creates metadiscourse as she explicitly reproduces and discusses the "language" of the original post. She links this language to Alma_Michelle's psychological state.

(10) sayif067 (post 19)

1 Because you put this out there to the masses, I am going to give you an honest
2 assessment. I think you are self-conscious about your weight and reacting extremely
3 defensively to your doc's recommendation. You are using language that is WAY more
4 melodramatic and forceful than the doctor used. You say you are being "punished" for
5 being at the upper part of a healthy BMI range and that you're being told you "NEED" to
6 lose weight when by your own admission, your doctor simply said she'd LIKE to see you
7 drop a few pounds. That language is far less harsh and punitive than you are interpreting
8 it.

This section is abundantly metadiscursive, and intertextual resources are prominent. Sayif067 begins by pointing out that her post is inspired by Alma_ Michelle's previous discourse—Alma_Michelle put her problem "out there to the masses" (line 1). She also metacommunicates about the remainder of her post: it will provide an "honest assessment" (lines 1–2). This helps mitigate the face threat that follows.

In the remainder, sayif067 reflects upon Alma_Michelle's description of what the doctor reportedly said, assessing her reaction as inappropriate: Alma_ Michelle should not feel "punished" (line 4). The word "punished" appears in quotation marks, and thus as a form of constructed dialogue, though Alma_ Michelle did not use this term; instead, she had indicated that she was feeling "forced" to lose more weight than she wanted to (extract 1c). Sayif067 reasons that Alma_Michelle should not feel "punished" because the doctor did not in fact indicate a "NEED" (line 5) to lose more weight (Alma_Michelle did use the term "need"), but just made a gentle suggestion.

Sayif067 also characterizes Alma_Michelle's original post as containing an "admission" that the doctor would "LIKE" to see her lose a little bit of weight (line 6). In that the term "admit" implies unwillingness (often to accept an unpleasant truth), this term negatively comments on the relationship between what the doctor was depicted as saying in original post versus Alma_Michelle's reaction. The capitalization of "need" and "like" draw connections between them and in creating connections also highlight contrast between the current post and Alma_Michelle's. In addition, sayif067 explicitly comments on

Alma_Michelle's word use, characterizing the "language" she has used in her post as "WAY more melodramatic and forceful" than the doctor's (lines 3–4). In other words, she metacommunicates about lexical choice. Thus, she indirectly advises a reinterpretation by the OP. (The post also includes a second paragraph that affirms a reframing offered by a previous poster: that the doctor made her recommendation based on Alma_Michelle's individualized exam; sayif067 also encourages Alma_Michelle to "get a thicker skin," which I address later.)

As shown in this section, constructed dialogue is used to create hypothetical utterances (i.e., of "normal doctors"), to recreate past utterances from outside of the thread, and to tie back to words used earlier in the thread. This intertexually links posts together, contributing to the problem-solving activity. It constructs metadiscourse that characterizes doctor–patient talk more broadly, while also emphasizing or suggesting reinterpretation of language, thereby accomplishing a reframing (or in other instances not shown here, a paraphrase) of what the interaction between the OP and her doctor actually meant.

Using the board's quotation function

A platform-enabled format of constructed dialogue also occurs on this thread: use of the quotation function available on this and other FIF boards, which exactly reproduces a previous post (marking it as such) and facilitates commentary on it, a strategy that has been highlighted in previous chapters and is repeatedly used on FIF (and in many other online contexts). As Severinson Eklundh (2010:n.p.) notes in her analysis of email communication and newsgroup discussions, "quoted text has a discourse-deictic relationship to the message from which it is taken" (see also Levinson 1983). Quoting is a "context-linking mechanism" that many computer-mediated platforms support; it constructs coherence without using paraphrase (Severinson Eklundh 2010:n.p.). In Severinson Eklundh's email data, lines of material automatically quoted from a previous message are marked by the ">" symbol, which she refers to as a "pointer"; this symbol can be layered to show quotations within quotations. As mentioned in previous chapters, FIF formats quotation by using a box that is shaded and smaller in size than the larger encompassing post. As in previous chapters, I use gray shading to indicate quoted material. (At the time this thread was originally posted, uses of the boards' quotation function were also marked explicitly with "QUOTE," but this format no longer appears on the site). The quotation function serves as a way of taking advantage of the affordances of the medium; it is an intertextuality-producing strategy that is essential to the metadiscourse that is fundamental to working through the OP's problem collaboratively, as well as other issues that emerge on the thread.

The following post by getgoinggogo represents a situation in which getgoinggogo himself had posted a message (of which I am showing an extract, beginning with "my point is"), and then Alma_Michelle quoted it and responded (beginning with "Again, when the doc came into the room"), and getgoinggogo quoted both and responded in turn (starting with "Sorry, I'm having a slow night"). Due to the multiply embedded quotation here, for clarity I indicate the person being quoted each time.

(11)   getgoinggogo (quoting and responding to the OP's quoting of him) (post 26)

> ((*quoted extract of post by getgoinggogo*)) my point is that your doc has actually evaluated you, while the BMI chart compares individuals to a population and doesn't give individualzed info, like your doc can.

> ((*post by Alma_Michelle that responds to getgoinggogo above and is quoted and responded to below by getgoinggogo*)) Again, when the doc came into the room, this was literally this very FIRST thing we talked about (and taking blood pressure and pulse, which is great). After she mentioned my height/weight that my nurse recorded, she then took my family history sheet. I wouldn't consider myself a health nut, but I am certainly health conscious and I would say that the majority oft he time I lead a healthy lifestyle. I will admit that during high stressed times during school (I'm a grad student) I can easily put on a few pounds if I'm not careful—but since I'm aware of this, I try to do what I can to avoid it. Sometimes I'm not as successful, but I always manage to get back on track. I've never had any health issues.

((*getgoinggogo quoting and responding to the above*))

1   Sorry, I'm having a slow night. So, in order it was:
2
3   Hello->BMI measurement & recommendation/BP/pulse->family history? And no (even
4   casual) discussion in between about metabolic disorders (like e.g. PCOS)?
5
6   In that case, I can see why you might be a bit miffed, esp if she was brusque. You should
7   actually give her feedback on this. She can't improve if no one tells her. Most people just
8   switch docs. (Or switch, and give feedback later, either way she should know.)

Getgoinggogo uses the quotation function to connect his post to one previous by Alma_Michelle in which she used the quotation function herself to respond to his earlier message. In doing this, the participants are able to achieve a shared sense of what happened to Alma_Michelle (the order of events, in particular when exactly the doctor told Alma_Michelle she should lose some weight, and whether the doctor gathered information such as about BP [blood pressure] and PCOS [polycystic ovary syndrome]), while simultaneously flagging their continued communication (i.e., intertextually linking their posts together, communicating that they are connected). Getgoinggogo also shares his current understanding of what happened—that the doctor suggested weight loss before examining Alma_Michelle. Interestingly, he states this in a form that depends on the use of symbols ("->" to represent an arrow to indicate sequence [line 3]); he boils down part of Alma_Michelle's experience into a series of events. He now sees why she might be upset ("a bit miffed" [line 6]). In other words, their metadiscourse has clarified things for him regarding what happened in the appointment Alma_Michelle had. He then moves to giving advice: she should give feedback to the doctor about her communication. Using the metadiscursive term "feedback" (line 7) is notable in that while it highlights the idea that difficulties in interaction can be solved through further communication (an idea I explore in more detail in Chapter 6), "feedback" is commonly given by those who are in positions of relative power. For example, when Yelp reviewers post negative reviews and thereby threaten a hotel's reputation (a powerful move), hotels respond by indicating that they value customer "feedback" (Zhang and Vásquez 2014). Using this term indirectly conceptualizes a doctor–patient encounter as a type of service encounter where "the customer is always right," though this may not have been getgoinggogo's intention.

There are many examples of the quotation function being used on the thread to link posts into an evolving process of meaning-making fundamental to the activity of collaborative problem-solving. Two more appear in the next section, both of which also involve the strategy of pointing.

Pointing

On several occasions the boards' quotation function is used in conjunction with pointing. The notion of "pointing" has already emerged in this chapter with Severinson Eklundh's (2010:n.p.) noting of the "discourse-deictic relationship" of a quotation to its source message; it also links back to previous chapters where the caret or a deictic pronoun is used to point, such as when "fixing" another's post, and that is the form of pointing I analyze here. For instance, alsoalso442, in the thread's 15th post, quotes Alma_Michelle's post and uses pointing. In the quoted portion (which I've redacted), Alma_Michelle explains that she did not have time to express her perspective on her weight before the doctor made the recommendation for her to lose weight.

(12) <u>alsoalso442 (post 15)</u>

> ((*beginning of quoted post by Alma_Michelle elided*)) I never shared with this doctor
> that I look too thin if I drop into the low 130s. She simply made this assumption that
> since my BMI according to my height/weight was in the higher healthy range, it wasn't
> healthy enough. I have no relationship with this doctor, as she is new, and this was
> essentially our first interaction.

1 Sounds like you didn't discuss any of this with your doctor. I would suggest you tell this
2 ^^^ to your doctor and see what she has to say. You might be pleasantly surprised.

Alsoalso442 uses the "^" symbol three times (line 2); it stands for "above,"
literally pointing to the quoted text so that she can communicate something
about it. In addition, she twice uses "this" (line 1) to refer to what Alma_
Michelle had posted, which is also intertextual and metadiscursive—"this"
merits a conversation with the doctor. This vivid intertextual linking connects
their posts while advancing the collaborative problem-solving activity cen-
tering around the OP's interaction with her doctor, leading to advice giving by
alsoalso442 and mention of a possible positive outcome.

A similar example occurs near the thread's end in an extract where getgoinggogo, in the 44th post, quotes Alma_Michelle (in gray), who has by then
displayed a modified understanding of her experience, and adds his own comment. In the quoted material, Alma_Michelle states that her reaction to the
doctor's comment might have been based on her own lack of experience with
this kind of interaction.

(13) <u>getgoinggogo (post 44)</u>

> Honestly, I think I've reacted so strongly because I've never had a doctor comment
> on my weight, even when I've asked their opinion with doctors I've had in the
> past. However, I don't think I'll go back, just because I like to feel comfortable with
> my provider. ((*explains that she recently relocated—elided*)) I did fill out a feedback
> from [form] at the office, I basically just said it wasn't a good fit- I'm not a fan
> of minimizing a professional's expertise/experience even if we didn't click on a
> relational level, I make a point to separate liking/disliking from a good doc/bad doc :)

1 This is fair enough. Hope you find someone competent & likeable. :)

Getgoinggogo uses the boards' quotation function to link his response directly
to a previous post by Alma_Michelle; he strengthens the link by referring to
the quoted text by beginning his post with the word "this." Repetition in general performs a similar (though not identical) pointing and tying function;
for instance, in the extract above, Alma_Michelle's mention of "feedback"
echoes the earlier post by getgoinggogo that explicitly suggested she give the

doctor "feedback" (the term surfaces in multiple posts across the thread). Getgoinggogo also expresses approval of Alma_Michelle's having indicated that she provided feedback and her plans for the future. Further, the smiley face emoticon used by Alma_Michelle (appearing within the quoted text) is repeated just below in getgoinggogo's response—he also ends his message with a smiley face emoticon. As scholars (e.g., Johnstone et al. 1994; Tannen 2007b) have pointed out, repeating in general (including in the form of quotation) directs people back to previous discourse. Here getgoinggogo shows that his perspective on the problem Alma_Michelle is working through has also been altered, and he conveys understanding and well wishes to her.

Advice giving

The final strategy I identified is advice giving, a mainstay in online support forums (and quite thoroughly examined in online contexts; see, e.g., Locher 2006, 2013; Morrow 2012). As mentioned, telling of some kind of problem in an online discussion board, as Alma_Michelle does in her initial post, is one way to elicit advice, and it is not surprising that advice appears prominently in this thread. Advice in turn can be provided indirectly through storytelling, as was seen in extract 7, where jcoffee3 offered Alma_Michelle a matching story describing her challenging interactions she has had with physicians owing to her "dense and thick" body frame. After telling her story, jcoffee3 reminds Alma_Michelle that she is in charge of her own body and life and adds, "I can almost guarantee if you tone up a little, even if you don't loose weight, you'll hit that BMI your doctor is looking for," which indirectly provides advice (and validates what the doctor advised). Extract 8, where Sparrow showed herself questioning her doctor—"but I don't have high blood pressure"—provides an example of communicating agentively with one's doctor, which presumably should be emulated. This thus also functions as indirect advice giving. As mentioned previously, Vehvilläinen (2009) conceives of advice itself as a problem-solving activity, and Sparrow's post contributes to the problem-solving activity with a story that has advice built into it.

Advice, like these other intertextual strategies I have examined, has links to prior discourse on the thread as well as to offline interaction. For example, as we saw in extract 3, camclaine advises, "if you disagree, then don't take pressure from" the doctor. The first part of this gives a paraphrase of one possible interpretation of Alma_Michelle's problem as she described it in her original post (she does not agree with her doctor), and the second provides the advice for what Alma_Michelle should now do offline. Sayif067 (in post 19, where she offers an "honest assessment," the first part of which was shown in excerpt 10) references the doctor's expertise before pivoting to advice, and how she gives advice involves mention of specific details from Alma_Michelle's original post:

(14)   sayif067 (post 19)
   1   She is the one with a decade of medical education under her belt. At the end of the day, if
   2   you're happy in the 140-145 range, then fine. It's your body. Own it. You're an adult.
   3   Get some thicker skin. Yes, your doctor is in a position of authority but you always have
   4   the right to say "thanks, but no thanks."

Noting the range of weight within which Alma_Michelle reported feeling comfortable, this poster offers bits of advice in a "tough love" style, including mention that Alma_Michelle is an "adult," and directly advising that she should "own" her body and also become less sensitive ("Get some thicker skin" [line 3]). The advice also includes hypothetical constructed dialogue (line 4): Alma_Michelle could literally say "thanks, but no thanks" during future doctor visits, or reply in a way that captures that expression's essence.

In fact, a number of instances of advice are explicitly metadiscursive. These advise that Alma_Michelle should communicate with the doctor, as well as how. For example, we have seen that alsoalso442 advised in post 15 of the thread, "I would suggest you tell this ^^^ to your doctor" (extract 12), and in post 26 getgoinggogo advised, "You should actually give her [the doctor] feedback on this" or switch doctors and "give feedback later" (extract 11). Cbitts32 notes that "The key is communication. Full disclosure. Not always comfortable but sometime it works. Make another appointment and talk to her again. Voice you concerns!" (post 12). Similarly, sayif067, in post 42, summarizes one of the thread's themes: "I think another big takeaway that others have mentioned is talking to your doctor. Next time you are in, bring it up—hey last time I was here this rubbed me the wrong way, can you explain more why you recommended that particular weight, etc." She not only identifies communication as important, and in so doing recognizes that others in the thread have brought this up, but also offers hypothetical constructed dialogue Alma_Michelle could use in the future. In addition, sayif067 indicates that she read a study that patients are hesitant to ask doctors questions and thus end up feeling frustrated (an example of locating the source of her information, though indirectly) and ends her post by making the proclamation, "Communication is key!"

These types of statements hark back to Craig's (2005) point that laypersons (as well as communication scholars) usually believe that communication is important, that bad communication is the cause of many problems for people, and that fixing communication issues is a means of improving the world. It echoes the idea that there is a contemporary cultural obsession with communication, which has been advanced by numerous scholars, as discussed in

Chapter 1. Providing advice about communication—be it recognizing its importance in general, or indicating how to communicate in particular ways—offers solutions that help bring closure to the problem-solving episode and, in theory, help Alma_Michelle improve her life in a small but meaningful way.

Summary of intertextual strategies

In this analysis of one problem-solving activity that occurs across disparate postings by various participants, I uncovered seven primary intertextual linking strategies that accomplished metadiscourse about an offline instance of doctor–patient communication, as well as about the unfolding online interaction, thereby helping solve the original poster's problem as outlined in her original post and expanded on in her subsequent posts: information about the offline doctor–patient encounter, and about the OP, is brought out through multiple posters' question asking; paraphrasing and reframing offer similar or (somewhat) different perspectives on what occurred; telling matching stories provides support and offers insight into different people's offline experiences; constructed dialogue displays other instances and types of doctor–patient communication and reconsiders earlier language on the thread itself; the boards' quotation function links posts to facilitate a more conversational exchange, which helps offer alternate and helps establish shared perspectives on the past communication context in the current one; pointing via a symbol or pronoun increases connection among posts, demonstrating understanding and facilitating advice giving; and advice giving again moves the online thread offline by suggesting actions the original poster might take (e.g., in terms of exercise), issues she should think about (e.g., her sensitivity), and ways she might think about and participate in future doctor–patient interactions. Through these strategies, which often co-occur and are intertwined, I suggest, participants construct metacommunication online that facilitates a collaborative exchange that works to help solve the OP's problem.

While it is not clear if Alma_Michelle's problem is completely solved to her satisfaction, in post 27, she reports that she has adjusted her perspective: responding in particular to sayif067's "tough love" post (excerpts of which were shown in extract 14), but also to suggestions from the thread more generally, Alma_Michelle agrees that she is "being really over sensitive" to the doctor's words, and that she has come to "re-evaluate how [she] reacted." She also notes that perhaps the doctor "truly only meant [what she said] as a recommendation and not as a condescending statement," though perhaps "she could have presented it in a better way." This voices multiple viewpoints put forth on the thread, including a revised version of her original formulation that the doctor's comment was inappropriate. This captures the interactive and collaborative nature of the problem-solving activity. In addition, Alma_

Michelle decides how to proceed: she will not see this doctor again but will also try not to be so sensitive in the future; she will look into getting her body fat percentage checked; and she will continue to use FIF.

In summary then, the linking strategies present in this thread take advantage of the intertextual possibilities of language and medium, facilitating the gradual gathering and sharing of information and personal experiences, of multiple perspectives on what happened in an instance of offline communication, and of ideas about how to proceed. Individuals also constructed identities for themselves and others—an underlying question is whether Alma_ Michelle and/or the doctor behaved in unreasonable ways—and in so doing revealed some expectations regarding institutional roles and responsibilities, which I briefly address next.

COMMUNICATION RESPONSIBILITIES AS EXPRESSED IN THE PROBLEM-SOLVING ACTIVITY

The case study analysis presented in this chapter involves a particular type of metadiscursive activity: participants communicating about, and trying to address, an instance of verbal communication that reportedly occurred between the original poster and her doctor. Thus far, I have shown how the thread can usefully be conceptualized as a metadiscursive problem-solving episode about the poster's problem, one that is undergirded by the idea that communicating about communication is valuable. The analysis of the contents of the discussion, however, additionally reveals that the participants work through a larger and common "problem" regarding doctor–patient communication, what Sarangi (2016) calls a role responsibility framework for medical care—in other words, the expected or ideal distribution of responsibilities between doctors and patients. For example, posters remark that the doctor's "bedside manner" was the problem, or that the doctor was not "very professional" because she spoke "bluntly," or that the doctor might have been "brusque." These comments imply that a doctor should be able to communicate about weight in a professional and affectively appropriate way (a finding that echoes existing research on healthcare provider communication about body weight, e.g., Kahan [2018]; Speer and McPhillips [2018]).

Examining the content and themes of posters' contributions, I identified the following responsibilities being attributed to doctors, either directly or indirectly. Doctors should: (1) assess/comment on a patient's weight but do so in professional and affectively appropriate ways (e.g., not be "brusque"); (2) gather all the relevant information before making such assessments (not only BMI measures); and (3) view and treat the patient as an individual (e.g., consider issues such as the patient's personal preferences regarding their body weight—which involves listening to the patient). Patients, especially those who are concerned about their weight, in turn, should: (1) interpret providers' assessments/comments without being overly sensitive (e.g., "get a thicker skin"); (2) give honest feedback to doctors about how their communication is perceived; and (3) understand that measures such as BMI are only indicators that need to be interpreted within the context of their own bodies, health history, and so on. These general observations fit well with previous research outlining expectations of doctor–patient communication responsibility distribution (e.g., Gordon et al. 2009) in that the ideology being advanced in the thread is that responsibilities are shared. Notably, doctor–patient communication is viewed as a two-way street. Particularly interesting is that weight is acknowledged as a sensitive topic for both doctors and patients, and that both parties have responsibilities in relation to that—doctors need to make affectively appropriate and professional comments, and patients need to be not too sensitive. This reifies a cultural conceptualization of communication breakdowns and difficulties as something that can be improved through communicating about communication, as argued by Craig (2005) among others, and as made evident by a plethora of research that aims to understand better, and ultimately improve, human communication and relationships (e.g., Gumperz [1982] regarding cross-cultural communication; Tannen [1990] regarding everyday interactions between women and men; and Jager and Stommel [2017] regarding online chat-based counseling). This theme will be further explored in the next chapter.

CONCLUSION

In conclusion, I have demonstrated how the activity of working through an original poster's problematic offline encounter centers around discourse about offline communication, notably the OP's interaction with her doctor, but also others' experiences that are brought into the thread. It also involves making connections to posts that constitute the online thread wherein the problem-solving activity plays out. I showed how seven strategies that exploit linguistic and online discussion interface affordances are used to create connections between posts and between online and offline interaction, allowing posters to refer back to prior communication, and, importantly, to communicate about it.

This chapter thus highlights connections between online support discourse and other realms of online posters' life experiences, such as doctor–patient encounters: meaning-making regarding everyday face-to-face encounters occurs in the moment, but there may also be collaborative sense-making that occurs afterward online or elsewhere in the form of metadiscursive activities that are displaced in space and time. This fact highlights how online and offline interactive experiences are interconnected (and in many ways inseparable);

that is, intertextual strategies are used online to link posts to posts, but also to link to offline experiences (such as when the OP quoted her doctor's words), so that these can be commented on, evaluated, and discussed.

In investigating one thread as an episode of collaborative problem-solving, this analysis also uncovered patients' perspectives on role responsibility distribution regarding talk about excess body weight, in other words, ideologies about how doctors and patients should communicate. The next chapter continues the exploration of online intertextuality and metadiscourse regarding offline communication, as well as communication expectations and ideologies, this time emerging from a thread started by one poster's report about offline communication with her partner about her use of the FIF app and website.

CHAPTER 6

"He's got a right to be upset if your phone is in your face when he's trying to spend time with you"

Constructing cultural discourses and Master Narratives

about digital communication technologies and

interpersonal communication and relationships

In the previous chapter, I examined how participants in one online discussion thread employed intertextual strategies to create metadiscourse as they worked together to help the OP, Alma_Michelle, solve a communicative dilemma—how she should interpret and react to a physician's comment about her body weight. In this chapter, I also consider how intertextual linking is used to accomplish metadiscourse in a single thread where offline interaction is brought onto the online discussion boards. However, in this thread, in discussing the reported problem, posters repeatedly put into relief multiple competing and opposing ideologies and expectations—or cultural discourses (Carbaugh 2007) or Master Narratives (Tannen 2008)—about appropriate use of FriendInFitness (FIF) as a digital communication technology platform housed on an electronic device, as well as about the nature of interpersonal communication and partner relationships. They do not engage in the metadiscursive activity of "problem-solving" so much as the metadiscursive activity of "constructing competing ideologies."

The data considered in this chapter consist of one lengthy thread started by an OP I call lexb. In her initial post, lexb reports that her partner "hates"

Intertextuality 2.0. Cynthia Gordon, Oxford University Press. © Oxford University Press 2023.
DOI: 10.1093/oso/9780197642689.003.0006

her use of the FIF app and that he says it has caused her to become obsessive. In contrast to the thread started by Alma_Michelle about her communication with her doctor, and the "clean eating" thread started by CuddleSmash that was examined in Chapter 2, lexb does not participate again after her initial post. In part owing to this, the thread does not manifest the same level of collaborative negotiation of meaning that we saw in CuddleSmash's "clean eating" thread, nor the joint problem-solving that emerged in Alma_ Michelle's. While posters do offer advice and different perspectives on the original poster's problem, the thread has a somewhat more "agonistic" shape, as the term is used by Tannen (1998:3): the posts work to create a "warlike atmosphere," in the sense that many posters manifest a recognizably "adversarial frame of mind" (which is not uncommon in many online contexts but seems less typical of threads on FIF; as mentioned in Chapter 2, the relatively few "personal attacks" that occurred in the "clean eating" thread stood out). Also, in lexb's thread, there does not seem to be any satisfying conclusion reached.

To explore how participants in this thread discursively engage in the meta-discursive activity of constructing and contesting ideologies about the interrelationships between digital communication technologies, interpersonal communication, and partner relationships, I primarily draw on theorizing from anthropologically oriented scholarship that has explored ideologies related to technology and media (e.g., Gershon 2010; Katriel 1999), cultural categories of communication (e.g., Carbaugh 2007; Katriel and Philipsen 1981; Philipsen 1992), and ideologies about personhood and relationships (e.g., Carbaugh 2007; Fitch 1998). I also draw on interactional sociolinguistic notions (e.g., Tannen 2013) and critical perspectives (e.g., Thurlow, Aiello, and Portmann 2020).

Katriel (1999:96) suggested over two decades ago that as new communication technologies are introduced into everyday life and relationships, it is important for ethnographers of communication (and, I would add, for scholars who analyze social interaction more generally) to conduct studies that explore how such technologies "subtly affect basic interactional expectations and practices." After all, "the introduction of cellular telephones into the fabric of everyday life" has "affected our sense of context, our sense of interactional accessibility, and, indeed, our very conception of what counts as social interaction" (p. 96). Building on such observations, I demonstrate how uses and understandings of new communication media—in this case the individual calorie-tracking feature of the FIF app as well as the online discussion boards I have been exploring in this book, both of which are housed on digital communication devices—intersect with the culturally assumed nature of personhood and relationships, as well as the needs of members of a couple to balance relational dimensions that have been illuminated in previous work, notably in linguistics (e.g., Tannen 1994) and communication studies (e.g., Baxter 2011;

Fitch 1998): connection and independence, along with the related issues of disclosure and privacy.

My analysis shows not only how posts in the thread are linked to one another through intertextual strategies—notably use of the quotation function, "constructed dialogue" (Tannen 2007b), advice (that includes the pronoun "you"), and lexical repetition—but also how the posts are thematically linked to one another and how the discourse of the thread is intertextually linked to broader cultural assumptions and ideologies via indexing (as discussed by Ochs 1992, 1993). Examination of this chapter's data ultimately reveals different expectations about how partners should try to create a balance between engaging with the FIF discussion boards and related app and interacting with their partners (which also indexes more general expectations about communication in intimate relationships). In other words, I show how participants define and negotiate their media ideologies (Gershon 2010) in relation to ideologies about "communication" as a cultural category (Katriel and Philipsen 1981) as well as "interpersonal ideologies" (Fitch 1998). Specifically, I demonstrate how the discourse of the thread is linked to and (re)creates three key themes, or what Tannen (2008) calls Big-N Narratives: that digital communication media are potentially disruptive to private, face-to-face conversations; that partners' different understandings of a single digital media technology can lead to interactional—and relationship—trouble; and that use of digital media such as the app and its connected discussion boards (re)animates inherent relationship tensions, notably struggles between independence and connection, privacy and disclosure. These in turn index larger cultural discourses (Carbaugh 2007) or Master Narratives (Tannen 2008): quality time and communication are important to partner relationships, partners should communicate (somewhat) openly about their technology use, and partners should strike the right balance between autonomy and connection in the context of an understanding that successful weight loss requires both self-focus and support from others.

IDEOLOGIES ABOUT TECHNOLOGY AND COMMUNICATION MEDIA

My analysis builds on and extends previous research investigating ideologies connected to the technologies that facilitate digital discourse and to individual platforms, along with studies that uncover ideologies about (appropriate) uses of digital communication technologies and platforms in the context of interpersonal communication, and how these are discursively realized.

Advocating for the importance of studying ideology in digital discourse, Thurlow and Mroczek (2011:xxvii) remark that "digital technologies are themselves inherently ideological" in terms of issues of access and control, as well as how technologies are used to reify or resist dominant voices. They also observe that scholars need to acknowledge "a certain *materiality* to communication technologies" as well as how they are "embedded in complex ways into the banal practices of everyday life" (Thurlow and Mroczek 2011:xxiv; italics in the original). Mobile phones have received a good deal of research attention in this regard. In a case study ethnography of one Anglo-European teenage girl's uses and perceptions of her iPhone, Carrington (2015) notes that the phone comes with built-in ideologies: it "demonstrates an intentionality and a script that prescribes use, and in so doing has the effect of amplifying or diminishing some aspects of [the teenager's] perception and action" (p. 167). For instance, that the phone needs continual updates presses the girl to understand technology as a cycle of non-stop change. Deumert (2014:16) describes how for one young South African woman who grew up in a rural area, her phone not only allows her to be mobile while also staying in touch with her family but also "symbolizes her status as a young professional and her nostalgia for home"; her screen pictures a traditional amaXhosa home, and her ringtone is a cockerel's call that reminds her of rural life at home.

Looking across cultural groups as well as gender identity categories, Gordon, Al Zidjaly, and Tovares (2017:9) observe that mobile phones are "situated in users' social, political, linguistic, and cultural contexts," and in turn how people use their phones helps create these contexts; similar perspectives are advanced by Caronia and Caron (2004) and Androutsopoulos and Juffermans (2014). Gordon et al.'s comparative, survey-based study (involving 393 participants) found that among college students in Ukraine, Oman, and the United States, phones were perceived differently. For instance, the Omani women overwhelmingly conceived of and reported utilizing their mobile phones as tools for identity expression; 90% agreed with a survey item indicating that they decorate the outside of their phones for this purpose, and 100% agreed with an item stating that they choose distinctive ring tones or a special screen saver or wallpaper to express themselves (this speaks to the "materiality" of the technologies, as discussed by Thurlow and Mroczek [2011]). The Ukrainian men, at the other end of the spectrum, overwhelmingly disagreed with these items on the survey. What is important for my purposes here is that "the same" technological artifact—a mobile phone—may carry with it different meanings and expectations of use for different users. This diversity is rarely represented in media depictions of mobile technology, however. For instance, Thurlow, Aiello, and Portmann (2020) find that stock photography images in commercial image banks (that are available for and are used by news media) represent "teens and technology" in ways that highlight teens' dependence on technology over their connections to other people; this "reinscribes the stereotype of kids unduly fixed on their technology and cut off from 'real' social interaction (c.f. Thurlow, 2007)" (Thurlow, Aiello, and Portmann 2020:541). But stereotypes and ideologies circulated by the media may not match the reality of people's everyday experiences. For example, Tovares, Gordon, and Al Zidjaly (2021) found that the majority of the Ukrainian, Omani, and American college students they surveyed reported using their mobile phones to connect with their family members (72% for Omanis, 78% for Ukrainians, and 97% for Americans) and friends (79% for Omanis, 78% for Ukrainians, and 97% for Americans). One of the dominant terms American women in the study used to describe their phones (just behind "useful," "convenient," and "helpful") was "connection."

Not only communication technologies but also individual platforms have ideologies that come to be attached to them. Boczkowski, Matassi, and Mitchelstein's (2018) interview and survey study shows that among some Argentinians, different social media platforms tend to be perceived and used differently; for instance, Facebook is for displaying a self that is socially acceptable, whereas Instagram is for a glossier presentation of self. Matassi, Boczkowski, and Mitchelstein (2019) find that the same platform holds diverse meanings for members of different age groups: again examining their data collected in Argentina, the authors find that for younger adults (ages 18–34), the messaging application WhatsApp represents a continuous flow of content that one must monitor to be socially included; for middle-aged adults (35–59), it is primarily a means of connecting to one's responsibilities (usually family and work); and for older adults (ages 60 and older), it is understood as less necessary to their everyday lives (though emblematic of, and a way of connecting with, younger people).

In *The Breakup 2.0*, Gershon (2010) examines how American college students disengage and disconnect from relationships via social media and texting (and some other options, such as face-to-face interaction, email, or a voice phone call), and how they talk about such experiences in interviews. In exploring her data, she uncovers these users' "media ideologies," or the "set of beliefs about communicative technologies with which users and designers explain perceived media structure and meaning" (p. 3). For instance, Gershon finds that college students often perceive email as a relatively formal medium of communication, a finding echoed by Tannen (2013, 2021), who also focuses on the perspectives and practices of American college students. Both scholars also observe that older people (such as the professors of these students) tend not to perceive email as a formal medium; as Gershon describes it, in general college students and older adults maintain different "idioms of practice" regarding email as a communication technology medium, meaning that they tend to differ in terms of their understanding of how it should be used, and what its use indicates. In line with this, many participants in Gershon's study reported that while texting was too informal for a breakup, email was also inappropriate in that it was too formal. In courtship, too, social media carried different meanings, as did switching between them: a switch from Facebook to texting, for example, signaled a new stage in the relationship.

Ideologies of digital communication technologies and their uses bridge online and offline encounters. This fits in with Bolander and Locher's (2020:n.p.) observation that there is a "blurring of borders between 'online' and 'offline'" and that this blurring is increasingly being identified as important by, and investigated in, discourse analytic and sociolinguistic research. Scholars in numerous disciplines have observed that mobile phones and computers alter aspects of face-to-face interaction, and that people also develop understandings of how technological devices, such as mobile phones, should be used in the physical presence of others. Individuals who procure a mobile phone (or tablet or laptop) enter into a "more or less continuous process of trying to place the object into the context of their everyday lives" as they consider "[w]here it is appropriate to use it, how it should be displayed, and when it should and should not be used" (Ling 2008:63). The presence of mobile phones means that many people are "always on" (Baron 2008) or in "perpetual contact" (Katz and Aakhus 2002; see also Ling 2008) with others through their phones. As Katriel (1999:97) notes, however, this might not always be welcomed, such as when a cell phone user, "[r]ather than engaging with or responding to his or her immediate environment," engages with a cell phone. She observes that this may lead people in the environment of a cell phone user who is engrossed in a call or text exchange to feel treated "as nonpersons" (p. 98).

Indeed, in the context of romantic relationships, research finds that a partner's mobile phone use when a couple is spending time together may lead to unhappiness and dissatisfaction. For example, Miller-Ott and Kelly (2016), in their analysis of the discourse of focus groups conducted with college students, uncover that while students evoked cultural expectations that people should always be available to contact through their mobile phones, they also voiced an expectation that partners in romantic relationships should be fully attentive to each other (and cell phone use on dates was thus described as "rude" and "disrespectful"). Lenhart and Duggan (2014), in a Pew report, found that 25% of married/partnered people surveyed and 42% of unmarried people surveyed reported feeling like their partner was distracted by their phone during their time together. A more recent Pew report by Vogels and Anderson (2020) found that for people in married or partner relationships, just over half reported that their partner is "often or sometimes distracted by their cellphone while they are trying to have a conversation with them, and four-in-ten say that they are at least sometimes bothered by the amount of time their partner spends on their mobile device" (n.p.). Among survey respondents whose partner was a social media user, 23% "felt jealous or unsure of their relationship because of the way their current partner interacts with others on these sites," even while other respondents (especially those between 18 and 29 years old) viewed social media platforms as valuable sites for showing affection and love.

To explore how people create meanings and construct identities in relation to communication technology use in situ, Robles, DiDomenico, and Raclaw (2018) analyze video-recorded conversational interactions (mostly among college-age friends), focusing on extracts wherein participants talk about the technology use of co-present or absent others. They found that participants discursively constructed ideologies regarding uses of communication technologies and social media by way of portraying themselves as average, or ordinary, users: they presented relatively uninterested, neutral stances toward social media; they quantified their social media use to make it seem unremarkable in the context of the current interaction; and they labeled the behaviors of themselves and others as (in)appropriate, attributing identities to users based on these described behaviors. For example, when a young woman is teased by her friends about the number of selfies that she takes and posts on Instagram during a usual drive to go shopping ("like twenty," in her friend's words), the woman counters that she has "like, FOUR selfies on Instagram." In other words, she interprets twenty as "too many" and does work to dispel the perception that her social media use is inappropriate or unusual. (When she takes out her phone moments later in the conversation and counts her selfies, however, she easily finds thirteen and says to her friends, "You win.") Through exchanges such as this one, young adults put forth and (re)negotiate their perspectives on appropriate, and even moral, uses of digital communication technologies and platforms.

In another study considering communication where digital communication technology is highlighted, İkizoğlu (2019) demonstrates how a mobile phone–based translation app is treated as participant-like in the video-recorded interactions of one multilingual family and facilitates interaction between members who do not speak a common language. This reflects the underlying ideology that technology is part of everyday (family) interaction, not necessarily a disturber of it, a finding that emerges in other studies as well (e.g., Choe 2020; Gordon 2013a; İkizoğlu 2021; Pigeron 2009; Tovares 2007). While many studies highlight how online and offline interactions are relatively seamlessly woven together in peer interaction (e.g., Aarsand 2008; DiDomenico and Boase 2013), others illuminate how expectations about how mobile communication technologies should be used (while) in face-to-face encounters differ across users owing to a variety of factors, including age, gender, and cultural background (e.g., Al Zidjaly and Gordon 2012; Axelsson 2010; Baron and Hård af Segerstad 2010; Campbell 2007, 2008; Forgays, Hyman, and Scheiber 2014). Ling (2008) suggests that a common understanding of mobile phones is that they constitute a kind of "secondary engagement," in Goffman's (1963) sense; DiDomenico and Boase (2013) take this perspective in their analysis of a video-recorded conversation among friends who repeatedly attend to their mobile phones. The authors observe that the primary/secondary involvement distinction is often not clear. Rowe (2018) reinforces this in her examination of how young adult friends engaging in video-computer-mediated communication (on FaceTime or Skype) manifest different ideologies regarding appropriate behaviors in this context, particularly about involvement in simultaneous activities such as texting.

In summary, ideologies about communication technologies and specific social media platforms vary. Uses of digital communication technologies in face-to-face encounters, and well as ideologies about their uses, may differ by a user's age or other social factors. Further, while such ideologies are constructed in public discourse contexts (e.g., in media representations of how people use mobile phones), they are also created and contested moment by moment in social interactions. Likewise, ideologies about communication and its role in social life in general and interpersonal relationships in particular emerge and are negotiated in everyday conversational exchanges, including online (and in the specific discussion thread I examine); I turn to these ideologies next.

IDEOLOGIES ABOUT COMMUNICATION AND RELATIONSHIPS

Carbaugh's (2007) notion of "cultural discourses" provides a useful entry point into how communication and relationships are interlinked; he describes these as shared, culturally inflected understandings of personhood and of communication that manifest in and influence how language is used. This concept emerges as part of cultural discourse analysis (or CuDA), Carbaugh's approach to studying how communication is "shaped as a cultural practice" and how "cultural commentary" is "imminent in practices of communication" (p. 168). This approach to discourse is closely related to the ethnography of communication, interactional sociolinguistics, and other primarily qualitative, interpretative approaches in that it views communication as constitutive of social reality, and in that it acknowledges that

> as people communicate, so they engage in a meta-cultural commentary, that is, they (and we) say things explicitly and implicitly about who they are, how they are related to each other, how they feel, what they are doing, and how they are situated in the nature of things. (p. 168)

CuDA thus reinforces and complements studies by Tannen (e.g., 1986, 1990, 2001, 2005, 2017) and other linguists (e.g., Gordon 2006; Yamada 1997) emphasizing how specific (para)linguistic features send what Bateson (1972) calls "metamessages" that pertain to relationships, and studies by communication scholars illuminating how relational communication is embedded in particular cultural contexts (e.g., Fitch 1991, 1998; Muñoz 2014; Philipsen

1987, 1992, 2002). Carbaugh remarks that within this framework, "terms for talk and communication generally" have been "especially productive as a focus for cultural explorations" (p. 170). An oft-cited example is Katriel's (1986, 2004) discussion of *dugri*, a frank, direct way of speaking in Israeli Sabra culture that is often misunderstood by outsiders. Other examples include Dori-Hacohen and Shavit's (2013) analysis of Israeli *tokbek* (talk-back online commenting regarding politics), which has come to have pejorative meanings as a "bashing ritual" that fails to promote civil exchange; Boromisza-Habashi's (2016) exploration of how Hungarian citizens talk about and evaluate *kommunikáció* ("communication") in the context of politics, including its veracity and artfulness; and Su's (2019) study of the metalanguage of Taiwanese *liamo* (politeness).

Carbaugh (2007:174) explains how CuDA views meaning as a kind of "ongoing commentary" that can be analyzed: through such commentary, people convey "cultural meanings—about personhood, relationships, action, emotion, and dwelling" that "are formulated in cultural discourse analyses as 'radiants of cultural meaning' or 'hubs of cultural meaning' which are active in communication practice." The "radiants" or "hubs" that Carbaugh describes can be illuminated by considering *cultural terms* (such as *dugri*, as already mentioned, or the Japanese notion of *amae*, or "sweet interdependence," as discussed by scholars including Yamada [1997]); *cultural propositions* (such as the assumption that in the United States, a person is a unique individual, as described, for example, by Carbaugh [2005]); and *cultural premises*, or how analysts formulate "participants' beliefs about the significance and importance of what is going on" (Carbaugh 2007:177). As Carbaugh (2007:178) explains, cultural premises "capture and explicate taken-for-granted knowledge which usually does not need to be stated by participants since it is believed to be part of common sense." Premises, along with terms and propositions, are important means of examining and illuminating cultural discourses regarding interpersonal communication and relationships. For example, Fitch (1998:18) illuminates how, among urban Columbians, "an interpersonal ideology of connectedness to people is a powerful symbolic resource" for dealing with difficulties, such as crime and violence, and the notion of *confianza*, which roughly captures the idea of "trust" or "closeness," is especially important.

Other studies highlight the US focus on individuality and independence (e.g., Carbaugh 1996), the Japanese focus on connection through hierarchy (e.g., Watanabe 1993), and the various linguistic and other communicative strategies that are used to negotiate all of these relational dimensions in interaction (e.g., Tannen 1994, 2003, 2007a). In a similar spirit, Tannen's (2008) analysis of narratives women tell about their sisters demonstrates how accounts of specific experiences (small-n narratives) are used to develop themes the narrator is conveying about her relationship with her sister (Big-N Narratives). These themes in turn speak to, and are shaped by, culture-wide ideologies (Master Narratives), typically not explicitly stated. Tannen finds that one prominent Master Narrative (or what Carbaugh might call a cultural discourse) is that sisters should be close and similar.

Existing scholarship reveals several Master Narratives or cultural discourses that are particularly relevant to this chapter. First, in the United States and many other sociocultural contexts, people in intimate partner relationships are generally expected to be close and interconnected but still maintain independence and autonomy as individuals. Thus, the issues of privacy and secret keeping are oft-discussed in research examining couples' communication, such as in Baxter and Wilmot's (1985) analysis of what topics couples keep taboo and how. Partners' shared investment in various kinds of relationship and/or family "work" also emerges as a topic of study; for example, Tannen (2006) demonstrates how members of one American couple, over the course of a single day's conversations, "reframe" a discussion about one partner's resistance to assist the other with a particular task to be about his involvement in household chores more generally, and then to be about his dependability in terms of emotionally supporting his partner. Equality is also often seen as an issue to be managed in many intimate partner relationships; for example, Kendall (2007) examines how in their everyday talk, two middle-class American women construct themselves and their husbands as coequal partners in childrearing (though their actual childrearing practices reflect inequality). Balance between these various relationship tensions is negotiated in everyday interaction and can be understood through what Tannen (e.g., 1994, 2001, 2007a) refers to as the relativity of linguistic strategies, a theory that highlights a contextualized understanding of discourse and demonstrates how the very same linguistic or discourse strategy can be used to construct power, solidarity, or both at once, and how power and solidarity mutually entail each other. Relational dialectics theory suggests that all relationships are animated by competing discourses, such as privacy versus disclosure and certainty versus uncertainty (e.g., Baxter 2011; Baxter and Montgomery 1996).

A second Master Narrative or cultural discourse that is important for this chapter is that members of couples are expected to communicate, and this communication is expected to be of a certain type and quality. Katriel and Philipsen (1981) examine the meaning of "communication" in American talk about interpersonal life. Focusing on case studies of the communication practices of two women, which included observations, interviews, and the women's logging of their own communication, and situating these case studies in observations of other speaking situations (such as the American talk show *The Phil Donahue Show*) and existing academic research, Katriel and Philipsen "develop a grounded theory of 'communication' as a cultural category" (p. 303). They find that "communication" (or "real communication," or "open communication") implies closeness and mutual support between participants, as well as flexibility, or the willingness to listen and understand the other's perspective.

In contrast, "mere talk" (or "small talk," or "chit-chat") is not seen as entailing closeness, being viewed as more neutral and rigid or conventionalized. This fits in with a broader understanding of communication, interpersonal relationships, and self-identity as "work" (p. 310). "Communication," in American interpersonal life, the authors explain, "is the solution to the problem of 'relationship' (love) and of 'self' (personhood)" (Katriel and Philipsen 1981:315). Communication about the relationship and its problems (including communication problems) can be perceived as part of a couple's "quality time" together, as revealed in previous research, for instance Baxter and Erbert's (1999) quantitative study regarding heterosexual romantic relationships among American college students. Partners may also differ in how they view the role of talk more generally in their relationship; Tannen's (e.g., 1990) qualitative research uncovers a tendency for women, more than men, to value private talk between couples at home, and to view it as a means of constructing closeness between partners.

In summary, existing research suggests that cultural discourses (or Master Narratives, or ideologies) pertaining to not only technology, but also communication, people, and relationships, are constituted by, and shape, everyday communicative practices. The analysis that follows examines how and in what forms these discourses or ideologies emerge in metadiscourse via intertextuality.

INTERTEXTUALITY, METADISCOURSE, AND IDEOLOGIES OF INTERPERSONAL COMMUNICATION AND RELATIONSHIPS

I analyze one lengthy online discussion thread that was posted on the "General Diet and Weight Loss Help" board. The thread consists of 274 postings, posted by 226 participants (168 women, 40 men, and 18 others whose gender identities were not foregrounded in their public profiles or posts). The majority of posters, 202 including lexb, the OP, posted only one time to the thread (which, again, makes it quite different from threads examined in previous chapters). Sixteen of the posters posted twice, four posted three times, two posted four times, one posted five times, and one posted eleven times.

In her original post, lexb describes a disagreement she had with her male partner. As in threads examined in previous chapters, the OP's post shapes the thread that unfolds, providing a primary touchstone for what follows. "Partner hates me using FIF :("is the title she gives the thread (as the emoticon in the thread title suggests, I collected this thread very early on in my data collection, in 2012). In the body of her post, lexb describes a "row" (or quarrel) with her partner over her use of FIF:

(1)   lexb (OP; post 1):

1   My partner and I have just had a huge row over me using FIF—he says it is making me
2   obsessive and doesn't understand why I can't just eat healthily and exercise like 'normal
3   people'. I log everything, down to a mint or cup of coffee, and he thinks it is crazy. I love
4   FIF, it helps me stay on track and I know that without it I would over eat because I
5   wouldn't be so conscious, but now I am thinking maybe I should stop using it and see
6   how I go just estimating calories and exercise—or as he suggests, stop thinking about it
7   and just 'exercise and stay away from burgers'-what do you guys think? Anyone ever feel
8   like logging everything is a bit obsessive?

The OP introduces her problem in the first sentence of her post, and she indicates that the main conflict that has emerged between herself and her partner regarding FIF is that her partner believes it causes her to be "obsessive" about food, to the point that she is using the tracking function of the app excessively (as lexb explains, she logs even very minor low- or no-calorie items, such as "a mint or cup of coffee" [line 3]). She then reports that her partner has evaluated her negatively based on this: he thinks her behavior is "crazy" (line 3) and that how she manages her weight is not "normal" (line 2). In her post, the OP seems to be mulling over her partner's belief that the app's logging function may encourage obsessive behavior, and she reaches out to the boards for input on this, reporting that she is considering not using the app even though she values it.

In her post, lexb creates intertextual links between her present online communication and previous offline communication numerous times and produces metadiscourse. She labels an interaction she had with her partner as "a huge row," metadiscursively framing it, and indicates, via constructed dialogue in the form of indirect reported speech, what he reportedly said ("he says" [line 1]) during the argument (that FIF makes her obsessive and he does not understand why she is not like "normal people," who do not use the weight loss app [lines 2–3]). The phrase "normal people" appears in quotation marks in the post and thus purportedly represents his exact words, emphasizing (and perhaps problematizing) them. Lexb also reports that her partner "suggests" that she should stop thinking about what she eats and that she should instead just "exercise and stay away from burgers" (line 7), which she again presents as constructed dialogue in the form of direct speech, using quotation marks. In her use of "suggests," lexb also communicates the mild level of forcefulness of her partner's request. Lexb thus uses constructed dialogue to bring (select) elements of her offline interaction into the online context, using (purportedly, sometimes exact) intertextual repetition to create links between the online and offline interactions. In addition, she labels the offline exchange using the activity label "huge row," which indicates a particular key for it but also characterizes her partner as saying and suggesting (rather than, for instance, yelling and ordering).

In the discussion thread that develops, users put forth their ideas about the OP's relationship, their own partner relationships, and intimate relationships in general. They also communicate about the various modes of communication they view as relevant to the OP's post: face-to-face communication with one's partner, as well as modes that are linked to the FIF app, including human–computer interaction (logging, or entering one's food intake and exercise into the app) and computer-mediated interaction with others (the online discussions). This results in some very rich online discourse about discourse online (on the FIF site in general) and offline (in the context of couples' conversations).

As mentioned, examining this thread through the lens of collaborative problem-solving used in the last chapter would seem to suggest that the OP's problem is not "solved" in any apparent way (in part due to the OP's lack of participation), even though a number of the intertextual linking strategies used there (e.g., constructed dialogue, the board's quotation function, and pointing by way of deictic pronouns) are also used in this thread. Notably, while posters do ask information-seeking questions, or attempt to paraphrase or reframe lexb's understanding of what happened, she does not respond. In post 180, after multiple posts have suggested that the OP break up with her partner, one participant notes that posters do not have enough knowledge about her situation to offer such advice: "In this particular thread, we don't have enough information to know about the OP's relationship to reasonably suggest she end it." This reflects how this thread does not achieve a high level of shared understanding about the offline situation at issue.

This thread also features many more posts as compared with the thread examined in the last chapter (274 as compared with 46) and involved many more participants (226 as compared with 24); these factors too may contribute to the construction of a thread consisting largely of advancing competing ideas and ideologies, rather than collaborative problem-solving and a displayed evolving perspective by the OP. And, as mentioned, most posters (202 of the 226) posted only once, which indicates that there was not a lot of sustained engagement.

In addition, many posters immediately offer advice very early on in the thread, which means that the thread does not include a lot of preliminary information gathering as compared with Alma_Michelle's thread from the last chapter (and again, even where posters query the OP here, she does not respond). Examples of advice giving in the first ten posts to lexb's thread include: "Tell him to mind his own business!" (post 2), "Tell him to build a bridge and get over it" (post 4), "Don't take it to heart" (post 5), "Can't you just make a joke of it, treat it lightly?" (post 6), "Ignore him" (post 7), "I agree with what [poster 6] says: try to make a little joke when you log your food/exercise, ask him to come join you at the computer and show him the site" (post 9), and "You can also have moments of meals that you decide not to log" (post 10).

In other words, people put forth their own opinions from the outset and put much less effort into soliciting more information from the OP. Further, there is a lot of assessment and name-calling of the partner throughout the thread that seems to encourage even more agonistic discourse: he is evaluated as being jealous (posts 7, 78, 135, 218, 231); insecure (e.g., "I wonder if the poor thing is feeling neglected? YAWN!!!" in post 80); "a real loser" (post 20), unsupportive (posts 20, 31, 72, 113, 204, 226); "immature and controlling" (post 244); "a brat" and "complete jerk" (post 22); "a bouchdag" (presumably an inversion of the word "douchebag"; post 31); a "HATERRRRR!!!!!" (post 165); and "a **** twit" (presumably the asterisks are blocking out "fuck" or "shit"; post 134). In post 194 a user named mariacat notes,

> I can't believe this thread is still going, but then again people loooove to give unwarranted 'relationship advice' and then fight about it like it makes any difference. Personally I feel worse for the OP having 8 pages of 'leave him!' 'no you're an idiot and she has to stay!' than her having her original problem.

This metadiscourse demonstrates awareness by at least one participant that this is not an especially productive thread.

Near the very end of the thread, Marvelucas (who posted eleven times in the thread, more than anyone else) summarizes all of this in his post (post 270):

(2) Marvelucas (post 270)
1   I'm staggered as to many of the responses on here! Essentially her partner has supported
2   her weight loss and healthy lifestyle by suggesting she eats better and exercises - but
3   thinks she is 'crazy' to log every single mint etc. Wow what a horrible person he must
4   be!!!
5
6   So this guy has now been labeled a 'real loser'
7   HE has been called obsessive
8   She has been told to ditch him
9   She has been told to kick him out on the street
10 He has been told to mind his own business (his partners health and well being isn't his
11 business???)
12 He has been labelled jealous and controlling
13 He has been called a douche
14 he has been called insecure
15
16 Many many others!
17
18 The other day my wife suggested that I was overdoing it down the gym - should I ditch
19 her? She is trying to control me! She is such a loser! Oh man, maybe she's jealous of the

20 girls down my gym! Hold on - what's it got to do with her anyway, she should mind her
21 own damn business!

In this post, Marvelucas criticizes the thread as a whole, calling attention to the harsh terms used to describe the OP's partner (e.g., *real loser*,
a douche, *insecure*) and the harsh nature of the advice the OP has been
given (e.g., *ditch him, kick him out on the street*). In lines 18–20, Marvelucas
comments that his own partner sometimes expresses concern about his
health habits (she "suggested" that he overdoes it at the gym), and he
creates the hypothetical "correct" response, based on the advice of the
thread, to leave her since she is a jealous loser. In so doing, he ridicules
previous posts while also echoing the phrase "mind [her] own damn business," which was originally posted as advice in the first response to the
OP's post (in post 2).

Marvelucas repeatedly uses intertextual repetition of words from other
posts and paraphrase of the content of posts in general to highlight some
of the problems he sees in the thread, thus producing negatively valanced
metadiscourse about it. Despite the fact that the thread is not as "helpful" as
Alma_Michelle's, it provides important, though more abstract, insights from
my perspective as an analyst (in Carbaugh's [2007] terms, it reveals cultural
premises and cultural discourses; in Tannen's [2008] terms, it points to and
constructs Master Narratives; in other words, it reveals ideologies). Themes
(Big-N Narratives) emerge in the metadiscursive activity of the thread that
suggest that digital communication media are potentially disruptive to private, face-to-face talk; that partners' different understandings of a single
digital media technology can lead to interactional trouble; and that apps (re)
animate tensions inherent in all intimate relationships. These in turn point to
three prominent cultural discourses (or ideologies): quality time and communication are important to partner relationships, partners should be somewhat
open about their technology use, and partners should strike some workable
balance between autonomy and connection (including in the context of weight
loss, which requires both self-focus and support from others). I address each
of these in turn.

Cultural discourse 1: Quality time and communication are important to partner relationships

This cultural discourse is evoked in posts discussing how digital communication media are potentially disruptive of interpersonal communication
and relationships, either in a general way or in the context of the poster's
relationship. In other words, in discussing how digital communication

media—notably use of the FIF app's calorie logging function (human–computer interaction) and discussion boards (computer-mediated human interaction)—may interrupt face-to-face interaction and lead to hurt feelings, a widespread ideology is advanced: quality time (which is expected to be [relatively] media free) and communication are important to partner relationships. Built into this is the assumption that relationships with other people (face-to-face) supersede involvement with technology in terms of importance—face-to-face communication should be the primary engagement.

For instance, xyntz quotes part of the original poster's post—"Anyone feel like logging everything is a bit obsessive?"—and responds to it by explaining that while to lose weight you need to log what you eat, there is a point where the behavior can become disruptive. (In line 5, BF refers to boyfriend.)

(3) xyntz (post 10):
1 No that is the name of the game, what you don't log you can't follow - but if you
2 interrupt life to log everything - dinner conversation, etc . . . it is obsessive and intrusive.
3 It's the intrusive part that is bothersome.
4
5 You can also have moments or meals that you decide not to log. If your BF inviting you
6 to dinner and you turn that down because of FIF logging? That isn't a good thing.
7
8 One can log a little more privately too.

This post presents an understanding of overuse of the app (which is not explicitly defined) as generally incompatible with positive relational communication (it's "intrusive," line 2). In other words, the poster suggests that the app and the mobile phone can be used in a "wrong" way and thereby hurt relationships. This view can be interpreted as an exemplar of the phenomenon identified in existing research where using technology, rather than engaging with a co-present interlocutor, can create bad feelings (e.g., Katriel 1999). However, xyntz suggests that this problem can be overcome if users are wise about their app use, such as by not logging calories during dinner conversation, and by logging "a little more privately" (line 8).

In fact, throughout the thread, various users offer strategies for avoiding using the logging function of the app in the presence of one's partner, family, or friends. These posts too index the idea that technology (when used wrongly) can hurt interpersonal relationships, and in turn they construct the cultural discourse that quality time and talk are important. In these cases, what is indicated is that human–human interaction should not be interrupted by human–computer interaction (logging via use of the app). For example, it is suggested that it is useful to preplan and enter calories in advance of meals, so as to not have to do so when one is with others (e.g., post 15: "Something that also worked for me was to spend some time in the morning pre-planning my days - that way I was not logging all the time"; post 44: "you can log while you're planning" the day). Another strategy that posters suggest is to remember what one ate and log the items later (e.g., post 16: "calculate in your head, add up the calories log them later when you can sneak away for a bit lol" [laughing out loud]; post 26: "I think you should just remember most of your food and do your logging in one big hit when your alone or not spending time with him"; post 64: "Snap a picture of your food as a reminder or jot it down or just get good at remembering"; post 201: "keep track but log when he isn't around?"). Still others simply suggest avoiding using the app too much in the partner's presence (post 155: "fine [find] a way to tone it down out of courtesy to him, when he's around."; post 89: "I try to stay away from FIF when he is around (as much as possible anyway) and log in when he is outside or gone out"; post 97: log calories "when he's playing with Facebook on his phone, lol."). In other words, many posters suggest logging away from the partner or when the partner is otherwise engaged; this presents an understanding of app use in the presence of a partner as disruptive. One woman even reports hiding her phone from her partner "under the duvet to log" (post 98), two others indicate that they enter their calories while in the bathroom (post 77 and 160), and one poster recommends that the OP just stop mentioning the app to her partner (post 149). These are all strategies that speak to the idea that mobile communication technology use can be harmful to interpersonal interaction, and subsequently, relationships.

In a similar example, another poster (goldlid) makes the link between technology use and relationships more explicit (while also providing the inspiration for the title of this chapter):

(4)   goldlid (post 123)

1   I think the question is . . . How much time are you spending logging? If you use your

2   phone, then are you on the phone constantly logging stuff? He's got a right to be upset if

3   you phone is in your face when he's trying to spend time with you.

4   If you're on the computer, it's the same thing too.

5   If it's taking away from your relationship, then you CAN find a way to adjust it.

6   There's nothing wrong with you logging your stuff. But if you're constantly on this

7   website . . . . then that's what his issue probably is!!!

8

9   Log your stuff no more than 2-3 times a day! See if that helps!

10

11 My husband thought I was texting or playing games. He had no idea that everytime we

12 ate, I was logging my meals. He still doesn't understand it. I just make sure to log my

13 stuff after our quality time.

Goldlid indicates it is reasonable for one member of a couple to be bothered by the other's involvement with their phone or computer during a conversation. This post also demonstrates use of the term "quality time" (line 13) in a way that prioritizes it over, and excludes, technological engagement. Like other posters, goldlid emphasizes the need to limit the amount of time spent not only logging calories ("How much time are you spending logging?," line 1; "Log your stuff no more than 2–3 times a day!", line 9), but also on the website ("But if you're constantly on this website. . . . Then that's what his issue probably is!!!," lines 6–7). (She additionally notes that her husband seems to have a different understanding of her phone use than she does; I address this in a later section.) Acknowledging the need for balance, post 217 advises, "you may want to try to make sure you are not putting FIF in.his face all the time. If it is the subject of every conversation and he has to be overly aware of everything you eat and shape his life around your eating habits, it may be a lot for him (. . .) Just make sure that FIF isn't the third person in your relationship. He may be missing all the old hobbies you two used to [do] together." While this poster is sympathetic to a partner who might be upset about the app, and simply want to spend more quality time together, she also indicates that lexb "may have found a dud," in which case she should "Keep FIF and lose the partner."

The examples discussed in this section represent how posters index the idea that digital communication media—and specifically the use of the FIF app, and to some extent, its associated website—are potentially disruptive to interpersonal communication and relationships. In describing their own strategies of managing human–computer interaction (e.g., their use of the app and/or website when the partner is not around), posters simultaneously address how communication between partners should work: One should spend "quality time" with one's partner and not let technology "interrupt" the talk that builds relationships.

Cultural discourse 2: Partners should communicate openly about their technology use, to some extent

The second primary cultural discourse I identified is the idea that there should be some "appropriate" amount of open communication between partners about one's use of technology (in this case, use of the logging function and online discussion board functions of FIF). This cultural discourse is evoked in posts that highlight the theme of how partners' different understandings, or idioms of practice, regarding a single digital media technology can lead to interactional and relational trouble, and how communicating about these can fix that trouble. This is a clear example of viewing "communication" as a means of solving problems, which helps motivate the omnipresence of metadiscourse in everyday life in general, and on these discussion boards (and this thread) in particular.

Various posters point out contrasts between how they understand, and how their partner understands, their use of FIF. For example, if a partner understands FIF to be a tool for self-monitoring, they might be surprised by their partner's use of the online social component (the discussion boards, group discussions one can join, and direct messages between users). Further, the social component itself can be misunderstood.

Multiple posters identify the online discussion boards as a place they go to for weight loss and healthy living "support." For example, in post 37 a user notes that she not only finds the logging feature of FIF helpful but also appreciates the "motivation and support from other like minded people" on the boards. Post 47 also identifies the site as a support resource; for this poster, this contrasts what she has at home ("Could it be we come here for support since we don't get it at home? Thats my case anyway"). Amnda11 also identifies the website as an ideal place to get weight loss support specifically, as this support may not be available "IRL" (in real life):

(5)   Amnda11 (post 136)
   1   For me it's a lot less about the logging and a lot more about the support and interaction
   2   with other people. Most people IRL DO NOT want to hear about or talk about your diet,
   3   your exercise or even mention doing anything to get healthy. It makes them feel guilty
   4   and insecure. At least here we have someone to talk to and won't be so judgmental.

This poster too suggests that her practices regarding FIF are to use the website for weight loss support, since others in her life seem to be resistant to the topic (in fact, this theme is identified by many users: people do not want to hear about their weight loss success because it makes them feel bad about themselves).

Another user, rudeygirl_a, suggests to the OP that it might be the community element of FIF (the discussion boards), not the human–computer interaction part (logging by using the app—discussed in the last section) that is the problem. She does this by referencing other users' (specifically men's) profile pictures and other photos.

(6)   rudeygirl_a (post 126)
   1   its prob not the logging, its all the ripped abs and muscley men makin appearances on
   2   your computer screen.

Rudeygirl_a indicates that it could be that lexb's partner in fact is not bothered by her use of the app to monitor her calorie intake, but rather by her participation in discussion boards that involve other users, including members of the opposite sex who might have nice abdominal muscles and attractive musculature overall (line 1, "ripped abs and muscley men"). This fits in with other participants' more general observations that lexb's partner could be jealous about the possibilities for social interaction FIF offers, or the idea that she is participating in interactions from which he is excluded. This suggests that while lexb may be using FIF for logging and weight loss support, he might see it as a threat to their relationship.

Another poster, larann, also addresses the idea that lexb's partner may not be troubled by the logging aspect of FIF, but by the fact that she might be using it to communicate with men (including one on one, which she refers to as "the chat side of it"). Larann explains her own situation in the extract from her post below:

(7) larann (post 7)

1   I think my husband was more worried about the chat side of it. So one night I sat with
2   him on couch n showed him friends etc . . . I even showed him a friend request from a
3   male that I ignored with a polite message of good luck. Once he realised I was only
4   sticking to women he's been fine

Larann suggests that initially, her partner might have misunderstood how FIF worked and what she was using it to do—she is not using it to flirt with other men, but rather to connect with other women who share her goal of losing weight. In addition, she suggests that metacommunicating is one solution, explaining how she showed her husband the (women) friends she was communicating privately with on the site, as well as an instance where a man tried to friend her for private communication and she declined. A similar perspective—that the partner may see use of FIF as an opportunity to communicate and flirt outside the relationship—is advanced in post 98 (the same post wherein the poster indicated she would hide her phone under the duvet to log her calories). This poster, caviargal, explains that her partner "keeps asking" if she is "flirting with other guys . . . I tell him for a start 99% of my FIF friends are female and if you call talking about 'thigh chaffing' is flirting well then we need to talk! Lol." Caviargal reports online the communication she had offline with her partner, indicating that she "tells" her partner how she uses the communicative aspects of FIF. Specifically, she uses it to communicate almost exclusively with other women, and further, from these women she looks for support, and with them she discusses seemingly uninteresting topics (such as how to manage the discomfort of one's thighs rubbing together, which she describes as "thigh chaffing" [chafing]).

Similarly, in post 36, the poster, also a woman, suggests that lexb invite her partner to join her on the site; this will provide him a way to understand the technology and how she is using it.

(8)   strongerhappyme (post 126)

    1   maybe ask him if he would like to join and that way will see that this site is for those that

    2   want to keep healthy and fit and not dating sex site that he might think it is so good luck

Strongerhappyme again suggests that the partner may misunderstand what the site is for, or how lexb is using it. Her recommendation is to communicate: "Ask" him to join, and that way, he can come to understand lexb's practices regarding FIF—she uses it for health reasons, not to connect with other men. (A quick Internet search indicates that there are websites specifically designed for dieting and dating, but FIF is not one of them. Of course, that does not mean this use is not possible. Indeed, in Chapter 3, I made mention of a thread titled "The Singles Hangout" that was posted on the Chit-Chat discussion board.)

In summary, the posts discussed in this section collectively highlight that partners and users might differently understand FIF. If partners have different understandings of the app and its associated website—as a logging tool versus a tool for social support, or as a website for support versus an opportunity to meet new, sexually attractive people—this can cause problems in the relationship. Communicating with one's partner is suggested as a solution to mismatched understandings (or, in Tannen and Wallat's [1993] terms, clashing "knowledge schemas") about the site. In other words, the overall message is: let your partner know enough about what you are doing so that he understands (that the partner is usually a "he" in this thread is beyond the scope of the analysis but will be pondered briefly near the end of the chapter). This is necessary because interpersonal relationships are affected by (lack of) shared understandings about what a particular platform is for, and how a partner is using it.

Cultural discourse 3: Partners need to strike a balance between autonomy and connection (as well as privacy and disclosure)

The previous section, which touches on how much a user of FIF needs to share with their partner about the platform's logging and discussion board aspects, leads directly into the third cultural discourse (or Master Narrative or ideology) that emerged in the thread—that partners need to strike some kind of happy balance between autonomy and connection—as well as to the related issues of privacy and disclosure. This emerges because use of the app and its connected discussion boards may (re)animate these tensions that, as shown by numerous scholars (e.g., Baxter 2011; Fitch 1998; Tannen 1990, 1994, 2005), are inherent in all interpersonal relationships. In other words, a person's app use highlights something about cultural understandings of the nature of human beings and relationships: a theme emerges that when one partner is using a weight loss app and its affiliated website, relationship tensions are brought into relief. Communication about this in the discussion thread demonstrates cultural discourses that reflect the existence of these tensions, and the need to find balance, while also creating the intertextual links that accomplish metadiscourse.

These tensions (and competing ideologies about what is the "proper" balance of independence and connection, and privacy and disclosure, all very controversial in this thread) can be seen in the post by the first person to post after the OP. Lizz123 writes, "Tell him to mind his own business!!" This suggests that online activities related to one's weight loss, and perhaps one's health and computer-related practices more generally, are private and should reflect autonomy. (This post is also generally representative of the tendency noted earlier in this chapter for posters to post advice without first gathering more information.)

The post by Lizz123 is quoted by BirdyJenn, who also adds the following:

(9) BirdyJenn (post 3)

> Lizz123
> Tell him to mind his own business!!

1 I agree!! If you want to get healthier, that is NONE OF HIS BUSINESS. Seriously, it is
2 not his place to tell you how to go about dieting and exercising. Do what feels right for
3 you and tell him to get over it.

Both Lizz123 and BirdyJenn speak to the theme that one's weight loss practices, including how one uses a weight loss app, are an individual's private business (which contrasts with posts examined in the previous section suggesting some openness with the partner regarding app use). These posters' parallel uses of multiple exclamation points ("Tell him to mind his own business!!" and "I agree!!") help emphasize this perspective, as does BirdyJenn's repetition of Lizz123's use of "business" (she not only quotes Lizz123's post but actually reproduces this word in agreeing with her), as well as her use of all caps line 1: "that is NONE OF HIS BUSINESS.")

This perspective is advanced by a number of the posters (and later hotly contested by others), thereby emphasizing the importance of autonomy and privacy as issues in relationships. While some posters acknowledge that it might be useful at times (for some people) to explain to their partners how they are using the app, others suggest that the whole endeavor of engaging in weight loss, including any online components, is not relevant to a partner. For example, post 8 indicates that it is inappropriate for lexb's partner to tell her what she "can and cant do," since it's unlikely that he seeks her "approval to see his friends, go out for a drink, or watch his favourite tv show!!!" (post 8); in other words, partners should have some independence and privacy (as well as equality). (Note that one partner keeping tabs on the other is framed in this comment as an act of control rather than connection; the act is ambiguous and polysemous when it comes to power and solidarity, in Tannen's [1994] terms.) In post 29 a user explains, "You are doing this for YOU!"—in other words, use of the app and trying to lose weight constitute an individual goal. This is echoed by others who note, "You are3 doing this for you and not for your partner" (post 69), "bottom line is do what you think is good and healthy in YOUR life" (post 87), "I find it strange that it's actually causing fights - who cares if you're obsessing over YOUR HEALTH" (post 139), and "your not doing this for him, its for you and YOUR health" (post 165). The idea that weight loss is something for the individual is made clear and explicit; the repeated use of second-person singular pronouns, often typed in capital letters, drives this home. Understanding weight loss as an individual choice and worthy goal also intertextually links to the broader self-transformation narrative offered in public and media discourse regarding weight loss (e.g., Gordon 2015b; Mishra 2017) and to neoliberal and capitalistic ideologies (e.g., Guthman 2011) in how self-determination and autonomy are emphasized.

Other posters are harsher in how they proclaim that one's weight loss efforts, as well as the entailed use of an online app to lose weight, are individual practices that do not involve a partner: "I'd tell your partner to STFU [shut the fuck up] and mind his own business!" (post 107); posts 112, 117, and 118 quote post 2 ("Tell him to mind his own business!!") and add "yep! I agree . . . none of his flipping business if he continues to be (what seems like) nasty to you about it," "This x 10000000," and "YEAH!! What she said!," respectively. In other words, numerous posters indicate that independence and privacy are part of weight loss as an activity and should also be expected in intimate relationships.

As mentioned, however, Marvelucas takes issue with this perspective, as was previously shown in excerpt 2 (post 270, near the end of the thread, where he mocks the attitude that a partner who wants to be involved with another's healthy lifestyle should "mind their own business" by demonstrating a hypothetical reaction to his wife's hypothetical observation that he has been "overdoing it" at the gym: "Hold on - what's it got to do with her anyways, she should mind her own damn business!"). Earlier in the thread, he quotes the "Tell him to mind his own business" post (post 2), which is itself embedded in another post (post 102) that agrees with that post ("I agree!! If you want to get healthier, that is NONE OF HIS BUSINESS. Seriously, it is not his place to tell you how to go about dieting and exercising do what feels right for you and tell him to get over it."). Marvelucas adds a response to this quoted text, shown below.

(10)   Marvelucas (128)

> ((*quoted posts not shown*))

1   Since when is someones health, well being, hobbies, pasttimes and interests been
2   none of a partner's business!
3
4   Of course he should be interested in what his partner does - ridiculous to think
5   otherwise.
6
7   "Hi darling, what have you been up to today?"
8   "None of your damn business!"

Here Marvelucas uses the board's quotation function to intertextually link to and disagree with the discourse of previous posters. In so doing, he not only puts forth the idea that partners should share certain things (and calls the idea of them not doing so "ridiculous" in line 4) but also reanimates the ongoing discussion of the relationship tensions of autonomy and connection, privacy and disclosure. This becomes clear in the imagined face-to-face dialogue he constructs between two partners: one asks how the other's day was in a way that shows caring and seeks connection, as is indexed by the endearment term "darling" (line 7: "Hi darling, what have you been up to today?"). However, the responding partner treats this as an invasion of privacy and perhaps as an attempt at control (line 8: "None of your damn business!"). This is a hyper-exaggerated example of the kind of miscommunication that can occur in couples' (and especially heterosexual couples') relationships, as identified by Tannen (e.g., 1990), resulting in a failure to achieve connection and closeness. What is seemingly intended as a "connection maneuver" is interpreted as a "power maneuver" (Tannen 2003, 2007a).

Later in the thread, in post 144, Marvelucas also pushes back against the idea that partners should be autonomous and keep information to themselves. He uses the quotation function to quote the poster who (in post 107) indicated, "I'd tell your partner to STFU [shut the fuck up] and mind his own business!," as well as a response by another poster, LondonReal (in post 140), who quoted that post and added, "I'm going to take a stab in the dark here and guess that you're single? That attitude doesn't fly in any long term relationship." Marvelucas agrees with that last point and elaborates.

(11)   Marvelucas (144)

> ((*quoted message not shown*))

1   exactly!
2
3   All he said was exercise, eat healthy and don't worry too much about logging

4   every mint! So he has to STFU!!

5

6   I've even seen people recommending she should dump him!

Here again Marvelucas disagrees with the idea that lexb's partner should keep quiet and that lexb should end the relationship just because he expressed his perspective on her weight loss practices involving the app. This again points to the importance of personal connection (as contrasted with autonomy) and disclosure (as compared with privacy), while also indexing the larger cultural discourse that these relationship tensions need to be balanced in some way.

Marvelucas is the primary person who pushes back against the idea that lexb should claim her independence from her partner regarding her use of FIF (as mentioned, he posts more than any other poster to the thread). However, he is not the only one. As seen earlier, RealLondon, in her post (post 140), suggests that telling a partner to "mind his own business" is not conducive to having a long-term relationship. Others emphasize that lexb may be misunderstanding her partner, and that her partner may be trying to be involved as a way of creating connection. As bellemary explains, the partner "may just feel left out and want attention from you," and it would be good to explain that "You are doing this for you, to live healthy for you AND your partner and in the end I am sure they will appreciate the new healthy you :)" (post 3). This fits in with the spirit of being open with one's partner about use of the app and the weight loss process more generally. The woman who posts post 203 gives a similar perspective: "Is he upset bc [because] your attention is on here and not on him? That can be fixed. You two need to have a talk and he needs to know this is important for you." In offering this, the poster also endorses the idea that communication is a solution to relationship woes. The woman in post 205 suggests to lexb that her partner may be acting out of care and concern: "Everyone is being so mean about your partner, but there is a possibility hes just trying to look out for you."

In sum, many posters use the thread as a chance to criticize lexb's partner and encourage her to understand weight loss as her own, independent journey that is separate from her partner, while some others (and notably one) suggest that this is not how intimate relationships work. Both groups of posters, however, point to the ongoing tensions within relationships of how independent and connected partners should be, and how much they should share and how much they should keep to themselves. In other words, in discussing a case where the OP had an argument with her partner about her use of FIF, the posters highlighted that partner relationships involve balancing these dimensions (in instances of weight loss app use, and beyond), and that this balance may not always be easy.

Gender on this thread

As mentioned, the gender of posters and their gendered patterns of interaction are not the focus of my analysis, as they were not in previous chapters where I anecdotally observed that the "flaming" posts I encountered were generally produced by users whose gender presentation was as men (and, as indicated, it is not always possible to categorize posters' gender presentations). However, it seems worth noting that many of the posters (but not all) criticizing lexb's partner, urging lexb to focus on herself, and even suggesting she reassess or end the relationship are posters who present themselves as women who are involved in a heterosexual intimate relationship or who do not indicate the gender of their partner. The poster who participates the most and advocates for the view that partners should be joined together in their activities, Marvelucas, self-presents as a man involved in an intimate relationship with a woman.

As demonstrated, participants manifest different ideas about the appropriate balance between autonomy and connection in partner relationships on this thread and advocate for their own ideas in the context of the original poster's stated problem. However (and perhaps related to gender), some seem also to have different understandings of the purpose of this thread, its situational definition, or what Tannen and Wallat (1993) call the "interactive frame." Specifically, some women seem to use the thread as a chance to assert the individual power of women in general, and to rally around a woman whose male partner is potentially standing in the way of her (individual) goals. Thus, what is taking place is "rallying around," or "celebrating" what is (colloquially, though often dismissingly) labeled "girl power." In contrast, Marvelucas and some other posters (both women and men) seem to orient to the thread as a context in which to provide specific and literal pieces of advice for the OP (in which case "dump him" could be seen as a bit extreme and could be seen as an attack on any partner who wants any level of involvement with a partner who is trying to lose weight). While this merits further exploration, the idea that different people might understand the thread differently is not surprising. As shown by Tannen and Wallat (1993), Watanabe (1993), Gordon (2008), and others, participants do not necessarily have a shared understanding of what is going on in their unfolding interaction or how that interaction should be structured. Further, the analysis in this chapter has revealed a multitude of different understandings and expectations, including about FIF and how and why a partner might use their cell phone around mealtime, the role of a partner in the relatively individualistic activity of weight loss, and the appropriate balance between independence and connection between members of a couple more generally. That people might have different understandings regarding an online discussion thread on such topics makes sense, especially given the overall shape of the thread (its many one-time participants, as well as its advice-oriented quality).

CONCLUSION

In conclusion, I have shown how identifying cultural discourses that emerge across posts to a single online discussion thread highlights the interconnectedness between interpersonal communication, partner relationships, and a particular digital communication technology (an app for weight loss that has mobile phone–based logging and online social components). The analytic approach I have used considers ideologies by drawing on Carbaugh's (2007) theorizing on cultural discourses and Tannen's (2008) on Master Narratives: I identified themes or what Tannen calls Big-N Narratives in the talk, notably that digital communication media, including use of FIF, may disrupt face-to-face communication and relationships; that mismatched knowledge schemas or ideologies of practice regarding a particular digital media technology can lead to interactional and interpersonal trouble; and that use of digital communication media (re)animates fundamental relationship tensions, such as between being an independent person while also being connected to one's partner. These themes, in turn, index three even larger cultural discourses or Master Narratives: that quality communication and time are important in intimate relationships, that partners should communicate with a certain amount of openness regarding their technology use, and that partners should find a balance of being an individual (engaged in the self-transformative activity of weight loss) and being a partner in a relationship. The first two of these are metadiscursive, while the third communicates about interpersonal relationships (which entail communication).

Using the app is viewed as impacting communication among members of a couple: it is potentially disruptive, though a savvy user can avoid this disruption. This echoes a range of prior research studies identifying mobile communication technology during face-to-face conversational exchanges as being problematic (e.g., Vogels and Anderson 2020) though as something that is also negotiated in context (e.g., Robles, DiDomenico, and Raclaw 2018). Further, because mobile phones, computers, and apps can be used for multiple purposes, use of the app can be ambiguous and may require a discussion explaining how the app is used and for what purposes. It may highlight or even disturb the independence and connection balance in the relationship as partners negotiate one person's use of the app and website, along with their weight loss practices. In general, then, app use is viewed as potentially problematic in relationships for various reasons (though a few posters mention that both partners use the app and that this has brought them closer together). These cultural discourses are realized intertextually in the metacommunicative posts of participants. Posters use the board's quotation function, as well as repetition of other types—such as word repetition from prior posts, constructed dialogue, and advice that uses the deictic pronoun "you" and is targeted at the OP's original post—to linguistically link to other posts, thus communicating in relation to and about them. Individual posts realize themes that I, as the analyst, was able to discern across posts. Individually but all the more apparent collectively, the posts also evoke more abstract ideologies, creating different radiants of meaning. Thus, as seen in previous chapters, the intertextuality within an individual thread not only constructs meanings in the posters' online interaction (which was the focus of Chapters 2–4) but also indexes or points to interactions (both general and specific) and ideologies that exist outside the thread (the focus of Chapters 5 and 6). This demonstrates the importance of Bolander and Locher's (2020) contention that the online/offline distinction is in many ways not sustainable, and that there is value in exploring the complexity of spaces where they seem inseparable, while also illuminating how online intertextuality and metadiscourse, when analyzed in tandem, reveal insights into an important sociolinguistic phenomenon: ideological (re)construction.

The identified cultural discourses or ideologies also seem to be influencing how posters (reportedly) have adapted FIF and the entailed mobile phone and/or computer use into their everyday lives. For example, logging "obsessively" or at least fairly consistently is a form of self-discipline that asserts one's independence (and hiding the phone or logging in secret could be seen as a way of maintaining independence and also not imposing on one's partner); reading and participating in the discussion boards can be viewed as a way of getting support in this endeavor, something the partner might not offer; and communicating about FIF with one's partner could be seen as a way of creating connection around the somewhat "individual" activity of tracking one's calories, and of being open enough to avoid misunderstandings of how FIF (especially the discussion board component) is being used. While exactly how cultural discourses emerge in and shape day-to-day use of the FIF website and its affiliated app merits further research, this chapter has revealed how examining metacommunicative activity in one discussion thread—which involved communication about face-to-face communication, computer-mediated communication, and human–computer interaction—highlights how these modes of communication are perceived as interrelated, as well as growing cultural conceptualizations of how interpersonal communication, relationships, and digital communication media intersect, and sometimes collide, both on and offline.

CHAPTER 7

Conclusion

Intertextuality 2.0: Constructing metadiscourse online

"Intertextuality" and "metadiscourse" are both far-reaching and multifaceted terms, with long histories of use in linguistics, communication studies, linguistic anthropology, and related fields. In this book, I have brought them together as "intertextuality 2.0," exploring intertextuality in the context of Web 2.0's interactive, multimodal, digital discourse, and demonstrating the value of elevating metadiscourse in the study of online intertextuality. In other words, I have advocated for an understanding of commonly recognized online intertextual linking strategies as resources for accomplishing metadiscourse in the form of metadiscursive activities or frames. This is important if we are to understand more fully the prominence and functionality of intertextuality online, as well as how intertextuality and metadiscourse are productively brought together in micro-level discourse analysis.

In what follows, I discuss how this book's chapters collectively show that intertextuality and metadiscourse are prominent, interconnected, and fundamental to the FriendInFitness (FIF) discussion boards. I first summarize the range of intertextual linking strategies I identified in my analysis, emphasizing their diversity and how they are shaped by the medium. Second, I discuss how these strategies make possible the accomplishment of the practical, goal-directed metadiscursive activities—targeted at various levels of discourse structure—through which posters weave the fabric of their online community of practice. Third, I summarize how this study contributes to our growing understanding of intertextuality and metadiscourse and their theoretical interrelationship, as well as to research on digital discourse. I conclude by "going meta" to address how this study, as an exercise that has been both intertextual

Intertextuality 2.0. Cynthia Gordon, Oxford University Press. © Oxford University Press 2023.
DOI: 10.1093/oso/9780197642689.003.0007

and metadiscursive, contributes to the interdisciplinary study of language and (online) social interaction.

INTERTEXTUALITY ONLINE

Intertextuality, or how meaning is created in texts and interactions through callbacks to (and in anticipation of) other texts and interactions, manifests in various forms that have been well documented by scholars interested in language and communication. Intertextuality has been argued to be omni-present in language use in the sense that all instances of language hark back to those prior (e.g., Bakhtin 1981, 1984, 1986; Becker 1994, 1995). Analyses of intertextuality in situated social interactions have reinforced and extended these ideas (e.g., Bauman and Briggs 1990; Tannen 2007b). With the develop-ment of the web and social media, researchers have produced an abundance of studies demonstrating that intertextuality is pervasive in digital discourse contexts and that it occurs in multiple forms (as summarized in Chapter 1). Intertextuality online has been explored through the study of posters' uses of hyperlinks and hashtags; their mobilization of platform-facilitated quota-tion functions; their uses of other forms of quotation of material from the unfolding interaction, some other digital interaction, offline conversation, or some other source; their repetition of words, symbols, emojis, memes, or GIFs within the same thread or to link to material outside of the thread; their direct and indirect references to other texts and interactions, both on-line and offline; their paraphrasing of other textual material; and their uses of deictic words and symbols. Texts are also linked to other (online) texts through shared genre features, which can be described as "interdiscursivity" (e.g., Fairclough 1992) or as "generic intertextuality" (e.g., Bauman 2004), or, in the case of memes, as membership in metaphorical "families" (Segev et al. 2015). This body of research has also demonstrated that intertextuality serves a variety of functions in online and social media discourse, extending earlier studies that focused on conversational interaction and traditional written texts, such as books. These functions include acknowledging another person's contribution, constructing interactional coherence, agreeing or disagreeing, joking or mocking, displaying expertise, constructing various types of identi-ties, demonstrating solidarity and community membership, and (re)creating · ideologies. There is a sense that the range of forms and functions of intertex-tuality is limitless.

Taking advantage of a multimodal textual record characterized by "per-sistence" (to use Herring's [1999] term), I analyzed online discussion board discourse and demonstrated how various intertextual strategies are woven together to accomplish metadiscourse. All of these strategies are based in what is at the heart of intertextuality: repetition (Tannen 2007b). "The same" item (though it is never exactly the same, as Tannen explains) appears again or is referenced again, connecting a current discourse to some prior discourse. In research on the "meta" of language, repetition has been identified as "a prime example of a metalinguistic resource available to speakers (and writers)" (Coupland and Jaworski 2004:29). This book provides an account for how intertextuality serves as a resource for engagement in metadiscursive activities.

Across this book's chapters, the boards' quotation function emerged as a primary means of creating the intertextuality inherent in metadiscursive activities: one poster quotes another's post linking the current post to that prior post and adds commentary (whether by adding their own text, adjusting the existing text through manipulation of graphical features, adding an emoji or GIF, and so on). This commentary may be directed at a specific word (or words) in the post, an idea or ideology advanced in the post, the tone of the post, a GIF or some other visual material in the post, or some combination. The quotation function is a very clear way of linking post to prior post, text to "prior text" (Becker 1995). Nonetheless, it is used in conjunction with other intertextual linking strategies, such as through uses of deictic pronouns and symbols to point to the prior post, the repetition of words from the prior post in the current post, quotation marks, and repetition of visual material such as an emoticon or emoji. Further, there are many instances where other forms of linking are used and the board's quotation function is not; while many users take advantage of this affordance, it is not necessary for participation on the boards. Intertextual links in the absence of the boards' quotation function may be more subtle, such as when language from an original poster's post is echoed later down the thread, when a post uses an emoji in a parallel way to a prior post, or when a GIF "rhymes" with a previous GIF. They may be related to layout or genre (as moderators' "letters" addressed to posters in the posts wherein they announce they are locking a thread, discussed in Chapter 4). Further, themes are intertextually repeated, such as the idea that digital communication technologies might interfere with interpersonal relationships (Chapter 6), or that the notion of "clean eating" is difficult to define (Chapter 2). Even larger ideologies (or "Master Narratives" [Tannen 2008] or "cultural discourses" [Carbaugh 2007])—such as that partners need to strike a balance between autonomy and connection (Chapter 6) or that doctors and patients have specific communicative responsibilities in their encounters (Chapter 5)—also re-emerge across posts, connecting them together. Such ideologies are in dialogue with other ideologies (such as those related to digital technology, individual autonomy, weight loss and morality, gender, and food). These ideologies, which emerged in this book but were not the book's focus, are ripe for research and are receiving increasing attention; for example, contributors to Tovares and Gordon's (2020) edited volume explore how food-related ideologies are realized in digital discourse contexts (e.g., Al Zidjaly, Al

Moqbali, and Al Hinai 2020; İkizoğlu and Gordon 2020; Mapes 2020; see also Mapes 2021). The interplay of intertextuality, metadiscourse, and ideology merits additional research, especially online.

Some of the intertextual linking strategies I identified are multimodal. While text is at the center of most of my examples—indeed the vast majority of the communication on the boards is done through language—the boards' affordances also facilitate the use of emoticons and emojis as well as the posting of GIFs, memes (image macros), and photographs (while these appear prominently on the boards, there is evidence that for some posters, taking advantage of this affordance is more challenging, as discussed in Chapter 3). While the FIF discussion boards are more limited in terms of multimodality than a context like VoiceThread—which Herring (2013) demonstrates to be a prime site for "convergence" of multiple media, including synchronous and asynchronous use of video, audio, and text—the discussion boards, like many Web 2.0 contexts, offer possibilities for multimodal intertextual linking, and, by extension, multimodal metadiscourse (as when an echo of a GIF comments in some way on a previous GIF, as shown in Chapter 4).

METADISCURSIVE ACTIVITIES ONLINE

As outlined in Chapter 1, there are many studies of the "meta" of language and a proliferation of terms to refer to this (e.g., metacommunication, meta-discourse, metapragmatics, metalinguistics, metalinguistic commentary, and meta-talk). While there are obvious similarities and connections between these terms—all address "meta" and some aspect of "language" or "commu-nication"—they have been used differently and with different analytic foci, such as to describe queries about word meanings and produce directives re-lated to appropriate language use (e.g., Blum-Kulka 1997); to explore various deictic phenomena (e.g., Hanks 1993); and to consider stylization, reported speech or what Tannen (2007a) calls "constructed dialogue," and talk about the talk of other people (e.g., Jaworski, Coupland, and Galasínski 2004a). Given my attention to several of these phenomena, which occur at different levels of discourse structure, I used the umbrella word "metadiscourse" in this book. While scholars have considered metadiscourse *about* the language of digital discourse (e.g., Thurlow 2006) and the use of metadiscourse *in* digital discourse contexts (e.g., Jager and Stommel 2017; Lanamäka and Päivärinta 2009), this is a burgeoning area of research, and one to which I have aimed to contribute.

Metadiscourse occurs "in a variety of ways and by units of varied length, from individual words to whole clauses or sentences" (Hyland 2017:18), and multimodally as well (e.g., Coupland and Jaworski 2004). It could be thought of as a bit of a "fuzzy" as a notion. I have attempted to embrace this fuzziness in order to highlight the ways in which meanings are created and alignments are negotiated at any given level (or multiple levels) of discourse structure, as well as the connections among different levels. In explicitly bringing metadiscourse together with the notion of intertextuality to analyze the discourse of online discussion boards centered on weight loss and health, I have illustrated how intertextual linking strategies are fundamental in the creation of discourse about discourse, and how metadiscourse constitutes a diverse array of activities online, communicating about all of the following:

- Word meanings (e.g., "clean eating"; "study");
- Discussions of word meanings (e.g., "Whose definition of 'clean' is used?");
- Word choice (e.g., by strikethrough of a word or replacement of one word with another) and thereby ideas (e.g., that a reduction of "calories" is responsible for weight loss, not "carbs");
- The appropriateness of an individual post in terms of content or tone (e.g., "That's not really helpful"; "no need to be rude");
- Appropriate participation on the boards in general (e.g., Community Guidelines such as "No Hi-Jacking, Trolling, or Flame-Baiting");
- The type of discourse in a specific post (e.g., "People can think for themselves and won't agree with you no matter how much you <u>bully</u> them");
- The appropriateness of multiple posts (e.g., "I'm staggered as to many of the responses on here!");
- The quality of whole threads (e.g., "dumpster fire"; "this thread has stayed relatively on topic");
- One's own use of language on the thread (e.g., I "fixed it for you"; "I ain't being ugly. I am pointing out facts . . .");
- Others' online practices in general (e.g., "You are the best thread closer . . . EVAH!"; "once again posting a conclusion with no support");
- Visual materials (e.g., a meme that says "Comment with another meme . . . or just say 'yes'?"; a moderator's explanation, "This thread seems as good as any for a Flash Gordon gif, it's not like we're running the risk of having it not make sense in context.");
- Specific instances of language use brought in from offline interactions (e.g., "It doesn't sound like the doctor was very professional");
- How people who hold particular identities should speak (e.g., a doctor should not be "brusque"); and
- More abstract cultural discourses or ideologies (which are usually not explicitly named).

Posters also communicate about discourse they anticipate (e.g., "I know there will be plenty of bro-science and hyperbole to sort through") and advocate for future discourse (e.g., "Tell him to mind his own business!"). All of these metadiscursive activities are marbled throughout the discourse of the boards.

By linking to and communicating about some prior discourse (and less frequently, imagined future discourse), posters undertake numerous metadiscursive activities on the boards, both those that are named by posters (such as the specific and highly routinized practice of "fixing," the general practice of "disagreeing," and the prohibited practice of "bullying") and those that are not (such as "negotiating ideologies about communication and relationships"). These activities, I argue, are essential to the functioning of this online community of practice that consists of "people who come together around mutual engagement in an endeavor" (Eckert and McConnell-Ginet 1992:464). The mutual endeavor of those who gather on these boards is losing weight (or otherwise attending to one's health and body), and specifically sharing information and support in relation to this. The practices of this online community—and, in consequence, the existence of the community itself—are born out of posters' interactions, including the metadiscursive activities I have identified and examined.

INTERTEXTUALITY AND METADISCOURSE IN AN ONLINE COMMUNITY OF PRACTICE

A strong motivation for this book was my noticing the many instances of intertextuality and metadiscourse present on the FIF discussion boards, and wanting to understand what they were doing there (i.e., I took a bottom-up approach typical of many discourse analytic, including interactional sociolinguistic, studies). This led me to identify and analyze the metadiscursive activities named earlier. This book was also motivated, however, by what I perceived as a gap in the literature: while it is widely acknowledged that intertextuality and metadiscourse are related and interconnected, the exact nature of their relationship in micro-level online interaction remains underexplored. "Intertextuality 2.0" represents my effort to demonstrate how metadiscourse and intertextuality are intertwined online in a particular way: intertextual linking strategies make possible the metadiscursive activities that constitute an important part of a community's everyday practices. More broadly, I wanted to elevate metadiscourse in the study of intertextuality, something I myself neglected to do in my prior research on communication in an entirely different context: everyday family conversations that were audio-recorded. In Gordon (2009), I note that Becker (1994, 1995) suggests that language use, or what he terms "languaging," involves "reshaping" "prior text" into current contexts. He also observes that "social groups seem to be bound primarily by a shared repertoire of prior texts" (Becker 1994:165). I found a prolific amount of intertextual repetition in the recordings of the families whose discourse I analyzed, and I found the idea that intertextuality binds people together into groups or communities compelling. I demonstrated how this binding occurs in how family members used intertextuality to co-construct the "interactive frames" (Tannen and Wallat 1993) that constitute a family's discursive world. Examining online data and intertextuality has expanded my perspective: intertextuality 2.0 elevates metadiscourse, which is essential if we are to examine intertextuality in digital discourse contexts. Maschler (2009) uses the word "metalanguaging" to capture the various ways people use language to communicate about using language. We need to attend to both "languaging" (which is based in intertextuality) and "metalanguaging" (which also relies on intertextuality) if we are to understand more fully online interactions and the role of intertextuality in digital contexts.

The importance of elevating metadiscourse in studies of online intertextuality owes to theory as well as empirical findings. While many researchers have observed theoretical connections between intertextuality and metadiscourse and have identified both as prominent in communication in various contexts, far fewer have rigorously put these theories into dialogue in empirical, micro-level analysis. This study helps to fill that gap: if we are to understand intertextuality and metadiscourse as theoretically interconnected, it is important to understand their interplay in actual language data. Further, the "persistence" (Herring 1999) of online discourse has long been recognized as encouraging the reproduction of previous uses of language (and image), and, more recently, Adami (2014:224) points out that digital contexts have afforded, "to an unprecedented extent," users' "multimodal representation and re-use of previous existing texts in new contexts." Ready access to previous discourse encourages awareness of and redflection on instances of language use (following Johnstone et. al 1994), and, following Herring and Adami, this shapes online interaction. My study, in uncovering not only an abundance of intertextual linking but also an abundance of metadiscursive activity, supports these contentions.

Specifically, it revealed how posters to online discussion boards about health and weight loss accomplish activities that are inherently metadiscursive, and I suggested that these function in practical, strategic ways. In other words, they make the groups' "endeavor" possible. Through engaging in metadiscursive activities, posters communicate about specific lexical items that are relevant for people who are interested in improving their diets (e.g., "'clean," "processed"); they negotiate the appropriateness of their own and other's posts, determining what kind of discourse the group values; they communicate about the content of other posts by "fixing" it, to construct disagreement or to create humor; and they communicate about offline communication that affects individuals' weight loss (and seems to motivate their turning to the boards for support). While some of the strategies speak to solidarity (e.g., creating humor), others seemingly do not (e.g., arguing about whether "calories" or "carbs" are meaningful for weight loss), and still others definitely do not (e.g., mocking another person's post). But underlying every metadiscursive activity is intertextuality, which, at least on some level, functions to bind discourse and people together.

Collectively, the intertextual strategies and metadiscursive activities I have explored enable posters to do the "work" that is the overall purpose of their online community of practice: to provide support to each other as they seek to improve their health and to manage their weight, as well as to exchange useful information and relevant experiences. Existing research has demonstrated how people participating in online support forums use a range of shared practices to construct themselves as a group, ranging from using group-specific vocabulary, to manifesting and enforcing particular patterns of interaction, to collaboratively deciding what constitutes authoritative sources of information (e.g., Armstrong, Koteyko, and Powell 2012; Stommel 2008). I have approached the FIF discussion boards as constituting a community of practice centered around participants communicating together online to exchange information and provide mutual support for their weight loss and related efforts. Note that this is not to say that FIF is a uniform group; individual boards may also constitute sub-communities; recall, for example,

Figure 7.1. Metadiscursive Grumpy Cat meme.

that there are different boards for weight loss versus bodybuilding, with the former group tending to deride the latter's approach to eating and exercise as "bro-science." Further, threads (such as the highly interactive "clean eating" thread) may be understood as constituting a more "fleeting" (sub-)community of practice, in line with scholarship suggesting that when people come together online, it sometimes constitutes a "light" (Blommaert 2019) or "ambient" (Zappavigna 2011) togetherness. With this in mind, metadiscursive activities seem all the more important. What FIF posters have together is online discourse (I do not have evidence that the posters know each other in offline, or on other online, contexts). Bakhtin theorizes "culture" as "discourses retained by collective memory" (Todorov 1984:x). Metadiscourse is the means by which posters reflect on their shared (online, persistent) discursive world and engage together. They highlight certain concepts, practices, values, and ideologies as important. And, posters, in producing metadiscourse, show a valuing of communication itself—which reflects what Craig (2005:661) refers to as a shared "cultural preoccupation with communication"; as Jaworski, Coupland, and Galasiński (2004b:6) observe, "metalinguistic sensitivity" is "a hallmark of contemporary social life." In bringing together intertextuality and metadiscourse as "intertextuality 2.0," this book has shown how metalinguistic sensitivity and activities occur in online discussion boards for weight loss support, and it suggests why they are especially important for this and other similar online communities of practice.

"GOING META"

Writing this book has demonstrated a valuing of communication (in Craig's [2005] sense) that is both cultural and disciplinary. It shows a valuing of intertextuality and metadiscourse as concepts and phenomena, too. Varenne (1992) observed that studying interaction (which traditionally, for many discourse scholars, involved recording interactions, transcribing them, interpreting the interactions in light of ethnography or follow-up interviews, and so on) is an inherently intertextual exercise. Writing this book has involved (among other activities) reading, citing, and summarizing existing scholarship; attempting to interweave findings of studies from across academic disciplines and approaches to discourse analysis; bringing disparate online discussion posts together into coherent sets; converting memes into series of still shots and embedding them into academic prose; linking specific instances of language use in the data to texts from popular culture as well as to broader cultural discourses or ideologies; addressing reviewers' comments and suggestions; and referring, in later chapters, to previous ones.

It also has been an exercise in metadiscourse. Scholars in linguistics, communication, and kin disciplines must communicate about communication in order to analyze, illuminate, and better understand it. Academic write-ups of findings involve summaries and evaluations of past studies and indications of the current study's place in that context, metadiscursive words and phrases such as "next" and "in conclusion," and metadiscursive brackets such as quotation marks and parentheses (both of which I tend perhaps to overuse). They also may communicate about discourse that is to come. In that spirit, I end by noting my hopes that this study not only contributes to our understanding of, but will also help encourage future research on, intertextuality 2.0, that is, intertextuality and metadiscourse together in digital discourse, in support discussion boards, and in other web-based contexts. Research into these individual topics spans disciplinary boundaries, and exploring where they intersect encourages new ways of connecting concepts, illuminates relationships between discourse and medium, and contributes to our understanding of how meaning- and group making are accomplished. Stitching together the concepts of intertextuality and metadiscourse lends insight into how language use involves not only intense recontextualizing of, but also ample communicating about, other texts and instances of language use. It thus sheds light on the very nature of communication. Finally, pursuing the study of the interconnections between intertextuality and metadiscourse illuminates how people, laypersons and academics alike, orient to previous instances of discourse as the thread that weaves meaning, and shows how such instances help us understand later instances, as for the meme with which I conclude this book (shown in Figure 7.1), an echo of the one with which I started.

REFERENCES

Aarsand, Pål André. 2008. "Frame Switches and Identity Performances: Alternating between Online and Offline." *Text & Talk 28*, no. 2: 147–165.

Abbott, Barbara. 2003. "Some Notes on Quotation." *Belgian Journal of Linguistics 17*, no. 1: 13–26.

Abdi, Reza. 2002. "Interpersonal Metadiscourse: An Indicator of Interaction and Identity." *Discourse Studies 4*, no. 2: 139–145.

Abdi, Reza. 2009. "Projecting Cultural Identity through Metadiscourse Marking; A Comparison of Persian and English Research Articles." *Journal of English Language Teaching and Learning 1*: 1–15.

Adami, Elisabetta. 2014. "Retwitting, Reposting, Repinning; Reshaping Identities Online: Toward a Social Semiotic Multimodal Analysis of Digital Remediation." *LEA—Lingue e letterature d'Oriente e d'Occidente 3*: 223–243.

Adami, Elisabetta, and Carey Jewitt. 2016. "Special Issue: Social Media and the Visual." *Visual Communication 15*(3): 263–270.

Allen, Graham. 2000. *Intertextuality*. London: Routledge.

Al Rashdi, Fathiya. 2018. "Functions of Emojis in WhatsApp Interaction among Omanis." *Discourse, Context & Media 26*: 117–126.

Al Zidjaly, Najma. 2010. "Intertextuality and Constructing Islamic Identities Online." In *Handbook of Research on Discourse Behavior and Digital Communication: Language Structures and Social Interaction*, edited by Rotimi Taiwo, 191–204. Hershey, NJ: IGI Global.

Al Zidjaly, Najma. 2011. "Managing Social Exclusion through Technology." *Disability Studies Quarterly 31*, no. 4. https://doi.org/10.18061/dsq.v31i4.1716

Al Zidjaly, Najma. 2015. *Disability, Discourse and Technology: Agency and Inclusion in (Inter)action*. Basingstoke, UK: Palgrave Macmillan.

Al Zidjaly, Najma. 2017. "Memes as Reasonably Hostile Laments: A Discourse Analysis of Political Dissent in Oman." *Discourse & Society 28*, no. 6: 573–594.

Al Zidjaly, Najma, and Cynthia Gordon. 2012. "Mobile Phones as Cultural Tools: An Arabian Example. *Intercultural Management Quarterly 13*, no. 2: 14–17.

Al Zidjaly, Najma, Einas Al Moqbali, and Ahad Al Hinai. 2020. "Food, Activism, and Chips Oman on Twitter." In *Identity and Ideology in Digital Food Discourse*, edited by Alla Tovares and Cynthia Gordon, 197–224. London and New York: Bloomsbury.

Andersen, Elisabeth Muth. 2017. "Typing Yourself Accountable: Objectifying Subjective Experiences in an Online Health Forum." *Linguistik Online 87*, no. 8: 43–68.

Androutsopoulos, Jannis. 2006. "Introduction: Sociolinguistics and Computer-Mediated Communication." *Journal of Sociolinguistics 10*, no. 4: 419–438.

Androutsopoulos, Jannis. 2013a. "Online Data Collection." In *Data Collection in Sociolinguistics: Methods and Applications*, edited by Christine Mallinson, Becky Childs, and Gerard Van Herk, 236–249. New York: Routledge.

Androutsopoulos, Jannis. 2013b. "Participatory Culture and Metalinguistic Discourse: Performing and Negotiating German Dialects on YouTube." In *Discourse 2.0: Language and New Media*, edited by Deborah Tannen and Anna Marie Trester, 47–71. Washington, DC: Georgetown University Press.

Androutsopoulos, Jannis. 2014. "Moments of Sharing: Entextualization and Linguistic Repertoires in Social Networking." *Journal of Pragmatics 73*: 4–18.

Androutsopoulos, Jannis, and Michael Beißwenger. 2008. "Introduction: Data and Methods in Computer-Mediated Discourse Analysis." *Language@Internet 5*: Article 2. urn:nbn:de: 0009-7-16090.

Androutsopoulos, Jannis, and Kasper Juffermans. 2014. "Digital Language Practices in Superdiversity: Introduction. *Discourse, Context & Media 4–5*: 1–6.

Angouri, Jo, and Theodora Tseliga. 2010. "'You Have No Idea What You Are Talking about!' From E-Disagreement to E-Impoliteness in Two Online Fora." *Journal of Politeness Research 6*, no. 1: 57–82.

Antaki, Charles, Rebecca Barnes, and Ivan Leudar. 2005. "Diagnostic Formulations in Psychotherapy." *Discourse Studies 7*, no. 6: 627–647.

Applegate, Liz. 2016. "Four Easy Ways for Runners to Eat Clean." *Runner's World*, January 20. https://www.runnersworld.com/nutrition-weight-loss/a20860046/four-easy-ways-for-runners-to-eat-clean/.

Arminen, Ilkka. 2004. "Second Stories: The Salience of Interpersonal Communication for Mutual Help in Alcoholics Anonymous." *Journal of Pragmatics 36*, no. 2: 319–347.

Armstrong, Natalie, Nelya Koteyko, and John Powell. 2012. "'Oh Dear, Should I Really Be Saying That on There?': Issues of Identity and Authority in an Online Diabetes Community." *Health 16*, no. 4: 347–365.

Aronsson, Karin, and Lucas Gottzén. 2011. "Generational Positions at a Family Dinner: Food Morality and Social Order." *Language in Society 40*, no. 4: 405–426.

Axelsson, Ann-Sophie. 2010. "Perpetual and Personal: Swedish Young Adults and Their Use of Mobile Phones." *New Media & Society 12*, no. 1: 35–54.

Ba, Sulin, and Lei Wang. 2013. "Digital Health Communities: The Effect of Their Motivation Mechanisms." *Decision Support Systems 55*, no. 4: 941–947.

Backett-Milburn, Kathryn C., Wendy J. Wills, Mei-Li Roberts, and Julia Lawton. 2010. "Food, Eating and Taste: Parents' Perspectives on the Making of the Middle Class Teenager." *Social Science & Medicine 71*, no. 7: 1316–1323.

Bakhtin, Mikhail M. 1981. *The Dialogic Imagination: Four Essays*, translated by Caryl Emerson and Michael Holquist, edited by Michael Holquist. Austin: University of Texas Press.

Bakhtin, Mikhail M. 1984. *Problems of Dostoevsky's Poetics*, translated and edited by Caryl Emerson. Minneapolis: University of Minnesota Press.

Bakhtin, Mikhail M. 1986. "The Problem of Speech Genres." In *Speech Genres and Other Late Essays*, translated by Vern W. McGee, edited by Caryl Emerson and Michael Holquist, 60–102. Austin: University of Texas Press.

Bakhtin, Mikhail M., and Pavel Nikolaevich Medvedev. 1978. *The Formal Method in Literary Scholarship: A Critical Introduction to Sociological Poetics*, translated by Albert J. Wehrle. Baltimore and London: Johns Hopkins University Press.

Bamberg, Michael, and Alexandra Georgakopoulou. 2008. "Small Stories as a New Perspective in Narrative and Identity Analysis." *Text & Talk 28*, no. 3: 377–396.

Baron, Naomi S. 2008. *Always On: Language in an Online and Mobile World.* New York: Oxford University Press.

Baron, Naomi S., and Ylva Hård af Segerstad. 2010. "Cross-Cultural Patterns in Mobile Phone Use: Public Space and Reachability in Sweden, the USA and Japan." *New Media & Society 12*, no. 1: 13–34.

Bateman, John A. 2014. *Text and Image: A Critical Introduction to the Visual/Verbal Divide.* London and New York: Routledge.

Bateson, Gregory. 1972. *Steps to an Ecology of Mind.* New York: Ballantine.

Baxter, Leslie A. 2011. *Voicing Relationships: A Dialogic Perspective.* Los Angeles: Sage.

Baxter, Leslie A., and Larry A. Erbert. 1999. "Perceptions of Dialectical Contradictions in Turning Points of Development in Heterosexual Romantic Relationships." *Journal of Social and Personal Relationships 16*, no. 5: 547–569.

Baxter, Leslie A., and Barbara M. Montgomery. 1996. *Relating: Dialogues and Dialectics.* New York: The Guilford Press.

Baxter, Leslie A., and William M. Wilmot. 1985. Taboo Topics in Close Relationships. *Journal of Social and Personal Relationships 2*, no. 3: 253–269.

Bauman, Richard. 2004. *A World of Others' Words: Cross-Cultural Perspectives on Intertextuality.* Malden, MA: Blackwell.

Bauman, Richard, and Charles L. Briggs. 1990. "Poetics and Performances as Critical Perspectives on Language and Social Life." *Annual Review of Anthropology 19*, no.1: 59–88.

Baym, Nancy K. 1996. "Agreements and Disagreements in Computer-Mediated Discussion." *Research on Language and Social Interaction 29*, no. 4: 315–345.

Beach, Wayne A. 1993. "Transitional Regularities for 'Casual' 'Okay' Usages." *Journal of Pragmatics 19*, no. 4: 325–352.

Beach, Wayne A., and Phyllis Japp. 1983. "Storifying as Time-Traveling: The Knowledgeable Use of Temporally Structured Discourse." In *Communication Yearbook VIII*, ed. Robert N. Bostrom, 867–888. New Brunswick, NJ: Transaction Books-ICA.

Becker, A. L. 1994. "Repetition and Otherness: An Essay." In *Repetition in Discourse: Interdisciplinary Perspectives*, vol. 2, edited by Barbara Johnstone, 162–175. Norwood, NJ: Ablex.

Becker, A. L. 1995. *Beyond Translation: Essays towards a Modern Philology.* Ann Arbor: University of Michigan Press.

Berger, John. 1972. *Ways of Seeing.* London: Penguin.

Blommaert, Jan. 2019. "From to Groups to Actions and Back in Online-Offline Sociolinguistics." *Multilingua 38*, no. 4: 485–493.

Blum-Kulka, Shoshana. 1997. *Dinner Talk: Cultural Patterns of Sociability and Socialization in Family Discourse.* Mahwah, NJ: Lawrence Erlbaum.

Boczkowski, Pablo J., Mora Matassi, and Eugenia Mitchelstein. 2018. "How Young Users Deal with Multiple Platforms: The Role of Meaning-Making in Social Media Repertoires." *Journal of Computer-Mediated Communication 23*: 245–259.

Bogetić, Ksenija. 2016. "'Metalinguistic Comments in Teenage Personal Blogs': Bringing Youth Voices to Studies of Youth, Language and Technology." *Text & Talk 36*, no. 3: 245–268.

Bolander, Brook, and Miriam A. Locher. 2020. "Beyond the Online Offline Distinction: Entry Points to Digital Discourse. *Discourse, Context & Media 35* (100383). https://doi.org/10.1016/j.dcm.2020.100383.

Boromisza-Habashi, David. 2013. *Speaking Hatefully: Culture, Communication, and Political Action in Hungary.* College Station: Pennsylvania State University Press.

Boromisza-Habashi, David. 2016. "What We Need Is Good Communication: Vernacular Globalization in Some Hungarian Speech." *International Journal of Communication* 10: 4600–4619.

Boromisza-Habashi, David, and Russell M. Parks. 2014. "The Communal Function of Social Interaction on an Online Academic Newsgroup." *Western Journal of Communication 78*, no. 2: 194–212.

Bourlai, Elli, and Susan Herring. 2014. "Multimodal Communication on Tumblr: 'I Have So Many Feels!'" In *Proceedings of the 2014 ACM Conference on Web Science*, 171–175. New York: ACM. https://doi.org/10.1145/2615569.2615697

Bova, Antonio, and Francesco Arcidiacono. 2014. "'You Must Eat the Salad because It Is Nutritious.' Argumentative Strategies Adopted by Parents and Children in Food-Related Discussions at Mealtimes." *Appetite 73*: 81–94.

Briggs, Charles L., and Richard Bauman. 1992. "Genre, Intertextuality, and Social Power." *Journal of Linguistic Anthropology 2*, no. 2: 131–172.

Brown, Penelope, and Stephen Levinson. (1978) 1987. *Politeness*. Cambridge: Cambridge University Press.

Bryant, Erin M., Jennifer Marmo, and Artemio Ramirez Jr. 2011. "A Functional Approach to Social Networking Sites." In *Computer-Mediated Communication in Personal Relationships*, edited Kevin B. Wright and Lynne M. Webb, 3–20. New York: Peter Lang.

Bryfonski, Lara, and Cristina Sanz. 2018. "Opportunities for Corrective Feedback during Study Abroad: A Mixed Methods Approach." *Annual Review of Applied Linguistics 38*: 1–32.

Bucholtz, Mary. 1999. "Why Be Normal?': Language and Identity Practices in a Community of Nerd Girls. *Language in Society 28*, no. 2: 202–233.

Buttny, Richard. 1996. "Clients' and Therapist's Joint Construction of the Client's Problems." *Research on Language and Social Interaction 29*, no. 2: 125–153.

Buttny, Richard. 2010. "Citizen Participation, Metadiscourse, and Accountability: A Public Hearing on a Zoning Change for Wal-Mart." *Journal of Communication 60*, no. 4, 636–659.

Buttny, Richard, and Jodi R. Cohen. 2007. "Drawing on the Words of Others at Public Hearings: Zoning, Wal-Mart, and the Threat to the Aquifer." *Language in Society 36*, no. 5: 735–756.

Buttny, Richard, and Azirah Hashim. 2015. "Dialogue on '1 Malaysia': The Uses of Metadiscourse in Ethnopolitical Accounting." *Discourse & Society 26*, no. 2: 147–164.

Campbell, Scott W. 2007. "A Cross-Cultural Comparison of Perceptions and Uses of Mobile Phone Telephony." *New Media & Society 9*, no. 2: 343–363.

Campbell, Scott W. 2008. "Social Implications of Mobile Telephony: The Rise of Personal Communication Society." *Sociology Compass 2*, no. 2: 371–387.

Cameron, Deborah. 1995. *Verbal Hygiene*. London: Routledge.

Cameron, Deborah. 2000. *Good to Talk? Living and Working in a Communication Culture*. London: Sage.

Cameron, Deborah. 2004. "Out of the Bottle: The Social Life of Metalanguage." In *Metalanguage: Social and Ideological Perspectives*, edited by Adam Jaworski, Nikolas Coupland, and Dariusz Galasiński, 311–321. Berlin and New York: Mouton de Gruyter.

Carbaugh, Donal. 1989. "Fifty Terms for Talk: A Cross-Cultural Study." In *International and Intercultural Communication Annual: Language, Communication, and Culture,* edited by Stella Ting-Toomey and Felipe Korzenny, 93–120. Thousand Oaks, CA: Sage.

Carbaugh, Donal. 1989/1990. "The Critical Voice in Ethnography of Communication Research." *Research on Language in Social Interaction* 23: 261–282.

Carbaugh, Donal. 1996. *Situating Selves: The Communication of Social Identities in American Scenes*. Albany: State University of New York Press.

Carbaugh, Donal. 2005. *Cultures in Conversation*. Mahwah, NJ: Lawrence Erlbaum Associates.

Carbaugh, Donal. 2007. "Cultural Discourse Analysis: Communication Practices and Intercultural Encounters." *Journal of Intercultural Communication Research 36*, no. 3: 167–182.

Caronia, Letizia, and André H. Caron. 2004. "Constructing a Specific Culture: Young People's Use of the Mobile Phone as a Social Performance." *Convergence 10*, no. 2: 28–61.

Carrington, Victoria. 2015. "'It's Changed My Life': iPhone as Technological Artefact. In *Discourse and Digital Practice: Doing Discourse Analysis in the Digital Age*, edited by Rodney H. Jones, Alice Chik, and Christoph A. Hafner, 158–174. New York: Routledge.

Castor, Theresa, and Mariaelena Bartesaghi. 2016. "Metacommunication during Disaster Response: 'Reporting' and the Constitution of Problems in Hurricane Katrina Teleconferences." *Management Communication Quarterly 30*, no. 4: 472–502.

Cazden, Courtney B. 1976. "Play with Language and Meta-Linguistic Awareness: One Dimension of Language Experience." In *Play: Its Role in Development and Evolution*, edited by Jerome S. Bruner, 603–608. New York: Penguin.

Choe, Hanwool. 2019. "Eating Together Multimodally: Collaborative Eating in *Mukbang*, a Korean Livestream of Eating." *Language in Society 48*, no. 2: 171–208.

Choe, Hanwool. 2020. *Instant Messaging in Korean Families: Creating Family through the Interplay of Photos, Videos, and Text*. PhD diss., Georgetown University, Washington, DC.

Chouliaraki, Lilie, and Norman Fairclough. 1999. *Discourse in Late Modernity: Rethinking Critical Discourse Analysis*. Edinburgh: Edinburgh University Press.

Chui, Kawai. 1996. "Organization of Repair in Chinese." *Text & Talk 16*, no. 3: 343–372.

Cinquergrani, Chelsea, and David H. K. Brown. 2018. "'Wellness' Lifts Us above the Food Chaos": A Narrative Exploration of the Experiences and Conceptualisations of Orthorexia Nervosa through Online Social Media Forums." *Qualitative Research in Sport, Exercise and Health 10*, no. 5: 585–603.

Collister, Lauren B. 2011. "*-Repair in Online Discourse." *Journal of Pragmatics 43*, no. 3: 918–921.Coupland, Justine, and Nikolas Coupland. 2009. "Attributing Stance in Discourses of Body Shape and Weight Loss." In *Stance: Sociolinguistic Perspectives*, edited by Alexandra Jaffe, 227–249. New York: Oxford University Press.

Coupland, Nikolas. 2004. "Stylised Deception." In *Metalanguage: Social and Ideological Perspectives*, edited by Adam Jaworski, Nikolas Coupland, and Dariusz Galasiński, 249–274. Berlin and New York: Mouton de Gruyter.

Coupland, Justine, and Nikolas Coupland. 2009. "Attributing Stance in Discourses of Body Shape and Weight Loss." In *Stance: Sociolinguistic Perspectives*, edited by Alexandra Jaffe, 227–250. New York: Oxford University Press.

Coupland, Nikolas, and Adam Jaworski. 2004. "Sociolinguistic Perspectives on Metalanguage: Reflexivity, Evaluation and Ideology." In *Metalanguage: Social and Ideological Perspectives*, edited by Adam Jaworski, Nikolas Coupland, and Dariusz Galasiński, 15–51. Berlin and New York: Mouton de Gruyter.

Craig, Robert T. 1999. "Metadiscourse, Theory, and Practice." *Research on Language in Social Interaction 32*, nos. 1&2: 21–29.

Craig, Robert T. 2005. "How We Talk about How We Talk: Communication Theory in the Public Interest." *Journal of Communication 55*, no. 4: 695–667.

Dabaja, Ali. 2019. "How to Talk to Your Doctor about Awkward Men's Health Issues." *The Detroit News*, June 17, 2019. https://www.detroitnews.com/story/sponsor-story/henry-ford-health-system/2019/06/17/how-talk-your-doctor-awkward-mens-health-issues/1423525001/.

Danesi, Marcel. 2017. *The Semiotics of Emoji: The Rise of Visual Language in the Age of the Internet*. London: Bloomsbury.

Darics, Erika. 2010. "Politeness in Computer-Mediated Discourse of a Virtual Team." *Journal of Politeness Research 6*, no. 1: 129–150.

Dawkins, Richard. 1976. *The Selfish Gene*. Oxford: Oxford University Press.

Demjén, Zsófia. 2018. "Complexity Theory and Conversational Humour: Tracing the Birth and Decline of a Running Joke in an Online Cancer Support Community." *Journal of Pragmatics 133*: 93–104

Deumert, Ana. 2014. *Sociolinguistics and Mobile Communication*. Edinburgh: Edinburgh University Press.

DiDomenico, Stephen M., and Jeffrey Boase. 2013. "Bringing Mobiles into the Conversation: Applying a Conversation Analytic Approach to the Study of Mobiles in Co-Present Interaction." In *Discourse 2.0: Language and New Media*, edited by Deborah Tannen and Anna Marie Trester, 119–132. Georgetown, Washington, DC: Georgetown University Press.

Dings, Abby. 2012. "Native Speaker/Nonnative Speaker Interaction and Orientation to Expert/Novice Identity." *Journal of Pragmatics 44*, no. 11: 1503–1518.

Dippold, Doris. 2014. "'That's Wrong': Repair and Rapport in Culturally Diverse Higher Education Classrooms." *The Modern Language Journal 98*, no. 1: 402–416.

Dori-Hacohen, Gonen, and Nimrod Shavit. 2013. "The Cultural Meanings of Israli Tokbek (Talk-Back Online Commenting) and Their Relevance to the Online Democratic Public Sphere." *International Journal of Electronic Governance 6*, no. 4: 361–379.

Dresner, Eli, and Susan C. Herring. 2010. "Functions of the Nonverbal in CMC: Emoticons and Illocutionary Force." *Communication Theory 20*, no. 3: 249–268.

Drew, Paul. 1997. "'Open' Class Repair Initiators in Response to Sequential Sources of Troubles in Conversation." *Journal of Pragmatics 28*: 69–101.

Durrington, Vance A., and Chien Yu. 2004. "It's the Same Only Different: The Effect the Discussion Moderator has on Student Participation in Online Class Discussions." *The Quarterly Review of Distance Education 5*, no. 2: 89–100.

Dynel, Marta. 2016. 'I Has Seen Image Macros!' Animal Advice Memes as Visual-Verbal Jokes." *International Journal of Communication 10*: 660–688.

Eckert, Penelope. 2006. "Communities of Practice." In *Encyclopedia of Language and Linguistics*, 2nd edition, edited by Keith Brown, 683–685. Amsterdam: Elsevier.

Eckert, Penelope, and Sally McConnell-Ginet. 1992. "Think Practically and Look Locally: Language and Gender as Community-Based Practice." *Annual Review of Anthropology 21*, 461–490.

Egbert, Maria M. 1997. "Some Interactional Achievements of Other-Initiated Repair in Multiperson Conversation." *Journal of Pragmatics 27*, no. 5: 611–634.

Ehrlich, Susan. 2021. "Semiotic Ideologies and Trial Discourse: Implications for Multimodal Discourse Analysis." In *Approaches to Discourse Analysis*, edited by Cynthia Gordon, 123–135. Washington, DC: Georgetown University Press.

Erickson, Frederick. 1986. "Listening and Speaking." In *Languages and Linguistics: The Interdependence of Theory, Data, and Application*, edited by Deborah Tannen and James E. Alatis, 294–319. Washington, DC: Georgetown University Press.

Erickson, Frederick. 2004. *Talk and Social Theory: Ecologies of Speaking and Listening in Everyday Life*. Cambridge: Polity Press.

Fägersten, Kristy Beers. 2012. "Intertextual Quotation: References to Media in Family Interaction." In *The Appropriation of Media in Everyday Life*, edited by Ruth Ayaß and Cornelia Gerhardt, 79–104. Amsterdam and Philadelphia: John Benjamins.

Fairclough, Norman. 1992. *Discourse and Social Change*. Cambridge: Polity Press.

Feenberg, Andrew. 1989. "The Written World: On the Theory and Practice of Computer Conferencing." In *Mindweave: Communication, Computers, and Distance Education*, edited by Robin Mason and Anthony Kaye, 22–39. Oxford: Pergamon Press.

Finn, Jerry. 1999. "An Exploration of Helping Processes in an Online Self-Help Group Focusing on Issues of Disabilities." *Health & Social Work 24*, no. 3: 220–231.

Fitch, Kristine. 1991. "The Interplay of Linguistic Universals and Cultural Knowledge in Personal Address: Columbian *Madre* Terms." *Communication Monographs 58*, no. 3: 254–272.

Fitch, Kristine. 1998. *Speaking Relationally: Cultural, Communication and Interpersonal Connection*. New York: Guilford Press.

Forgays, Deborah Kirby, Ira Hyman, and Jessie Schreiber. 2014. "Texting Everywhere for Everything: Gender and Age Differences in Cell Phone Etiquette and Use." *Computers in Human Behavior 31*: 314–321.

franzke, aline shakti, Anja Bechmann, Michael Zimmer, Charles Ess, and the Association of Internet Researchers. 2020. Internet Research: Ethical Guidelines 3.0. https://aoir.org/reports/ethics3.pdf.

Fryer, Daniel Lees. 2021. "#AllCatsAreBeautiful: Ambient Affiliation and the Visual-Verbal Representation and Appreciation of Cats in Online Subversive Discourses. *Discourse & Society 33*, no. 1: 3–33. https://journals.sagepub.com/doi/pdf/10.1177/09579265211048727.

Fuller, Janet M., Janelle Briggs, and Laurel Dillon-Sumner. 2013. "Discourses about Food and Gender in *Men's Health* and *Women's Health* Magazines." In *Culinary Linguistics: The Chef's Special*, edited by Cornelia Gerhardt, Maximiliane Frobenius, and Susanne Ley, 261–280. Amsterdam/Philadelphia: John Benjamins.

Gailey, Jeannine A. 2021. "The Violence of Fat Hatred in the 'Obesity Epidemic' Discourse." *Humanity and Society*. https://doi.org/10.1177/0160597621995501.

Garfinkel, Harold, and Harvey Sacks. 1970. "On Formal Structures of Practical Actions." In *Theoretical Sociology; Perspectives and Developments*, edited by John C. McKinney and Edward A. Tiryakian, 337–366. New York: Appleton-Century-Crofts.

Gavin, Jeff, Karen Rodham, and Helen Poyer. 2008. "The Presentation of 'Pro-Anorexia' in Online Group Interactions." *Qualitative Health Research 18*, no. 3: 325–333.

Georgakopoulou, Alexandra. 2006. Postscript: Computer-Mediated Communication in Sociolinguistics. *Journal of Sociolinguistics 10*, no. 4: 458–557.

Georgakopoulou, Alexandra. 2007. *Small Stories, Interaction and Identities*. Amsterdam: John Benjamins.

Georgakopoulou, Alexandra. 2011. "'On for Drinkies?': Email Cues of Participant Alignments." Language@internet 8: Article 4. https://nbn-resolving.de/urn:nbn:de:0009-7-32155.

Gershon, Ilana. 2010. *The Breakup 2.0: Disconnecting over New Media*. Ithaca, NY: Cornell University Press.

Giaxoglu, Korina. 2017. "Story Leaks for Sharing: The Case of Leaking the 'Moscovici Draft' on Twitter." *Discourse, Context & Media 19*: 22–33

Gibson, James J. 1979. *The Ecological Approach to Visual Perception*. London: Houghton Mifflin.

Gillison, Samantha. 2018. "'Clean Eating' Has Become Such a Sham that Fast Food Chains Are Pushing It." *Think: Opinion, Analysis, Essays*. Accessed August 8, 2019. https://www.nbcnews.com/think/opinion/clean-eating-has-become-such-sham-fast-food-chains-are-ncna845081.

Goffman, Erving. 1955. "On Face-Work: An Analysis of Ritual Elements in Social Interaction." *Psychiatry: Journal for the Study of Interpersonal Processes 18*: 213–231.

Goffman, Erving. 1963. *Behavior in Public Places: Notes on the Social Organization of Gatherings*. New York: Free Press.

Goffman, Erving. 1967. *Interaction Ritual: Essays on Face-to-Face Behavior*. New York: Pantheon.

Goffman, Erving. 1974. *Frame Analysis: An Essay on the Organization of Experience*. Cambridge, MA: Harvard University Press.

Goffman, Erving. 1981. "Footing." Chapter 3 in *Forms of Talk*, 124–159. Philadelphia: University of Pennsylvania Press.

Goodwin, Charles. 1986. "Audience Diversity, Participation and Interpretation." *Text 6*, no. 3: 283–316.

Goodwin, Charles. 2018. *Co-Operative Action*. Cambridge: Cambridge University Press.

Goodwin, Marjorie Harness. 1983. "Aggravated Correction and Disagreement in Children's Conversations." *Journal of Pragmatics 7*: 657–677.

Goodwin, Marjorie H. 1990. *He-Said-She-Said: Talk as Social Organization among Black Children*. Bloomington: Indiana University Press.

Gordon, Cynthia. 2002. "'I'm Mommy and You're Natalie': Role-Reversal and Embedded Frames in Mother-Child Discourse." *Language in Society 31*, no. 5: 679–720.

Gordon, Cynthia. 2005. "Hypothetical Narratives and 'Trying on' the Identity of 'Big Sister' in Parent-Child Discourse." In *Language in Use: Cognitive and Discourse Perspectives on Language and Language Learning*, edited by Andrea Tyler, Mari Takada, Yiyoung Kim, and Diana Marinova, 191–201. Washington, DC: Georgetown University Press.

Gordon, Cynthia. 2006. "Reshaping Prior Text, Reshaping Identities." *Text & Talk 26*, nos. 4–5: 545–571.

Gordon, Cynthia. 2008. "A(p)parent Play: Blending Frames and Reframing in Family Talk." *Language in Society 37*, no. 3: 319–49

Gordon, Cynthia. 2009. *Making Meanings, Creating Family: Intertextuality and Framing in Family Interaction*. New York: Oxford University Press.

Gordon, Cynthia. 2011. "Impression Management on Reality TV: Emotion in Parental Accounts." *Journal of Pragmatics 43*, no. 14: 3551–3564.

Gordon, Cynthia. 2013a. "Beyond the Observer's Paradox: The Audio-Recorder as a Resource for the Display of Identity." *Qualitative Research 13*, no. 3: 299–317.

Gordon, Cynthia. 2013b. "'You Are Killing Your Kids': Framing and Impoliteness in a Health Makeover Reality TV Show." In *Real Talk: Reality Television and Discourse Analysis in Action*, edited by Nuria Lorenzo-Dus and Pilar Garcés-Conejos Blitvich, 245–265. London: Palgrave Macmillan.

Gordon, Cynthia. 2015a. "'I Would Suggest You Tell This ^^^ to Your Doctor': Online Narrative Problem-Solving Regarding Face-to-Face Doctor-Patient Interaction about Body Weight." In *Narrative Matters in Medical Contexts across Disciplines*, edited by Franziska Gygax and Miriam A. Locher, 117–140. Amsterdam: John Benjamins.

Gordon, Cynthia. 2015b. "'We Were Introduced to Foods I Never Even Heard of': Parents as Consumers on Reality TV." In *The Motherhood Business: Consumption, Communication and Privilege*, edited by Anne Teresa Demo, Jennifer L. Borda, and Charlotte H. Krøløkke, 95–120. Tuscaloosa: University of Alabama Press.

Gordon, Cynthia. 2019. "'You Might Want to Look Up the Definition of 'Continental Breakfast'": Other-Initiated Repair and Community-Building in Health and Weight Loss Blogs. *Multilingua 38*, no. 4: 401–426.

Gordon, Cynthia, and Ho Fai Cheng. 2017. "'Our Society Is Definitely Expecting Large Portions Nowadays': Negotiating Accountability for American Obesity in an Online Discussion Thread." (unpublished manuscript).

Gordon, Cynthia, and Didem İkizoğlu. 2017. "'Asking for Another' Online: Membership Categorization and Identity Construction on a Food and Nutrition Discussion Board." *Discourse Studies 19*, no. 3: 253–271.

Gordon, Cynthia, and Melissa Luke. 2013. "Re- and Pre-Authoring Experiences in Email Supervision: Creating and Revising Professional Meanings in an Asynchronous Medium." In *Discourse 2.0: Language and New Media*, edited by Deborah Tannen and Anna Marie Trester, 167–181. Washington, DC: Georgetown University Press.

Gordon, Cynthia, and Melissa Luke. 2016. "Metadiscourse in Group Supervision: How School Counselors-in-Training Construct Their Transitional Professional Identities." *Discourse Studies 18*, no. 1: 25–43.

Gordon, Cynthia, and Deborah Tannen (2021). "Interactional Sociolinguistics: Foundations, Developments, and Applications to Language, Gender, and Sexuality." In *The Routledge Handbook of Language, Gender and Sexuality*, edited by Jo Angouri and Judith Baxter, 181–196. London and New York: Routledge.

Gordon, Cynthia, Ellen Barton, Kathleen L. Meert, Susan Eggly, Murray Pollack, Jerry Zimmerman, K. J. S. Anand, Joseph Carcillo, Christopher J. L. Newth, J. Michael Dean, Douglas F. Willson, Carol Nicholson, and Eunice Kennedy Shriver National Institute of Child Health and Human Development Collaborative Pediatric Critical Care Research Network. 2009. "Accounting for Medical Communication: Parents' Perceptions of Communicative Roles and Responsibilities in the Pediatric Intensive Care Unit." *Communication & Medicine 6*, no. 2: 177–188.

Gordon, Cynthia, Najma Al Zidjaly, and Alla V. Tovares. 2017. "Mobile Phones as Cultural Tools for Identity Construction among College Students in Oman, Ukraine, and the U.S." *Discourse, Context & Media 17*: 9–19.

Graham, Sage. 2007. "Disagreeing to Agree: Conflict, (Im)politeness and Identity in a Computer-Mediated Community." *Journal of Pragmatics 39*, no. 4: 742–759.

Graham, Sage L. 2019. "'A Wink and a Nod': The Role of Emojis in Forming Digital Communities. *Multilingua 38*, no. 4: 377–400.

Graham, Sage L., and Scott Dutt. 2019. "'Watch the Potty Mouth': Negotiating Impoliteness in Online Gaming." In *Approaches to Videogame Discourse: Lexis, Interaction, Textuality*, edited by Astrid Ensslin and Isabel Balteiro, 201–223. London and New York: Bloomsbury.

Grice, H. Paul. 1975. "Logic and Conversation." In *Syntax and Semantics, vol. 3*, edited by Peter Cole and Jerry L. Morgan, 41–58. New York: Academic Press.

Gumperz, John J. 1982. *Discourse Strategies*. Cambridge: Cambridge University Press.

Gumperz, John J. 2009. "The Speech Community." In *Linguistic Anthropology: A Reader* (second edition), edited by Alessandro Duranti, 66–73. Malden, MA: Blackwell. (Originally published in *International Encyclopedia of the Social Sciences*. New York: Macmillan, 1968: 381–386.)

Gumperz, John. 2015. "Interactional Sociolinguistics: A Personal Perspective." In *The Handbook of Discourse Analysis*, edited by Deborah Tannen, Heidi E. Hamilton, and Deborah Schiffrin, 309–323. Chichester, UK: Wiley Blackwell.

Gürsimsek, Ödül Akyapi. 2016. "Animated GIFs as Vernacular Design: Producing Tumblr Blogs." *Visual Communication* 15(3): 329–349.

Guthman, Julie. 2011. *Obesity, Food Justice, and the Limits of Capitalism*. Berkeley and Los Angeles: University of California Press.

Gutzmann, Daniel, and Erik Stei. 2011. "How Quotation Marks What People Do with Words." *Journal of Pragmatics* 43, no. 10: 2650–2663.

Hall, Kira. 2005. "Intertextual Sexuality: Parodies of Class, Identity, and Desire in Liminal Delhi." *Journal of Linguistic Anthropology* 15, no. 1: 125–144.

Halliday, M. A. K. 1978. *Language as Social Semiotic: The Social Interpretation of Language and Meaning*. London: Edward Arnold.

Halliday, Michael A. K., and Ruqaiya Hasan. 1976. *Cohesion in English*. London: Longman.

Hamilton, Heidi E. 1998. "Reported Speech and Survivor Identity in On-Line Bone Marrow Transplantation Narratives." *Journal of Sociolinguistics* 2, no. 1: 53–67.

Hamilton, Heidi E. 2003. "Patients' Voices in the Medical World: An Exploration of Accounts of Noncompliance." In *Linguistics, Language, and the Real World: Discourse and Beyond*, edited by Deborah Tannen and James E Alatis, 147–165. Washington, DC: Georgetown University Press.

Hamilton, Heidi E. 2004. "Symptoms and Signs in Particular: The Influence of the Medical Concern on the Shape of Physician-Patient Talk" *Communication and Medicine* 1, no. 1: 59–70.

Hanks, William F. 1993. "Metalanguage and Pragmatics of Deixis." In *Reflexive Language: Reported Speech and Metapragmatics*, edited by John A. Lucy, 127–158. New York: Cambridge University Press.

Harrison, Sandra, and Julie Barlow. 2009. "Politeness Strategies and Advice-Giving in an Online Arthritis Workshop." *Journal of Politeness Research* 5, no. 1: 93–111.

Haugh, Michael, and Wei-Lin Melody Chang. 2015. "Troubles Talk, (Dis)affiliation, and the Participation Order in Taiwanese-Chinese Online Discussion Boards." In *Participation in Public and Social Media Interactions*, edited by Marta Dynel and Jan Chovanec, 99–133. Philadelphia/Amsterdam: John Benjamins.

Heritage, John. 2021. "How Linguistic Anthropologists Conceptualize Relations among Different Forms of Discourse." In *Approaches to Discourse Analysis*, edited by Cynthia Gordon, 104–122. Washington, DC: Georgetown University Press.

Herring, Susan. 1994. "Politeness in Computer Culture: Why Women Thank and Men Flame." In Cultural Performances: Proceedings of the Third Berkeley Women and Language Conference, edited by Mary Bucholtz, A. C. Liang, Laurel A. Sutton, and Caitlin Hines, 278-294. Berkeley, CA: Berkeley Women and Language Group.

Herring, Susan C. 1999. "Interactional Coherence in CMC." *Journal of Computer-Mediated Communication 4*, no. 4: 0–0. https://doi.org/10.1111/j.1083-6101.1999.tb00106.x

Herring, Susan C. 2004. "Computer-Mediated Discourse Analysis: An Approach to Researching Online Communities. In *Designing for Virtual Communities in the Service of Learning*, edited by Sasha A. Barab, Rob Kling, and James H. Gray, 338–376. Cambridge: Cambridge University Press.

Herring, Susan C. 2013. "Discourse in Web 2.0: Familiar, Reconfigured, and Emergent." In *Discourse 2.0: Language and New Media*, edited by Deborah Tannen and Anna Marie Trester, 1–25. Washington, DC: Georgetown University Press.

Herring, Susan C., and Jannis Androutsopoulos. 2015. "Computer-Mediated Discourse 2.0." In *The Handbook of Discourse Analysis*, edited by Deborah Tannen, Heidi E. Hamilton, and Deborah Schiffrin, 127–151. Chichester, UK: Wiley Blackwell.

Hill, Jane. 2005. "Intertextuality as Source and Evidence for Indirect Indexical Meanings." *Journal of Linguistic Anthropology 15*, no. 1: 113–124.

Ho, Victor. 2011. "What Functions Do Intertextuality and Interdiscursivity Serve in Request E-Mail Discourse?" *Journal of Pragmatics 43*, no. 3: 2253–2261.

Ho, Victor. 2018. "Using Metadiscourse in Making Persuasive Attempts through Workplace Request Emails." *Journal of Pragmatics 134*: 70–81.

Hockett, Charles F. 1958. *A Course in Modern Linguistics*. New York: Macmillan.

Hodges, Adam. 2011. *The "War on Terror" Narrative*. New York: Oxford University Press.

Hodsdon-Champeon, Connie. 2010. "Conversations within Conversations." Language@ Internet 7: Article 10. urn:nbn:de: 0009-7-28206, ISSN 1860-2029.

Hosoda, Yuri. 2000. "Other-Repair in Japanese Conversations between Nonnative and Native Speakers." *Issues in Applied Linguistics 11*, no. 1: 39–63.

Hosoda, Yuri. 2001. "Conditions for Other-Repair in NS/NNS Conversation." *The Language Teacher 25*(11): 29–31.

Howard, Kathryn M. 2009. "Breaking in and Spinning Out: Repetition and Decalibration in Thai Children's Play Genres." *Language in Society 38*, no. 3: 339–363.

Hübler, Axel, and Wolfram Bublitz. 2007a. "Introducing Metapragmatics in Use." In *Metapragmatics in Use*, edited by Wolfram Bublitz and Axel Hübler, 1–26. Amsterdam: John Benjamins.

Hübler, Axel, and Wolfram Bublit, eds. 2007b. *Metapragmatics in Use*. Amsterdam: John Benjamins.

Hugo, Victor. 1862. *Les Misérables*. New York: Carleton.

Hutchby Ian. 2001. *Conversation and Technology: From the Telephone to the Internet*. Cambridge: Polity Press.

Hyland, Ken. 1998. "Persuasion and Context: The Pragmatics of Academic Metadiscourse." *Journal of Pragmatics 30*, no. 4: 437–455.

Hyland, Ken. 2005. *Metadiscourse: Exploring Interaction in Writing*. London/New York: Continuum.

Hyland, Ken. 2017. "Metadiscourse: What Is It and Where Is It Going?" *Journal of Pragmatics 113*: 16–29.

Hymes, Dell. 1972. "Models of the Interaction of Language and Social Life." In *Directions in Sociolinguistics: The Ethnography of Communication*, edited by John J. Gumperz and Dell Hymes, 35–71. New York: Holt, Rinehart and Winston.

Ifantidou, Elly. 2005. "The Semantics and Pragmatics of Metadiscourse." *Journal of Pragmatics 37*: 1325–1353.

İkizoğlu, Didem. 2019. "'What Did It Say?': Mobile Phone Translation App as Participant and Object in Family Discourse." *Journal of Pragmatics 147*: 1–16.

İkizoğlu, Didem. 2021. *Agency and Participation in Multilingual Family Interaction*. PhD diss., Georgetown University, Washington, DC.

İkizoğlu, Didem, and Cynthia Gordon. 2020. "'Vegetables as a Chore': Constructing and Problematizing a "Picky Eater" Identity Online." In *Identity and Ideology in Digital Food Discourse*, edited by Alla Tovares and Cynthia Gordon, 13–32. London and New York: Bloomsbury.

Inoue, Miyako. 2003. "Speech without a Speaking Body: 'Japanese Women's Language' in Translation." *Language & Communication 23*, no. 3: 315–330.

Jackson, Cathy, and Carol Gray. 2005. "The Dog's Too Fat and so Is the Client: How to Handle Delicate Consultations." *In Practice 27*, no. 4: 219–221.

Jager, Margot, and Wyke Stommel. 2017. "The Risk of Metacommunication to Manage Interactional Trouble in Online Chat Counseling." *Linguistik Online 87*, no. 8: 191–212.

Jakobson, Roman. 1960. "Closing Statement: Linguistics and Politics." In *Style in Language*, edited by Thomas A. Sebok, 350–377. Cambridge, MA: MIT Press.

Jaworski, Adam, Nikolas Coupland, and Dariusz Galasiński, eds. 2004a. *Metalanguage: Social and Ideological Perspectives*. Berlin and New York: Mouton de Gruyter.

Jaworski, Adam, Nikolas Coupland, and Dariusz Galasiński. 2004b. "Metalanguage: Why Now?" In *Metalanguage: Social and Ideological Perspectives*, edited by Adam Jaworski, Nikolas Coupland, and Dariusz Galasiński, 3–8. Berlin and New York: Mouton de Gruyter.

Jaworski, Adam, and Dariusz Galasiński. 2002. "The Verbal Construction of Non-Verbal Behaviour: British Press Reports of President Clinton's Grand Jury Testimony Video." *Discourse & Society 13*(5): 629–648.

Jaworski, Adam, and Itesh Sachdev. 2004. "Beliefs about Silence in the Classroom." *Language and Education 12*(4): 273–292.

Jaworski, Adam, and Crispin Thurlow. 2009. "Taking an Elitist Stance: Ideology and Discursive Production of Social Distinction." In *Stance: Sociolinguistic Perspectives*, edited by Alexandra Jaffe, 195–226. New York: Oxford University Press.

Jaworski, Adam, Crispin Thurlow, Sarah Lawson, and Virpi Ylänn-McEwen. 2003. "The Uses and Representations of Local Languages in Tourist Destinations: A View from British TV Holiday Programmes." *Language Awareness 12*, no. 1: 5–29.

Jefferson, Gail. 1974. "Error Correction as an Interactional Resource." *Language in Society 3*: 181–199.

Jefferson, Gail. 1987. "On Exposed and Embedded Correction in Conversation." In *Talk and Social Organization*, edited by Graham Button and John R. E. Lee, 86–100. Clevedon, UK: Multilingual Matters.

Johnstone, Barbara. 1997. "'He Says . . . so I Said': Verb Tense Alternation and Narrative Depictions of Authority in American English." *Linguistics 25*: 33–52.

Johnstone, Barbara, et al. 1994. "Repetition in Discourse: A Dialogue." In *Repetition in Discourse: Interdisciplinary Perspectives,* edited by Barbara Johnstone, 1–20. Norwood, NJ: Ablex Publishing Corporation.

Jones, Graham H., Bambi B. Schieffelin, and Rachel E. Smith. 2011. "When Friends Who Talk Together Stalk Together: Online Gossip as Metacommunication." In *Digital Discourse: Language in the New Media*, edited by Crispin Thurlow and Kristine Mroczek, 26–47. New York: Oxford University Press.

Jones, Rodney H. 2004. "The Problem of Context in Computer-Mediated Communication." In *Discourse and Technology: Multimodal Discourse Analysis*, edited by Philip LeVine and Ron Scollon, 22–33. Washington, DC: Georgetown University Press.

Jones, Rodney H. 2009. "Dancing, Skating and Sex: Action and Text in the Digital Age." *Journal of Applied Linguistics and Professional Practice* 6(3): 283–302.

Jones, Rodney H., Alice Chick, and Christoph A. Hafner, eds. 2015. *Discourse and Digital Practices: Doing Discourse Analysis in the Digital Age*. New York: Routledge.

Kahan, Scott I. 2018. "Practical Strategies for Engaging Individuals with Obesity in Primary Care." *Mayo Clinic Proceedings 93*, no. 3: 351–359.

Karrebæk, Martha Sif. 2012. "'What's in Your Lunch Box Today?': Health, Respectability, and Ethnicity in the Primary Classroom." *Journal of Linguistic Anthropology 22*, no. 1: 1–22.

Kasper, Gabriele. 1985. "Repair in Foreign Language Teaching. *Studies in Second Language Acquisition 7*: 200–215.

Kasper, Gabriele, and Matthew T. Prior. 2015. "'*You Said That?*': Other-Initiations of Repair Addressed to Represented Talk." *Text & Talk 35*, no. 6: 815–844.

Katriel, Tamar. 1986. *Talking Straight: Dugri Speech in Israeli Sabra Culture*. Cambridge: Cambridge University Press.

Katriel, Tamar. 1999. "Rethinking the Terms of Social Interaction." *Research on Language and Social Interaction 32*, nos. 1–2: 95–101.

Katriel, Tamar. 2004. *Dialogic Moments: From Soul Talks to Talk Radio in Israeli Culture*. Detroit: Wayne State University Press.

Katriel, Tamar, and Gerry Philipsen. 1981. "'What We Need Is Communication': 'Communication' as a Cultural Category in Some American Speech." *Communication Monographs 48*, no. 4: 301–317.

Katz, James E., and Mark Aakhus, eds. 2002. *Perpetual Contact: Mobile Communication, Private Talk, Public Performance*. Cambridge: Cambridge University Press.

Kendall, Shari. 2007. "Father as Breadwinner, Mother as Worker: Gendered Positions in Feminist and Traditional Discourses of Work and Family." In *Family Talk: Discourse and Identity in Four American Families*, edited by Deborah Tannen, Shari Kendall, and Cynthia Gordon. 123–164, New York: Oxford University Press.

Kim, Mary Shin, and Stephanie Hyeri Kim. 2014. "Initiating Repair with and without Particles: Alternative Formats of Other-Initiation of Repair in Korean Conversations." *Research on Language and Social Interaction 47*, no. 4: 331–352.

Kinloch, Karen, and Sylvia Jaworska. 2020. "'Your Mind Is Part of Your Body': Negotiating the Maternal Body in Online Stories of Postnatal Depression on Mumsnet." *Discourse, Context & Media 39*, 100456. https://doi.org/10.1016/j.dcm.2020.100456

Knobel, Michele, and Colin Lankshear. 2007. "Online Memes, Affinities and Cultural Production." In *A New Literacies Sampler*, edited by Michele Knobel and Colin Lankshear, 199–227. New York: Peter Lang.

Koenig, Christopher J., Mohan J. Dutta, Namratha Kandula, and Latha Palaniappan. 2012. "'All of Those Things We Don't Eat': A Culture-Centered Approach to Dietary Health Meanings for Asian Indians Living in the United States." *Health Communication 27*: 818–828.

Kouper, Inna. 2010. "The Pragmatics of Peer Advice in a LiveJournal Community." Language@Internet 7: Article 1. www.languageat internet.de, urn:nbn:de: 0009-7-24642.

Kress, Gunther. 2010. *Multimodality: A Social Semiotic Approach to Contemporary Communication*. London: Routledge.

Kress, Gunther, and Theo van Leeuwen. (1996) 2006. *Reading Images: The Grammar of Visual Design*. London: Routledge.

Kristeva, Julia. (1967) 1980. "Word, Dialogue, and Novel." In *Desire in Language: A Semiotic Approach to Literature and Art*, translated by Thomas Gora, Alice Jardine, and Leon S. Roudiez, edited by Leon S. Roudiez, 64–91. New York: Columbia University Press.

Kumpf, Eric P. 2000. Visual Metadiscourse: Designing the Considerate Text. *Technical Communication Quarterly 9*, no. 4: 401–424.

Kurtz, Liza C., Sarah Trainer, Melissa Bresford, Amber Wutich, and Alexandra Brewis. 2017. "Blogs as Elusive Ethnographic Texts: Methodological and Ethical Challenges in Qualitative Online Research." *International Journal of Qualitative Methods 16*, no. 1: 1–12.

Labov, William. 1972. *Language in the Inner City: Studies in the Black English Vernacular*. Philadelphia: University of Pennsylvania Press.

Lanamäka, Arto, and Tero Päivärinta. 2009. "Metacommunication Patterns in Online Communities." In *Online Communities and Social Computing: 5th International conference, OCSC 2013, Held as Part of HCI International 2013, Las Vegas, NV, USA, July 21–26, 2013. Proceedings*, edited by A. Ant Ozok and Panayiotis Zaphiris, 236–245. Berlin: Springer-Verlag Heidelberg.

Lapadat, Judith C. 2003. "Teachers in an Online Seminar Talking about Talk: Classroom Discourse and School Change." *Language and Education 17*, no. 1: 21–41.

Lave, Jean, and Etienne Wenger. 1991. *Situated Learning: Legitimate Peripheral Participation*. Cambridge: Cambridge University Press.

Lawson, Nigella. 2015. *Simply Nigella: Feel Good Food*. New York: Flatiron Books.

Lay, Ethna D. 2014. "Re/Collections: From Books to Blogs." *Scholarly and Research Communication 5*, no. 2: 1–16.

Ledin, Per, and David Machin. 2018. *Doing Visual Analysis: From Theory to Practice*. London: Sage.

Lee, Carmen. 2013. "'My English Is So Poor . . . so I Take Photos': Metalinguistic Discourses about English on Twitter." In *Discourse 2.0: Language and New Media*, edited by Deborah Tannen and Anna Marie Trester, 73–83. Washington, DC: Georgetown University Press.

Leighter, James L., and Laura Black. 2010. "'I'm Just Raising the Question': Terms for Talk and Practical Metadiscursive Argument in Public Meetings." *Western Journal of Communication 74*, no. 5: 547–569.

Lemke, Jay. 2002. "Travels in Hypermodality." *Visual Communication 1*, no. 3: 299–325.

Lemke, Jay. 2009. "Multimodal Genres and Transmedia Traversals: Social Semiotics and the Political Economy of the Sign." *Semiotica 173*: 283–297.

Lenhart, Amanda, and Maeve Duggan. 2014. "Couples, the Internet, and Social Media," February 14. https://www.pewresearch.org/internet/2014/02/11/couples-the-internet-and-social-media/.

Lenihan, Aoife. 2011. "'Join Our Community of Translators': Language Ideologies and/in Facebook." In *Digital Discourse: Language in the New Media*, edited by Crispin Thurlow and Kristine Mroczek, 48–64. New York: Oxford University Press.

Lerner, Gene H. 1996. "Finding 'Face' in the Preference Structures of Talk-in-Interaction." *Social Psychology Quarterly 59*, no. 4: 303–321.

Levinson, Stephen C. 1983. *Pragmatics*. Cambridge: Cambridge University Press.

Linell, Per, and Margareta Bredmar. 1996. "Reconstructing Topical Sensitivity: Aspects of Face-Work in Talks between Midwives and Expectant Mothers." *Research on Language and Social Interaction 29*, no. 4: 347–379.

Ling, Rich. 2008. *New Tech, New Ties: How Mobile Communication Is Reshaping Social Cohesion*. Cambridge, MA: The MIT Press.

Linn, Susan. 2004. *Consuming Kids: The Hostile Takeover of Childhood*. New York: New Press.

Locher, Miriam A. 2006. *Advice Online: Advice-Giving in an American Internet Health Column*. Amsterdam and Philadelphia: John Benjamins.

Locher, Miriam A. 2013. "Internet Advice." In *Pragmatics of Computer-Mediated Communication*, edited by Susan Herring, Dieter Stein, and Tuija Virtanen, 339–362. Boston: De Gruyter, Inc.

Locher, Miriam, and Richard Watts. 2005. "Politeness Theory and Relational Work." *Journal of Politeness Research 1*, no. 1: 9–33.

London, Jaclyn. 2017. "Q What's Clean Eating'? It's All over Facebook." *Good Housekeeping*, April 5, p. 100. http://link.galegroup.com/apps/doc/A485748484/BIC?u=wash43584&sid=BIC&xid=bf382968.

Lovecraft, H. P. 1928. "The Call of Cthulhu." *Weird Tales 11*, no. 2 (February).

Lucy, John A. 1993a. "Metapragmatic Presentationals: Reporting Speech with Quotatives in Yucatec Maya." In *Reflexive Language: Reported Speech and Metapragmatics*, edited by John A. Lucy, 91–125. Cambridge: Cambridge University Press.

Lucy, John A. 1993b. "Reflexive Language and the Human Disciplines." In *Reflexive Language: Reported Speech and Metapragmatics*, edited by John A. Lucy, 9–32. Cambridge: Cambridge University Press.

Lucy, John A., ed. 1993c. *Reflexive Language: Reported Speech and Metapragmatics*. Cambridge: Cambridge University Press.

Lundström, Ragnar. 2018. "Spaces for Support: Discursive Negotiations of Supporter Positions in Online Forum Discussions about Suicide." *Discourse, Context & Media 25*: 98–105.

Lutfey, Karen, and Douglas W. Maynard. 1998. "Bad News in Oncology: How Physician and Patient Talk about Death and Dying without Using Those Words." *Social Psychology Quarterly 61*, no. 4: 321–341.

Machin, David. 2004. "Building the World's Visual Language: The Increasing Global Importance of Image Banks in Corporate Media." *Visual Communication 3*, no. 3: 316–336.

Machin, David, and Adam Jaworski. 2006. "Archive Footage in the News: Creating a Likeness and Index of the Phenomenal World." *Visual Communication 5*, no. 3: 345–366.

Mackey, Alison, Hae In Park, and Katlyn M. Tagarelli. 2016. "Errors, Corrective Feedback, and Repair: Variations and Learning Outcomes." In *The Routledge Handbook of English Language Teaching*, edited by Graham Hall, 499–512. London and New York: Routledge.

Madianou, Mirca, and Daniel Miller. 2012. "Polymedia: Towards a New Theory of Digital Media in Interpersonal Communication." *International Journal of Cultural Studies 15*, no. 2: 169–187.

Maingueneau, Dominique. 1987. *Nouvelles Tendances en Analyse du Discours*. Paris: Hachette.

Mandelbaum, Jennifer. 1987. "Couples Sharing Stories." *Communication Quarterly 35*, no. 2: 144–171.

Mapes, Gwynne. 2020. "Mediatizing the Fashionable Eater in @nytfood #tbt Posts." *In Identity and Ideology in Digital Food Discourse*, edited by Alla Tovares and Cynthia Gordon, 59–84. London and New York: Bloomsbury.

Mapes, Gwynne. 2021. *Elite Authenticity: Remaking Distinction in Food Discourse*. Oxford and New York: Oxford University Press.

Markham, Annette, and Elizabeth Buchanan. 2012. *Ethical Decision-Making and Internet Research: Recommendations from the AoIR Ethics Working Committee (Version 2.0)*. Accessed July 5, 2019. http://aoir.org/reports/ethics2.pdf.

Maschler, Yael. 2009. *Metalanguage in Interaction: Hebrew Discourse Markers*. Amsterdam and Philadelphia: John Benjamins.

Matassi, Mora, Pablo J. Boczkowski, and Eugenia Mitchelstein. 2019. "Domesticating WhatsApp: Family, Friends, Work, and Study in Everyday Communication." *New Media & Society 21*, no. 10: 2183–2200.

Matley, David. 2020. "'I Miss My Old Life': Regretting Motherhood on Mumsnet." *Discourse, Context & Media 37*, 100417. https://doi.org/10.1016/j.dcm.2020.100417

Meinhof, Ukrike Hanna. 2004. "Metadiscourses of Culture in British TV Commercials." In *Metalanguage: Social and Ideological Perspectives*, edited by Adam Jaworski, Nikolas Coupland, and Dariusz Galasiński, 275–288. Berlin and New York: Mouton de Gruyter.

Meinhof, Ulrkie H., and Jonathan Smith. 2000. "Spitting Image: TV Genre and Intertextuality." In *Intertextuality and the Media: From Genre to Everyday Life*, edited by Ulrike H. Meinhof and Jonathan Smith, 43–60. Manchester, UK: Manchester University Press.

Mendoza-Denton, Norma. 2011. "The Semiotic Hitchhiker's Guide to Creaky Voice: Circulation and Gendered Hardcore in a Chicana/o Gang Persona." *Journal of Linguistic Anthropology 21*, no. 2: 261–280.

Meredith, Joanne, and Elizabeth Stokoe. 2014. "Repair: Comparing Facebook 'Chat' with Spoken Interaction." *Discourse & Communication 8*, no. 2: 181–207.

Miller-Ott, Aimee E., and Lynne Kelly. 2016. "Competing Discourses and Meaning Making in Talk about Romantic Partners' Cell-Phone Contact with Non-Present Others." *Communication Studies 67*, no. 1: 58–76.

Milner, Ryan M. 2013. "Pop Polyvocality: Internet Memes, Public Participation, and the Occupy Wall Street Movement." *International Journal of Communication 7*: 2357–2390.

Miltner, Kate M., and Tim Highfield. 2017. "Never Gonna GIF You Up: Analyzing the Cultural Significance of the Animated GIF." *Social Media & Society 3*, no. 3: 1–11.

Mishra, Suman. 2017. "From Self-Control to Self-Improvement: Evolving Messages and Persuasion Techniques in Weight Loss Advertising (1930–1990)." *Visual Communication 16*, no. 4: 467–494.

Mitra, Ananda. 1999. "Characteristics of WWW Text: Tracing Discursive Strategies." *Journal of Computer-Mediated Communication 5*, no. 1. https://doi.org/10.1111/j.1083-6101.1999.tb00330.x

Mondada, Lorenza. 2009. "The Methodical Organisation of Talking and Eating: Assessments in Dinner Conversations." *Food Quality and Preference 20*, no. 8: 558–571.

Morrow, Phillip R. 2006. "Talking about Problems and Giving Advice in an Internet Discussion Forum: Some Discourse Features." *Discourse Studies 8*, no. 4: 531–548.

Morrow, Phillip R. 2012. "Online Advice in Japanese: Giving Advice in an Internet Discussion Forum." In *Advice in Discourse*, edited by Holger Limberg and Miriam Locher, 255–279. Philadelphia: John Benjamins.

Morson, Gary Saul, and Caryl Emerson. 1990. *Mikhail Bakhtin: Creation of a Prosaics.* Stanford, CA: Stanford University Press.

Mortensen, Janus. 2017. "Transient Multilingual Communities as a Field of Investigation: Challenges and Opportunities." *Journal of Linguistic Anthropology* 27, no. 3: 271–288.

Mudry, Tanya E., and Tom Strong. 2013. "Doing Recovery Online." *Qualitative Health Research 23*, no. 3: 313–325.

Muñoz, Kristine L. 2014. *Transcribing Silence: Culture, Relationships, and Communication.* Walnut Creek, CA: Left Coast Press.

Musolino, Connie, Megan Warin, Tracey Wade, and Peter Gilchrist. 2015. "'Healthy Anorexia': The Complexity of Care in Disordered Eating." *Social Science & Medicine 139*: 18–25.

Myrendal, Jenny. 2019. "Negotiating Meanings Online: Disagreements about Word Meaning in Discussion Forum Communication." *Discourse Studies 21*, no. 3: 317–339.

N.A. 2008. "Taste, Ties, and Time: Facebook Data Release." *Berkman Klein Center for Internet & Society.* No longer available online. https://dataverse.harvard.edu/dataverse/t3.

Nguyen, Naomee-Minh. 2021. "'This Is similar to Vincent Chin': Intertextuality, Referring Expressions, and the Discursive Construction of Asian American Activist Identities in an Online Messaging Community. *Discourse & Society 32*, no. 1: 98–118.

Norrick, Neal. 1989. "Intertextuality in Humor." *Humor 2*, no. 2: 117–139.

Norrick, Neal R. 2019. "Collaborative Remembering in Conversational Narration." *Topics in Cognitive Science 11*: 733–751.

Norris, Sigrid, and Rodney H. Jones, eds. 2005. *Discourse in Action: Introducing Mediated Discourse Analysis.* London and New York: Routledge.

Ochs, Elinor. 1992. "Indexing Gender." In *Rethinking Context: Language as an Interactive Phenomenon*, edited by Alessandro Duranti and Charles Goodwin, 335–358. Cambridge: Cambridge University Press.

Ochs, Elinor. 1993. "Constructing Social Identity: A Language Socialization Perspective." *Research on Language and Social Interaction 26*, no. 3: 287–306.

Ochs, Elinor, Clotilde Pontecorvo, and Alessandra Fasulo. 1996. "Socializing Taste." *Ethnos 61*, nos. 1–2: 7–46.

Ochs, Elinor, Ruth Smith, and Carolyn Taylor. 1989. "Detective Stories at Dinnertime: Problem-Solving through Co-Narration." *Cultural Dynamics 2*, no. 2: 238–257.

Ochs, Elinor, Carolyn Taylor, Dina Rudolph, and Ruth Smith. 1992. "Storytelling as a Theory-Building Activity." *Discourse Processes 15*, no. 1: 37–72.

Page, Ruth. 2010. "Re-Examining Narrativity: Small Stories in Status Updates." *Text & Talk 30*, no. 4: 423–444.

Page, Ruth E. 2012. "Second Stories Told in Discussion Forums." In *Stories and Social Media: Identities and Interaction*, 24–48. New York: Routledge.

Paugh, Amy, and Carolina Izquierdo. 2009. "Why Is This a Battle Every Night?: Negotiating Food and Eating in American Dinnertime Interaction." *Journal of Linguistic Anthropology 19*, no. 2: 185–204.

Philips, Susan. 1998. *Ideology in the Language of Judges: How Judges Practice Law, Politics and Courtroom Control.* New York: Oxford University Press.

Philips, Susan U. 2021. "How Linguistic Anthropologists Conceptualize Relations among Different Forms of Discourse." In *Approaches to Discourse Analysis*, edited by Cynthia Gordon, 8–20. Washington, DC: Georgetown University Press.

Philipsen, Gerry. 1987. "The Prospect for Cultural Communication." In *Communication Theory: Eastern and Western Perspectives*, edited by D. Lawrence Kincaid, 245–254. San Diego, CA: Academic Press.

Philipsen, Gerry. 1992. *Speaking Culturally: Explorations in Social Communication.* Albany: State University of New York Press.

Philipsen, Gerry. 2002. "Cultural Communication." In *Handbook of International and Intercultural Communication*, edited by William B. Gudykunst and Bella Mody, 51–67. Newbury Park, CA: Sage.

Pigeron, Elisa. 2009. "The Technology-Mediated Worlds of American Families." PhD diss., University of California, Los Angeles.

Pilař, Ladislav, Lucie Kvasničková, Roman Stanislavská, Richard Hartman, and Ivana Ticá. 2021. "Healthy Food on Instagram Social Network: Vegan, Homemade and Clean Eating." *Nutrients 13*, no. 6. doi: 10.3390/nu13061991.

Pollak, Kathryn I., Stewart C. Alexander, Truls Østbye, Pauline Lyna, James A. Tulsky, Rowena J. Dolor, Cynthia Coffman, Rebecca J. Namenek Brouwer, Iguehi Esoimeme, Justin R. E. Manusov, and Terrill Bravender. 2009. "Primary Care Physicians' Discussions of Weight-Related Topics with Overweight and Obese Adolescents: Results from the Teen CHAT Pilot Study." *Journal of Adolescent Health 45*, no. 2: 205–207.

Pounds, Gabrina, Daniel Hunt, and Nelya Koteyko. 2018. "Expression of Empathy in a Facebook-Based Diabetes Support Group." *Discourse, Context & Media 25*: 34–43.

Puhl, Rebecca, Jamie Lee Peterson, and Joerge Luedicke. 2013. "Motivating or Stigmatizing? Public Perceptions of Weight-Related Language Used by Health Providers." *International Journal of Obesity 37*: 612–619.

Rampton, Ben. 1995. *Crossing: Language and Ethnicity amongst Adolescents.* London: Longman.

Robinson, Jeffrey D. 2006. "Managing Trouble Responsibility and Relationships during Conversational Repair." *Communication Monographs 73*, no. 2: 137–161.

Robinson, Jeffrey D., and Heidi Kevoe-Feldman. 2010. "Using Full Repeats to Initiate Repair on Others' Questions." *Research on Language and Social Interaction 43*, no. 3: 232–259.

Robles, Jessica S., and Teresa Castor. 2019. "Taking the Moral High Ground: Practices for Being Uncompromisingly Principled." *Journal of Pragmatics 141*: 116–129.

Robles, Jessica S., Stephen DiDomenico, and Joshua Raclaw. 2018. "Doing Being an Ordinary Technology and Social Media User." *Language & Communication 60*: 150–167.

Rowe, Margaret Anne. 2018. "Friendship across Distance: Media Ideologies in Threatening Face and Building Solidarity over Video Calls." Unpublished senior honors thesis, Department of Linguistics, Georgetown University, Washington, DC.

Rushdie, Salman. 1990. *The Satanic Verses.* New York: Viking.

Sacks, Harvey. 1972. "On the Analyzability of Stories by Children." In *Directions in Sociolinguistics: The Ethnography of Communication*, edited by John J. Gumperz and Dell Hymes, 325–345. New York: Holt, Rinehart and Winston.

Sacks, Harvey. 1992. "April 24: Second Stories." In *Lectures on Conversation*, Vol. 1, edited by Gail Jefferson, 764–722. Oxford: Basil Blackwell.

Sampietro, Agnese. 2016. "Exploring the Punctuating Effect of Emoji in Spanish WhatsApp Chats." *Lenguas Modernas 47*, no. 1: 91–113.

Sarangi, Srikant Kumar. 2016. "Owning Responsible Actions/Selves: Role-Relational Trajectories in Counselling for Childhood Genetic Testing." In *Discourse and Responsibility in Professional Contexts*, edited by Jan-Ola Östman and Anna Solin, 37–63. London: Equinox.

Sass, Cynthia. 2017. "5 Things Not to Say to Your Partner about Losing Weight." *HuffPost*, December 6. https://www.huffpost.com/entry/help-partner-spouse-husband-wife-lose-weight_n_4731806.

Saunders, Benjamin, Julius Sim, Tom Kingstone, Shula Baker, Jackie Waterfield, Bernadette Bartlam, Heather Burroughs, and Clare Jinks. 2018. "Saturation in Qualitative Research: Exploring Its Conceptualization and Operation." *Quality & Quantity 52*: 1893–1907.

Saussure, Ferdinad de. 1916. *Cours de linguistique générale*. Paris: Payot.

Schegloff, Emanuel A. 1992. "Repair after Next Turn: The Last Structurally Provided Defense of Intersubjectivity in Conversation." *American Journal of Sociology 97*, no. 5: 1295–1345.

Schegloff, Emanuel A. 1997. "Practices and Actions: Boundary Cases of Other-Initiated Repair." *Discourse Processes 23*, no. 3: 499–545.

Schegloff, Emanuel A. 2000. "When 'Others' Initiate Repair." *Applied Linguistics 21*, no. 2: 205–243.

Schegloff, Emanuel A., Gail Jefferson, and Harvey Sacks. 1977. "The Preference for Self-Correction in the Organization of Repair in Conversation." *Language 53*, no. 2: 361–382.

Schiffrin, Deborah. 1980. "Meta-Talk: Organizational and Evaluative Brackets in Discourse." *Sociological Inquiry 50*, nos .3–4: 199–236.

Schiffrin, Deborah. 1987. *Discourse Markers*. Cambridge: Cambridge University Press.

Schiffrin, Deborah. 1994. *Approaches to Discourse*. Cambridge, MA: Blackwell.

Schiffrin, Deborah. 2006. *In Other Words: Variation in Reference and Narrative*. Cambridge: Cambridge University Press.

Schönfeldt, Juliane, and Andrea Golato. 2003. "Repair in Chats: A Conversation Analytic Perspective." *Research on Language and Social Interaction 36*, no. 3: 241–284.

Scollon, Ron. 2001. *Mediated Discourse: The Nexus of Practice*. London and New York: Routledge.

Scollon, Ron, and Suzie Wong Scollon. 2003. *Discourses in Place: Language in the Material World*. London: Routledge.

Seargeant, Philip, Caroline Tagg, and Wipanan Ngampramuan. 2012. "Language Choice and Addressivity Strategies in Thai-English Social Network Interactions." *Journal of Sociolinguistics 16*, no. 4: 510–531.

Segev, Elad, Asaf Nissenbaum, Nathan Stolero, and Limor Shifman. 2015. "Families and Networks of Internet Memes: The Relationship between Cohesiveness, Uniqueness, and Quiddity Concerns." *Journal of Computer-Mediated Communication 20*: 417–433.

Severinson Eklundh, Kerstin. 2010. "To Quote or Not to Quote: Setting the Context for Computer-Mediated Dialogues." Language@Internet 7: Article 5. https://www.languageatinternet.org/articles/2010/2665.

Sharf, Barbara F. 1997. "Communicating Breast Cancer On-Line: Support and Empowerment on the Internet." *Women & Health 26*, no. 1: 65–84.

Sherman, Brett. 2018. "'According to' Phrases and Epistemic Modals." *Natural Language and Linguistic Theory 36*: 627–636.

Shifman, Limor. 2013. "Memes in a Digital World: Reconciling with a Conceptual Troublemaker." *Journal of Computer-Mediated Communication 18*, no. 3: 362–377.

Shrikant, Natasha. 2020. "Metadiscourse and the Management of Relationships during Online Conflict among Academics." *Text & Talk 40*, no. 4: 513–535.

Shukrun-Nagar, Pnina. 2009. "Quotation Markers as Intertextual Codes in Electoral Propaganda." *Text & Talk 29*, no. 4: 459–480.

Sierra, Sylvia. 2016. "Playing Out Loud: Videogame References as Resources in Friend Interaction for Managing Frames, Epistemics, and Group Identity." *Language in Society 45*, no. 2: 217–245.

Sierra, Sylvia. 2019. "Linguistic and Ethnic Media Stereotypes in Everyday Talk: Humor and Identity Construction among Friends. *Journal of Pragmatics 152*: 186–199.

Sierra, Sylvia. 2021. *Millennials Talking Media: Creating Intertextual Identities in Everyday Conversation*. New York: Oxford University Press.

Silverman, Robyn. 2017. "How to Talk to Kids about Picky Eating & Good Nutrition with Jill Castle." Audio podcast post. How to Talk to Kids About Anything, December 19, 2017. Accessed July 16, 2019. https://drrobynsilverman.com/how-to-talk-to-kids-about-picky-eating-good-nutrition-with-jill-castle/.

Silverstein, Michael. 1993. "Metapragmatic Discourse and Metapragmatic Function." In *Reflexive Language: Reported Speech and Metapragmatics*, edited by John A. Lucy, 33–58. Cambridge: Cambridge University Press.

Sixsmith, Judith, and Craig D. Murray. 2001. "Ethical Issues in the Documentary Data Analysis of Internet Posts and Archives." *Qualitative Health Research 11*, no. 3: 423–442.

Skovholt, Karianne, Anette Grønning, and Anne Kankaanranta. 2014. "The Communicative Functions of Emoticons in Workplace E-Mails::-)." *Journal of Computer Mediated Communication 19*: 780–197.

Smith, Angela. 2020. "Clean Eating's Surprising Normalisation: The Case of Nigella Lawson." *Discourse, Context & Media 35* (2020): Article number 100376. https://doi.org/10.1016/j.dcm.2020.100376

Smithson, Janet, Siobhan Sharkey, Elaine Hewis, Ray B. Jones, Tobit Emmens, Tamsin Ford, and Christabel Owens. 2011a. "Membership and Boundary Maintenance on an Online Self-Harm Forum." *Qualitative Health Research 21*, no. 11: 1567–1575.

Smithson, Janet, Siobhan Sharkey, Elaine Hewis, Ray Jones, Tobit Emmens, Tamsin Ford, and Christabel Owens. 2011b. "Problem Presentation and Responses on an Online Forum for Young People Who Self-Harm." *Discourse Studies 13*, no. 4: 487–501.

Sneijder, Petra, and Hedwig F. M. te Molder. 2004. "'Health Should Not Have to Be a Problem': Talking Health and Accountability in an Internet Forum on Veganism." *Journal of Health Psychology 9*, no. 4: 599–616.

Sneijder, Petra, and Hedwig F. M. te Molder. 2006. "Disputing Taste: Food Pleasure as an Achievement in Interaction." *Appetite 46*: 107–116.

Sneijder, Petra, and Hedwig te Molder. 2009. "Normalizing Ideological Food Choice and Eating Practices. Identity Work in Online Discussions on Veganism." *Appetite 52*, no. 3: 621–630.

Solin, Ana. 2004. "Intertextuality as Mediation: On the Analysis of Intertextual Relations in Public Discourse." *Text 24*, no. 2: 267–296.

Søndergaard, Bent. 1991. "Switching between Seven Codes within One Family—a Linguistic Resource." *Journal of Multilingual and Multicultural Development 12*, nos. 1–2: 85–92.

Speer, Susan A., and Rebecca McPhillips. 2018. "Initiating Discussions about Weight in a Non-Weight-Specific Setting: What Can We Learn about the Interactional

Consequences of Different Communication Practices from an Examination of Clinical Consultations?". *British Journal of Health Psychology 23*, no. 4: 888–907.

Squires, Lauren. 2011. "Voicing 'Sexy Text': Heteroglossia and Erasure in TV News Representations of Detroit's Text Messages Scandal." In *Digital Discourse: Language in the New Media*, edited by Crispin Thurlow and Kristine Mroczek, 3–25. New York: Oxford University Press.

Squires, Lauren. 2014. "From TV Personality to Fans and Beyond: Indexical Bleaching and the Diffusion of a Media Innovation." *Journal of Linguistic Anthropology 24*, no. 1: 42–64.

Stephens, Mark B. 2009. "Clinical Commentary: Take a Direct Approach to Excess Weight." *The Journal of Family Practice 58*: 431.

Stommel, Wyke. 2008. "Conversation Analysis and Community of Practice as Approaches to Studying Online Community." Language@Internet 5: Article 5. https://www.languageatinternet.org/articles/2008/1537.

Stommel, Wyke, and Lynn de Rijk. 2021. "Ethical Approval: None Sought. How Discourse Analysts Report Ethical Issues around Publicly Available Online Data." *Research Ethics*. doi.org/10.1177/1747016120988767.

Stommel, Wyke, and Tom Koole. 2010. "The Online Support Group as a Community: A Micro-Analysis of the Interaction with a New Member." *Discourse Studies 12*, no. 3: 357–378.

Stoner, Mark. R. 2007. "PowerPoint in a New Key." *Communication Education 55*, no. 3: 354–381.

Streeck, Jürgen. 2021. "Gesture, Mimesis, and the Linguistics of Time." In *Approaches to Discourse Analysis*, edited by Cynthia Gordon, 37–54. Washington, DC: Georgetown University Press.

Su, Hsi-Yao. 2019. "The Metapragmatics of Taiwanese (Im)politeness: Conceptualization and Evaluation of *limao*." *Journal of Pragmatics 148*: 26–43.

Svennevig, Jan. 2008. "Trying the Easiest Solution First in Other-Initiation of Repair." *Journal of Pragmatics 40*: 333–348.

Tagg, Caroline. 2012. *Discourse of Text Messaging: Analysis of SMS Communication*. London: Continuum.

Tannen, Deborah. 1986. *That's Not What I Meant! How Conversational Style Makes or Breaks Your Relations with Others*. New York: Morrow.

Tannen, Deborah. 1990. *You Just Don't Understand: Women and Men in Conversation*. New York: Morrow.

Tannen, Deborah, ed. 1993. *Framing in Discourse*. New York: Oxford University Press.

Tannen, Deborah. 1994. "The Relativity of Linguistic Strategies: Rethinking Power and Solidarity in Gender and Dominance." In *Gender and Discourse*, 19–52. New York: Oxford University Press.

Tannen, Deborah. 1998. *The Argument Culture: Moving from Debate to Dialogue*. New York: Random House.

Tannen, Deborah. 2001. *I Only Say This Because I Love You: How the Way We Talk Can Make or Break Family Relationships throughout Our Lives*. New York: Random House.

Tannen, Deborah. 2003. "Power Maneuvers or Connection Maneuvers? Ventriloquizing in Family Interaction." In *Linguistics, Language, and the Real World: Discourse and Beyond: Georgetown University Round Table on Languages and Linguistics 2001*, edited by Deborah Tannen and James E. Alatis, 50–62. Washington, DC: Georgetown University Press.

Tannen, Deborah. 2004. "Interactional Sociolinguistics." In *Sociolinguistics: An International Handbook of the Science of Language and Society*, edited by Ulrich Ammon, Norbert Dittmar, Klaus J. Mattheier, and Peter Trudgill, 76–88. Berlin and New York: De Gruyter.

Tannen, Deborah. (1984) 2005. *Conversational Style: Analyzing Talk among Friends*. New York: Oxford University Press.

Tannen, Deborah. 2006. "Intertextuality in Interaction: Reframing Family Arguments in Public and Private." *Text & Talk 26*, nos. 4–5: 597–617.

Tannen, Deborah. 2007a. "Power Maneuvers and Connection Maneuvers in Family Interaction." In *Family Talk: Discourse and Identity in Four American Families*, edited by Deborah Tannen, Shari Kendall, and Cynthia Gordon, 27–69. New York: Oxford University Press.

Tannen, Deborah. (1989) 2007b. *Talking Voices: Repetition, Dialogue, and Imagery in Conversational Discourse*. Cambridge: Cambridge University Press.

Tannen, Deborah. 2008. "'We've Never Been Close, We're Very Different': Three Narrative Types in Sister Discourse." *Narrative Inquiry 18*, no. 2: 206–229.

Tannen, Deborah. 2013. "The Medium is the Metamessage: Conversational Style in New Media Interaction." In *Discourse 2.0: Language and New Media*, edited by Deborah Tannen and Anna Marie Trester, 99–117. Washington, DC: Georgetown University Press.

Tannen, Deborah. 2017. *You're the Only One I Can Tell: Inside the Language of Women's Friendships*. New York: Ballantine Books.

Tannen, Deborah. 2021. "The Ambiguity and Polysemy of Power and Solidarity in Professor-Student Emails and Conversations among Friends." In *Approaches to Discourse Analysis*, edited by Cynthia Gordon, 55–68. Washington, DC: Georgetown University Press.

Tannen, Deborah, Shari Kendall, and Cynthia Gordon, eds. 2007. *Family Talk: Discourse and Identity in Four American Families*. Oxford: Oxford University Press.

Tannen, Deborah, and Anna Marie Trester, eds. 2013. *Discourse 2.0: Language and New Media*. Washington, DC: Georgetown University Press.

Tannen, Deborah, and Cynthia Wallat. 1993. "Interactive Frames and Knowledge Schemas in Interaction: Examples from a Medical Examination/Interview." In *Framing in Discourse*, edited by Deborah Tannen, 55–76. New York: Oxford University Press.

Tanskanen, Sanna-Kaisa. 2007. "Metapragmatic Utterances in Computer-Mediated Interaction." In *Metapragmatics in Use*, edited by Wolfram Bublitz and Alex Hübler, 87–106. Amsterdam: John Benjamins.

Thalheimer, Judith C. 2016. "Hottest Nutrition Trends of 2016: Clean Eating." *Today's Dietitian 18*, no. 6: 37. https://www.todaysdietitian.com/newarchives/0616 p37.shtml.

Theodoropoulou, Irene. 2015. "Politeness on Facebook: The Case of Greek Birthday Wishes." *Pragmatics 25*, no. 1: 23–45.

Thurlow, Crispin. 2006. "From Statistical Panic to Moral Panic: The Metadiscursive Construction and Popular Exaggeration of New Media Language in the Print Media." *Journal of Computer-Mediated Communication 11*: 667–701.

Thurlow, Crispin. 2007. "Fabricating Youth: New-Media Discourse and the Technologization of Young People. In *Language in the Media: Representation, Identities, Ideologies*, edited by Sally Johnson and Astrid Ensslin, 213–233. London: Continuum.

Thurlow, Crispin. 2017. "'Forget about the Words'? Tracking the Language, Media and Semiotic Ideologies of Digital Discourse: The Case of Sexting." *Discourse, Context & Media 20*: 10–19.

Thurlow, Crispin, Giorgia Aiello, and Lara Portmann. 2020. "Visualizing Teens and Technology: A Social Semiotic Analysis of Stock Photography and News Media Imagery." *New Media & Society 22*, no. 3: 528–549.

Thurlow, Crispin, and Adam Jaworski. 2011. "Banal Globalization? Embodied Actions and Mediated Practices in Tourists' Online Photo Sharing." In *Digital Discourse: Language in the New Media*, edited by Crispin Thurlow and Kristine Mroczek, 220–250. New York: Oxford University Press.

Thurlow, Crispin, and Kristine Mroczek. 2011. "Introduction: Fresh Perspectives on New Media Sociolinguistics." In *Digital Discourse: Language in the New Media*, edited by Crispin Thurlow and Kristine Mroczek, xix–xliv. New York: Oxford University Press.

Todorov, Tsvetan. (1981) 1984. *Mikhail Bakhtin: The Dialogical Principle*, translated by Wlad Godzich. Minneapolis: University of Minnesota Press.

Tolins, Jackson, and Patrawat Samermit. 2016. "GIFs as Embodied Enactments in Text-Mediated Conversation. *Research on Language and Social Interaction 49*, no. 2: 75–91.

Tovares, Alla V. 2007. "Family Members Interacting while Watching TV." In *Family Talk: Discourse and Identity in Four American Families*, edited by Deborah Tannen, Shari Kendall, and Cynthia Gordon, 283–309. New York: Oxford University Press.

Tovares, Alla V. 2010. "'All in the Family': Small Stories and Narrative Construction of a Shared Family Identity That Includes Pets." *Narrative Inquiry 20*, no. 1: 1–19.

Tovares, Alla V. 2012. "A Television Quiz Show as a Resource in Family Interaction." In *The Appropriation of Media in Everyday Life*, edited by Ruth Ayaß and Cornelia Gerhardt, 105–130. Amsterdam and Philadelphia: John Benjamins.

Tovares, Alla V. 2019. "Negotiating 'Thick' Identities through 'Light' Practices: YouTube Metalinguistic Comments about Language in Ukraine." *Multilingua 38*, no. 4: 459–484.

Tovares, Alla V. 2020a. The Art of the Insult: (Re)creating Zaporizhian Cossacks' Letter-Writing on YouTube as Collective Creative Insurgency. In *Language of Conflict: Discourse of the Ukrainian Crisis*, edited by Natalia Knoblock, 213–232. London: Bloomsbury.

Tovares, Alla V. 2020b. "The Public Loneliness of Endurance Athletes: Creating Ambient Affiliation through Involvement Strategies on Twitter." *Discourse, Context & Media 34*. https://doi.org/10.1016/j.dcm.2020.100380.

Tovares, Alla, and Cynthia Gordon, eds. 2020. *Identity and Ideology in Digital Food Discourse*. London and New York: Bloomsbury.

Tovares, Alla V., Cynthia Gordon, and Najma Al Zidjaly. 2021. "Mobile Phones in Classrooms and in Professor-Student Communication: Ukrainian, Omani, and U.S. American College Students' Perceptions and Practices." *International Journal of Interactive Mobile Technologies (iJim) 15*, no. 10: 118–137.

Van Leeuwen, Theo. 1996. "The Representation of Social Actors." In *Texts and Practices: Readings in Critical Discourse Analysis*, edited by Carmen Rosa Caldas-Coulthard and Malcolm Coulthard, 32–70. London: Routledge.

Van Leeuwen, Theo. 2004. "Metalanguage in Social Life." In *Metalanguage: Social and Ideological Perspectives*, edited by Adam Jaworski, Nikolas Coupland, and Dariusz Galasiński, 107–130. Berlin and New York: Mouton de Gruyter.

Van Nijnatten, Carolus. 2006. "Meta-Communication in Institutional Talks." *Qualitative Social Work 5*(3): 333–349.

Varenne, Hervé, with the collaboration of Clifford Hill and Paul Byers. 1992. *Ambiguous Harmony: Family Talk in America*. Norwood, NJ: Ablex.

Vásquez, Camilla. 2010. "Examining Two Explicit Formulations in University Discourse." *Text & Talk 30*, no. 6: 749–771.

Vásquez, Camilla. 2014. *The Discourse of Online Consumer Reviews*. New York: Bloomsbury.

Vásquez, Camilla. 2015a. "'Don't Even Get Me Started . . .': Interactive Metadiscourse in Online Consumer Reviews." In *Digital Business Discourse*, edited by Erika Darics, 19–39. London: Palgrave Macmillan: London.

Vásquez, Camilla. 2015b. "Intertextuality and Interdiscursivity in Online Consumer Reviews." In *Discourse and Digital Practice: Doing Discourse Analysis in the Digital Age*, edited by Rodney H. Jones, Alice Chik, and Christoph A. Hafner, 66–80. New York: Routledge.

Vásquez, Camilla. 2019. *Language, Creativity and Humour Online*. London and New York: Routledge.

Vayreda, Agnès, and Charles Antaki. 2009. "Social Support and Unsolicited Advice in a Bipolar Disorder Online Forum." *Qualitative Health Research 19*: 931–942.

Veen, Mario, Hedwig te Molder, Bart Gremmen, and Cees van Woerkum. 2010. "Quitting is Not an Option: An Analysis of Online Diet Talk between Celiac Disease Patients." *Health 14*, no. 1: 23–40.

Vehviläinen, Sanna. 2009. "Student-Initiated Advice in Academic Supervision." *Research on Language and Social Interaction 42*, no. 2: 163–190.

Verschueren, Jef. 1995. "Metapragmatics." In *Handbook of Pragmatics Manual*, edited by Jef Verschueren, Jan-Ola Ostman, and Jan Blommaert, 367–371. Amsterdam: John Benjamins.

Verschueren, Jef. 1999. *Understanding Pragmatics*. New York: Oxford University Press.

Verschueren, Jef. 2004. "Notes on the Role of Metapragmatic Awareness in Language Use." In *Metalanguage: Social and Ideological Perspectives*, edited by Adam Jaworski, Nikolas Coupland, and Dariusz Galasiński, 53–73. Berlin and New York: Mouton de Gruyter.

Verschueren, Jef. 2013. "Ethnography of Communication and History: A Case Study of Diplomatic Intertextuality and Ideology." *Linguistic Anthropology 23*, no. 3: 142–159.

Vogels, Emily A., and Monica Anderson. 2020. "Dating and Relationships in the Digital Age," May 8. https://www.pewresearch.org/internet/2020/05/08/dating-and-relationships-in-the-digital-age/.

Walther, Joseph B. 2012. "Interaction through Technological Lenses: Computer-Mediated Communication and Language." *Journal of Language and Social Psychology 31*, no. 4: 397–414.

Waring, Hansun Zhang. 2005. "The Unofficial Businesses of Repair Initiation: Vehicles for Affiliation and Disaffiliation." In *Language in Use: Cognitive and Discourse Perspectives on Language and Language Learning*, edited by Andrea Tyler, Mari Takada, Yiyoung Kim, and Diana Marinova, 163–175. Washington, DC: Georgetown University Press.

Watanable, Suwako. 1993. "Cultural Differences in Framing. American and Japanese Group Discussions." In *Framing in Discourse*, edited by Deborah Tannen, 176–209. Oxford: Oxford University Press.

Webb, Helena. 2009. "'I've Put Weight on Cos I've Bin Inactive, Cos I've'ad Me Knee Done': Moral Work in the Obesity Clinic." *Sociology of Health & Illness 31*, no. 6: 854–871.

Weber, Brenda R. 2009. *Makeover TV: Selfhood, Citizenship and Celebrity*. Durham, NC: Duke University Press.

Weber, H. L. 2011. "Missed Cues: How Disputes Can Socialize Virtual Newcomers." Language@Internet *8*: Article 5. https://www.languageatinternet.org/articles/2011/Weber.

Wesemann, Dorette, and Martin Grunwald. 2008. "Online Discussion Groups for Bulimia Nervosa: An Inductive Approach to Internet-Based Communication between Patients." *International Journal of Eating Disorders 41*, no. 6: 527–534.

West, Laura, and Anna Marie Trester. 2013. "Facework on Facebook: Conversations on Social Media." In *Discourse 2.0: Language and New Media*, edited by Deborah Tannen and Anna Marie Trester, 133–154. Washington, DC: Georgetown University Press.

White, Peter R. R. 1998. *Telling Media Tales: The News Story as Rhetoric*. Doctoral thesis, University of Sydney, Sydney, Australia.

Wiggins, Bradley E., and G. Bret Bowers. 2015. "Memes as Genre: A Structural Analysis of the Memescape. *New Media & Society 17*, no. 11: 1886–1906.

Wiggins, Sally. 2004a. "Good for 'You.' Generic and Individual Healthy Eating Advice in Family Mealtimes." *Journal of Health Psychology 9*, no. 4: 535–548.

Wiggins, Sally. 2004b. "Talking about Taste. Using a Discursive Psychological Approach to Examine Challenges to Food Evaluations." *Appetite 43*: 29–38.

Wiggins, Sally. 2013. "The Social Life of 'Eugh.' Disgust as Assessment in Family Mealtimes." *The British Journal of Social Psychology 52*, no. 3: 480–509.

Wiggins, Sally. 2014. "Adult and Child Use of Love, Like, Don't Like and Hate during Family Mealtimes. Subjective Category Assessments as Food Preference Talk." *Appetite 80*: 7–15.

Wiggins, Sally. 2016. "Producing Infant Food Preferences during Weaning: The Role of Language and Gesture in Parent-Child Interaction." *Appetite 101*: 224.

Wiggins, Sally, and Jonathan Potter. 2003. "Attitudes and Evaluative Practices. Category vs. Item and Subjective vs. Objective Constructions in Everyday Food Assessments." *The British Journal of Social Psychology 42*: 513–531.

Wiggins, Sally, Jonathan Potter, and Aimee Wildsmith. 2001. "Eating Your Words: Discursive Psychology and the Reconstruction of Eating Practices." *Journal of Health Psychology 6*, no.1: 5–15.

Wilson, Bee. 2017. "Why We Fell for Clean Eating. *The Guardian*, August 11, 2017. Accessed August 8, 2019. https://www.theguardian.com/lifeandstyle/2017/aug/11/why-we-fell-for-clean-eating.

Wilson, Brian, and Michael Atkinson. 2005. "Rave and Straightedge, the Virtual and the Real: Exploring Online and Offline Experiences in Canadian and Youth Subcultures." *Youth & Society 36*, no. 3: 276–311.

Witmer, Diane F., and Sandra Lee Katzman. 1997. "On-Line Smiles: Does Gender Make a Difference in the Use of Graphic Accents?" *Journal of Computer-Mediated Communication 2*, no. 4: 0.0. https://doi.org/10.1111/j.1083-6101.1997.tb00192.x

Woolard, Kathryn A., and Bambi B. Schieffelin. 1994. "Language Ideology." *Annual Review of Anthropology 23*: 55–82.

Wortham, Stanton E. F. 2005. "Socialization beyond the Speech Event." *Journal of Linguistic Anthropology 15*, no. 1: 95–112.

Woude, Judith Vander, and Ellen Barton. 2001. "Specialized Corrective Repair Sequences: Shared Book Reading with Children with Histories of Specific Language Impairment." *Discourse Processes 32*, no. 1: 1–27.

Wright, Scott. 2009. "The Role of the Moderator: Problems and Possibilities for Government-Run Online Discussion Forums." In *Online Deliberation: Design, Research, and Practice*, edited by Todd Davies and Seeta Peña Gangadharan, 233–242. Stanford, CA: CLSI Publications.

Yahr, Emily. 2021. "'An Absolute Legend': Fans and Co-Stars Mourn Jessica Walter, Actress and Star of the Internet's Favorite GIFs." *The Washington Post*, March 25, 2021. https://www.washingtonpost.com/arts-entertainment/2021/03/25/jessica-walter-dies-fan-reaction/.

Yamada, Haru. 1997. *Different Games, Different Rules: Why Americans and Japanese Misunderstand Each Other*. New York: Oxford University Press.

Yang, Robin Ruowei. 2009. "Other-Repair in Chinese Conversation: A Case of Web-Based Academic Discussion." *Intercultural Pragmatics 6*, no. 3: 315–343.

Zappavigna, Michele. 2011. "Ambient Affiliation: A Linguistic Perspective on Twitter." *New Media & Society 13*, no. 5: 788–806.

Zappavigna, Michele. 2012. *Discourse of Twitter and Social Media: How We Use Language to Create Affiliation on the Web*. London: Bloomsbury.

Zappavigna, Michele. 2014. "CoffeeTweets: Bonding around the Bean on Twitter." In *The Language of Social Media*, edited by Philip Seargeant and Caroline Tagg, 139–160. Basingstoke, UK: Palgrave.

Zappavigna, Michele. 2018. *Searchable Talk: Hashtags and Social Media Metadiscourse*. London: Bloomsbury.

Zhang, Man. 2016. "A Multidimensional Analysis of Metadiscourse Markers across Written Registers." *Discourse Studies 18*, no. 2: 204–222.

Zhang, Yi, and Camilla Vásquez. 2014. "Hotels' Responses to Online Reviews: Managing Consumer Dissatisfaction." *Discourse, Context and Media 6*: 54–64.

Zimmer, Michael. 2010. "'But the Data Is Already Public': On the Ethics of Research in Facebook." *Ethics and Information Technology 12*, no. 4: 313–325.

VIDEO MATERIALS REFERENCED

Aladdin. 1992. Directed by Ron Clements and John Musker.

American Psycho. 2000. Directed by Mary Harron.

Arrested Development. 2003–2006 (on Fox) and 2013, 2018–2019 (on Netflix).

Basketball Wives LA (Season 4). 2015 (on VH1).

Beetlejuice. 1988. Directed by Tim Burton.

Bill and Ted's Excellent Adventure. 1989. Directed by Stephen Herek.

Bridesmaids. 2011. Directed by Paul Feig.

Flash Gordon. 1980. Directed by Mike Hodges.

Futurama. 1999-2023.

Wayne's World. 1992. Directed by Penelope Spheeris.

INDEX

For the benefit of digital users, indexed terms that span two pages (e.g., 52–53) may, on occasion, appear on only one of those pages.

Figure are indicated by *f* following the page number